D0230723

European Gastronomy into the 21st Century

European Gastronomy into the 21st Century

Cailein Gillespie
The Scottish Hotel School

Contributing Editor: John Cousins
The Food and Beverage Training Company

BUTTERWORTH
HEINEMANN

OXFORD AUCKLAND BOSTON JOHANNESBURG MELBOURNE NEW DELHI

Butterworth-Heinemann
Linacre House, Jordan Hill, Oxford OX2 8DP
225 Wildwood Avenue, Woburn, MA 01801-2041
A division of Reed Educational and Professional Publishing Ltd

℞ A member of the Reed Elsevier plc group

First published 2001

British Library Cataloguing in Publication Data
Gillespie, Cailein
    European gastronomy into the 21st century
    1. Gastronomy   2. Cookery, European
    I. Title   II. Cousins, John A.
    641'.013'094

ISBN 0 7506 5267 5

For information on all Butterworth-Heinemann
publications visit our website at www.bh.com

Composition by Genesis Typesetting, Rochester, Kent
Printed and bound in Great Britain

FOR EVERY TITLE THAT WE PUBLISH, BUTTERWORTH-HEINEMANN
WILL PAY FOR BTCV TO PLANT AND CARE FOR A TREE.

Contents

Figures

Tables

Preface

Gastronomy is the art and science of good eating. Within the context of current studies however it has a broader definition. It covers the study of, and the development of understanding of, the origins of food traditions (and this includes all types of beverages) within social, economic and geographical contexts.

Food is central to daily life, tradition, culture and civilization. It also is about life skills and citizenship, being as much concerned with nutrition, food hygiene and health promotion as it is with the pleasures of eating and drinking.

The subject of gastronomy has appeared throughout all hospitality courses and more recently is receiving a boost through the development of HNDs, higher education diplomas and undergraduate degrees in culinary arts. The importance of culinary arts is also recognized in the National Vocational Qualifications (and SVQs) up to level 4. In addition the subject is now becoming a legitimate focus for postgraduate studies.

The renewed interest in gastronomy, and related subjects, as a legitimate topic for research, necessitates the use of more academically sound approaches. There is a need for a range of new texts, which, although more narrow in their coverage, can provide sound logical structures, and well-researched information, which will guide those wishing to broaden their knowledge of the subject. This text attempts to meet some of these needs.

This book aims to provide a structured approach and supporting information for those wanting to develop their knowledge and understanding of European gastronomy at the beginning of the 21st century. The book considers the social, economic and geographical influences on the development of gastronomy within Europe. It is designed to meet the needs of students and practitioners who want to acquire underpinning knowledge and skills at undergraduate degree levels 2 and 3, NVQ level 4, HCIMA Professional Diploma and the City and Guilds Higher Diploma. It is also designed to provide a sound foundation and a framework on which to extend further studies.

The content of the book is based on research carried out from 1985 at The Scottish Hotel School. The focus of the book is specifically on European gastronomy in order to allow for a depth of coverage. A particular feature of the book is the inclusion of the views and profiles of some key contributors to the development of gastronomy for the 21st century and it offers an insight into the business of managing some of the world's most prestigious destination restaurants. The text also considers traditional and modern influences on gastronomy including restaurant design and wine and food harmony.

The book is structured into five chapters. Each chapter has an aim, and the objectives that might be achieved through study are also identified. A summary is provided at the end of each chapter. The chapters are then supported by a range of other material. A bibliography is given which includes both references made in the text as well as a listing of sources that have been consulted. There is a glossary of terms and also two appendices: the people mentioned in the text are identified in Appendix A and Appendix B gives a listing of trade, professional and gastronomic contacts.

Chapter 1 provides the foundation for the subject and for the book. The status of gastronomy in society is discussed as well as considering how gastronomic knowledge is disseminated. In section 1.5 various approaches to the study of gastronomy are outlined and section 1.6 contains an identification and description of the essential skills, including organoleptic skills, which are necessary for the exploration of gastronomy. Finally, although there is a word of caution about sensible eating and drinking, there is also encouragement for the explorative endeavour.

Chapter 2 provides a review of the historical gastronomic development within Europe and examines the contribution of some of the founding fathers of gastronomy. Chapter 3 considers the gastronomic experience of modern Europe. It extends the foundations laid in Chapters 1 and 2, and also focuses on contemporary developments including design, menu and beverage list construction, food and wine harmony, the advance of concept and fusion cuisines and also considers the importance, in gastronomy, of symbols, signs and senses. Chapter 4 focuses on profiles of those who have laid the foundations of modern gastronomy, together with some of the key contemporary contributors to the development of modern cuisine and gastronomy – the potential coverage of others being limited only by the space available and the opportunities of access to information.

Chapter 5 looks initially at influences on cuisine and gastronomic exploration into the 21st century. The status of chefs in society is examined, and design, vision and leadership are explored. The book then ends, in Chapter 5, with consideration of the emergence of the inter-relationship between gastronomy and philosophy. It is clear that the key contributors to the development of cuisine and tradition over the years have not been cooks alone. Geographic location, economic development and social change have all had impacts on gastronomic developments. In addition though it is those individuals who observe, think and have something to say about food who have contributed the most to the development of European gastronomic culture. These people have been more than gastronomes. They are also philosophers and again more than that. The literature combines these characteristics and qualities and provides the term of gastrosophers, which recognizes the fusion of all of them, and through that the recognition of gastrosophy as the new science.

The subject of gastronomy is rich in history and provides a wide range of memorable experiences. These experiences are the rewards for those who are curious and, with genuinely open minds, are seeking learning and appreciation. These experiences also, together with the research associated with them, lead to better understanding and to a never-ending wonderment. This book is about contributing to this enduring fascination.

Cailein Gillespie
2001

Acknowledgements

The preparation of this text has drawn upon a variety of research and experience. I would like to express my grateful thanks to all the organizations and individuals who gave so much assistance and support.

I would like to sincerely thank John Cousins, Author, Consultant and Director, The Food and Beverage Training Company, London, for being the contributing editor of this text. I am indebted to John for his friendship and for his capacity to ignite, sustain and champion similar academic interests in the sphere of hospitality and in food and beverage in particular. The partnership has been educative, productive and synergistic and if a modicum of our enthusiasm for this fertile subject sparks interest in the readers we will have fulfilled one of our ambitions in creating this text.

In particular we would also like to thank: Mr Matthew Alexander, Food and Beverage Manager, The Scottish Hotel School, University of Strathclyde in Glasgow; Mr Andy Anderson, Vice President and Partner, Sales and Business Development, Foresthills Hotels and Resorts, for an interview in July (2000); Professor Tom Baum, Head of Department, The Scottish Hotel School, for practical support and academic freedom during the production of this book; Mr Derek Bulmer, Editor, Michelin Travel Publications; Nina Colls, Communications Manager, Mandarin Oriental Hyde Park, London, for permission to use all of the images displayed on the cover of this book and for other images inside the book; Richard Congreve, I.S. (Information Systems) Manager, Scotland, Justerini and Brooks Edinburgh; Mr Paul Farrell, Assistant Food and Beverage Manager, The Scottish Hotel School; Mr Georg Fong, Vice President of Engineering and Construction and Partner, Foresthills Hotels and Resorts, Dallas, for an interview in July (2000); Malcolm Gee, Subject Head, Hospitality Operations, Thames Valley University; Mr Michael Hughes, Chef, The Scottish Hotel School; Hans Matthias Kann, Executive Assistant Manager, Food and Beverage, Oberoi Hotels Mumbai, for a brainstorming session in 1999; Liam Lambert, Director and General Manager, Mandarin Oriental Hyde Park, London; Mr Atef Mankarios, Chairman and Chief Executive, Foresthills Hotels and Resorts, Dallas, for an interview in July (2000); Gisela Moohan, Librarian-in-charge, Goethe-Institut, Glasgow; personnel in the Goethe-Institut München for kindly tracking down vital information; Margaret Mary Moran, Careers Service, The

University of Strathclyde; Mr Marco Rosetti (student), The Scottish Hotel School; Valerie Salis-Samaden (student), The Scottish Hotel School; Jean Finlayson, Secretary, The Scottish Hotel School, for typing the original manuscript; Caroline Whitlock, P.A. to Anton Mosimann, Mosimann's, London; Mr John Winkler, Publisher, The Hospitality Review, Threshold Press Ltd, for allowing excerpts to be printed from *Hospitality Review*, July 2000 issue, 'Anton Mosimann: from cook to chef to businessman' by C. Gillespie; for also kindly allowing excerpts from, *Hospitality Review*, April 2000 issue, 'Symbol, sign and senses: a challenge to traditional market communication', by C. Gillespie and A. Morrison; and a special thank you to Professor Roy C. Wood, Professor of Hospitality Management, The Scottish Hotel School, for his inspirational and supportive assistance in supervising the initial research which provided the foundation for this work.

And finally my very special thanks and appreciation go to the people without whom some of the thinking within this book, and the majority of the content of Chapter 4, would never have been possible. These are the modern culinary masters who gave of their time, provided information which enabled their profiles to be written and also provided copies of, and gave permission for the inclusion of, examples of their menus and photographs. Although profiled in Chapter 4, and having their summarized details given in Appendix A, it would be wrong of me not to mention them again here. These very special people are: Raymond Blanc, Paul Bocuse, Michel Guérard, Paul, Mark and Jean Pierre Haeberlin, Marc Meneau, Anton Mosimann, Dieter Müller, Dominique Nahmias (Olympe Versini), Pierre Troisgros, Roger Vergé and Eckart Witzigmann.

CHAPTER 1

Introducing gastronomy

This chapter aims to set the scene for the rest of the text.

This chapter is intended to help you to:

- develop a working definition of gastronomy
- explore the breadth of the subject
- determine the gastronomic way of living
- identify both amateur and professional approaches to gastronomy
- identify the major means by which gastronomic knowledge is disseminated
- determine what can be learned from gastronomy
- consider a range of possible approaches to the study of gastronomy
- identify and develop the essential skills, including organoleptic skills, necessary for the systematic study of gastronomy from a variety of perspectives.

1.1 What is gastronomy?

Gastronomy is not easy to define, as can be seen from the number of authors who have declined to attempt definition. Gastronomy can often be ill defined. There are difficulties in applying the term and consequently there are difficulties in the application of gastronomic values to the alimentary experiences and also to the hospitality industry in general. There is also confusion caused by pseudo gastronomy (or food and wine snobbism). So as a starting point for this book, gastronomy is defined as *the art, or science, of good eating*.

An intention of this book is to present a collection of contemporary practices in cuisine and gastronomy. One important aspect is to pose various questions about gastronomy. The key question is about the gifts of gastronomy. Is the principal gift simply a quality eating experience? If gastronomy is to be seen as more than this then we also need to explore:

- what comprises the gastronomic experience and way of living;
- who are the gourmets and gastronomes, and from what backgrounds and professions do they come;
- who are the driving forces behind gastronomy, and what is it that motivates them; and also,
- what can be learned from them?

A simple and easily manageable explanation of gastronomy is that it is concerned with the enjoyment of food and beverages. In this case, it is nearly everybody's subject! We all know what we enjoy, and we would like to think we understand why we enjoy a given food or drink. These individual gastronomic values are generally based on many foundations, for example cultural, geographical, social and alimentary socialization. Learning goes on unconsciously, though cultural assumptions are being made about what is good to eat and drink.

Gastronomy is for many individuals, a hypothetical construct. That is, one where the existence of it is merely inferred, and for which unambiguous objective evidence is not fully available. However there are many critical theoretical entities that are hypothetical constructs. In the case of gastronomy it is not currently a clearly defined subject with a beginning, middle and end. Indeed there is a great deal of overlap with many other subjects, callings, professions and trades. To illustrate this, Table 1.1 is an attempt to identify examples of these.

This book exploits the lack of definition, and strict adherence to classical discipline, and sets out areas, but not boundaries, involved in the subject. This eclecticism forms part of the total enjoyment, which can be obtained when gourmets and gastronomes, armed with their cognitive catholicism, allow themselves free rein across these disciplines.

A useful working definition of gastronomy can be *the study of food*. In most uses of the word gastronomy, food is the pre-eminently held factor. However, for the gourmet and gastronome, it essentially requires a broader definition: this is the enjoyment of good food and good beverage, in good company. It is also evident that there appears to be a dichotomy as there is both an amateur and a professional gastronomer. This is explored throughout this book and is specifically examined in Chapter 5.

Gastronomy can be subdivided into four main areas (Harrison, 1982). These are:

1 practical gastronomy

2 theoretical gastronomy

3 technical gastronomy

4 food gastronomy.

Table 1.1 Gastronomy can overlap with differing subjects, callings, professions and trades

Title	Author	Date
Anthropology	Arnott, Farb and Armagelos	1975, 1980
Archaeology	Tannahill	1973
Biology	Kracknell and Nobis	1985
Baker	Hanneman	1981
Butcher	Leto and Bode	1985
Brewer	Jackson	1992
Caterer	Kracknell, Kaufman and Nobis	2000
Chef	Kracknell, Kaufman and Nobis	2000
Cookery	Ceserani, Kinton and Foskett	1999
Commodities	Davis	1983
Confectioner	Lodge	1992
Consumer Studies	Cannon and Walker	1984
Dietician	Montignac	1989
Distiller	Cooper	1983
Economics	Medlik	1989
Farmer	McGee	1991
Finance	Kotas	1986
Florist	Titterington	1987
Geography	Hunter	1973
Herbalist	Titterington	1987
History	Mennell, Tannahill	1985, 1973
Horticulturalist	Arcier, Titterington	1990, 1987
Hospitality	Lashley and Morrsion	2000
Management	Cousins, Foskett and Gillespie	2001
Marketing	Buttle	1996
Medicine	Hinchcliff and Montague	1988
Nutrition	Balmforth	1992
Oenology	Robinson, Johnson	1999, 1990
Patisserie	Nicolello and Dinsdale	1991
Psychology	Weinburg	1972
Philosophy	Brillat Savarin, Telfer	1899, 1996
Physiology	Ramanumurthy	1969
Politics	Mitchell	1975
Scientist	McGee	1991
Service	Lillicrap, Cousins and Smith	1998
Sociology	Menell, Murcott and van Otterloo	1992
Sommelier	Durkan and Cousins	1995
Vintner	Peynaud	1996

Practical gastronomy

Practical gastronomy is concerned with the practice and study of the preparation, production and service of the various foods and beverages, from countries around the world, i.e. the cuisines. Practical gastronomy then has to do with the techniques and standards involved in the conversion of raw produce into aesthetic, nationally, regionally and culturally specific edible products. Practical gastronomers comprise chefs and all guest contact personnel including food service staff, sommeliers, trancheurs (carvers), and chefs-de-rang (station waiters).

The conversion of foods and beverages into complete dishes, menus and accompanying drinks as used in various countries, is one of practical gastronomy's specialist areas. It is also an area where the chef and the food and beverage professional are supremely active.

Theoretical gastronomy

Theoretical gastronomy supports practical gastronomy. It is concerned with a systems and process approach, focused on recipes, cookery books and other writing. It records various procedures that must be carried out in order to maximize success. Theoretical planning for the physical processes individuals have to go through, when formulating and preparing events, menus, dishes and drinks, are all part of the business concern of theoretical gastronomy.

Theoretical gastronomy is the source of creativity that has inspired and upheld the classical and national dishes of the world for centuries. This again is the field for chefs and other food and beverage professionals, who are combining their practical abilities, with theoretical input in order to maximize learning and efficiency.

Technical gastronomy

Technical gastronomy brings rigour and underpins practical gastronomy. It is much more than the mere knowledge of specifications for plant and machinery, and how they can effect production and service (spatial engineering). It looks at the systematic evaluation of anything in the gastronomic field that demands appraisal. It is also much more than the multiplication of recipes to achieve bulk preparation for any given event, with its subsequent subdivision into portions. It is a link between the small-scale operation and mass manufacture.

Menu engineering, which is defined as a sales mix analysis view, also advances this approach (Kasavana and Smith, 1982) and therefore forms part of the technical approach in gastronomy. It is an example of one of the tools, which can be utilized to ensure success, where observing, recording and analysing the performance of a number of variables can be used to maximize potential.

Technical gastronomy is also about the evaluation of convenience foods, new and evolutionary plant, newer production methods like *sous vide*, and the skills and equipment required to place these into production and safely monitor performance of them over trial periods. The technical side also assesses the validity of specific foods to given organizations. Research and development technicians, development chefs and food scientists, and operational specialists work in this area. Consultant chefs also specialize here, as do group chef executives.

Food gastronomy

Food gastronomy is concerned with food and beverages and their genesis. Fundamentally, the role of wine, and other beverages, in relation to food is to harmonize, in order to maximize the enjoyment to be had from both: although wine can also be more readily appreciated by itself. Traditional styles of catering necessitate a wide variety of foodstuffs in their production. The greater the complexity employed in the menu, the greater the likely number of commodities will be necessitated. Those working with foodstuffs and beverages require up-to-date product knowledge and continual learning, for food products and beverages change over time and with the seasons. Actively assessing demand, quality and storage considerations, even for all preserved foods such as dried goods and frozen food, will maximize return. Time is also a prime consideration in food gastronomy. As Anthony Worrall Thompson (1991) noted: 'So many chefs come out of full-time chefs' colleges and they just haven't got a clue about the speed of work or service. They are technically correct and know how to carve a chicken or cut through some meat, but they can't get used to the pace.'

Gastronomy, then, comprises the study and appreciation of all food and beverages. It can involve detailed knowledge of some of the well-known national dishes and beverages of the major countries of the world. It is also very possible to be a gourmet or a gastronome solely through appreciation.

Gastronomy provides a platform for an understanding of how food' and beverage resources are used in a particular situation. Through gastronomy it is possible to build a picture of the similarities of approach used in various countries and cultures in terms of their foods and beverages. What may be also important however, is the contrasting of approaches in the use of the same or similar foods and beverages in different countries.

Gastronomy is about the recognition of a variety of factors relevant to the foods and beverages eaten and consumed by a group, in a locality, region or even a nation. The study of gastronomy also involves a study of the factors impinging upon the delectation of food and how such delectation can be maximized. Gastronomy is also an examination of the terms 'good food' and 'good wine' (or other beverages), and in 'whose terms'. If in terms of the provider, what are the measures used in assessing what will be eaten? In terms of the consumer, then the question of level of appreciation, quality, ease of service and price need to be considered.

Gastronomy is also concerned with the quality of wine and all other beverages, and the way in which the totality of food and wine, i.e. the meal as a whole, complements the situation and those at the table. Accepting that the quality of the food and beverages is all-important, then gastronomy is concerned with the assessment and improvement of that quality in the context of the occasion.

Gastronomy is a subject without a clearly defined boundary. It is a field with extending horizons open to all interested parties, providers and consumers. From the consumer's point of view gastronomy is something that is generally seen to apply to the wealthy customer in the restaurant, and has focused primarily on the ability of consumers to enjoy the meal. Though economic elements are very apparent in the generally held concept that all gourmets and gastronomes must be well off, this is not necessarily the case. By truly recognizing and appreciating good food and beverage in good company, or by carefully developing their own personal diet, in a gastronomic sense, individuals can also consider themselves as having a gastronomic approach to living.

1.2 The status of gastronomy in society

Gastronomy and the development of a gastronomic culture have traditionally been of limited interest to the majority of individuals. The transmission of gastronomic culture has, to a large extent, been confined to, associated with, and fostered by a small but socially prominent élite. This élite has banded together in many European countries to promote eating as a social activity, which cultivates refined taste in the pleasures of the table. Gastronomy as an activity is highly stratified, and takes the form of a hierarchy headed by gastronomes, who are much more than gourmets, for gastronomes have a distinctive social role. In general they are arbiters of taste and also theorists of the social role of food and eating, and as Mennell (1985) succinctly stated, they are usually though not always 'propagandist concerning culinary taste'.

A problem then exists in that gastronomes have often been perceived as being élitist. It can be a strongly held belief, which many gastronomic organizations do little to refute, and much to reinforce. It is that many people do not understand what gastronomy is about, save the fact that those who are pronouncing on that which is gastronomic clearly have the ability to pay what is viewed by many as inflated prices for food and beverages.

Any association that the term gastronomy may have had with everyday food has been obscured. To some extent this process has been accelerated by the decline of domestic cooking and through less time being spent in the kitchen by modern families, in comparison with the past. Convenience foods have taken precedence over the fresh product. Understanding of the alimentative, psychological and cultural value of the family meal is potentially being lost. More individuals are tending to live in non-family groupings or on their own and do not always eat a nutritionally conceived diet.

If an appreciation of individual ingredients, not to mention food combining in the diet, is not accepted at such a basic level, it is hardly surprising that the majority of the population understand gastronomy as being concerned with élite forms of dining. For many, gastronomy is also viewed as potentially sinful. In Britain there is still a touch of Puritanism which makes it wrong to be seen indulging in the gastronomic. Such views are reinforced by gastronomic organizations. Membership of the largest academies and guilds is limited to those with capital, to prominent public figures, and to those who can do something for the organization or its membership. Often where the title gastronomic is up-front, an 'old boy' regime is also in force. Events are used principally for networking and for conferring cachet on a visible élite, since membership is next to impossible for those who may possess limited funds and/or are not among the 'in' crowd able to present the organization in a good light externally.

At the same time as gastronomy is élitist, there has also been, paradoxically, a dilution and devaluation of many of the images associated with it. This can be seen in the context of change in the meaning of the word gourmet. The word 'gourmet' (precisely a noun) has, over the last decade or so, become adjectival. In this new formation it is mainly used to falsely confer some distinction or exoticism on foods and food products not normally associated with traditional gastronomic views, but which have acquired some gastronomic legitimacy.

The contemporary status of gastronomy in society, then, is relative. It no longer applies purely to the classically inspired French *répertoire* of dishes, or those of other nationalities, nor does it adhere to traditional and hierarchically stratified foodstuffs. Thus there are gourmet soups, biscuits and cookies, and gourmet ice-cream (Häagen-Dazs for example). Gourmet Cheddar with pizza herbs, gourmet Cheddar with onions and chive, and many more exist, on the premise that the use of the term will confer some kind of distinction to the product. There is a craze for gourmet foods, which confer cachet. This is taking a similar path as the trend for foodie one-upmanship, which took hold of Europe's favoured restaurants in the mid to late 1970–80s, as part of the rise of nouvelle cuisine. If gastronomy has done one important thing in contemporary times, it has been to popularize itself, in a manner generally unsuited to most ordinary people.

Accepted standards of what gastronomy comprises have never been established, even within the gastronomic élite. Determining what areas within the field are fit for study and research; what is right to eat and drink at a gastronomic event and what tastes good, varies with specialism, environment, culture and subculture, as well as from one gastronomic organization to another (some gastronomic organizations have as their foci one particular foodstuff or range of foodstuffs), and individual to individual.

Anton Mosimann does not think that gastronomes are a dying breed. He says 'There are still many people who believe in the product and believe in the best, who want to give pleasure to other people, who are optimistic about what they are doing, and are motivated as I am. Everyday I get up I can't wait to get to work, I feel very much ready to go, and that of course is exactly what is important in our business.'

Michel Bourdin is, however, more sceptical, feeling that gastronomes who frequent places of quality are a dying breed, in the sense that they fail to recognize themselves as connoisseurs. 'There is more of a tendency today for people to speak what they read rather than speak what they think. If there is a lack of a dedicated literature for those who might individually consider themselves to be connoisseurs, they are much less likely to attempt to express those feelings.'

Although today's clientele are much more widely travelled through exposure to other countries' foods, restaurants and hotels, cuisine is constantly being shaped and transformed through such leverage as: the availability of ingredients, customer demands, chefs' experimentation, stimulation from various media etc., but there is still a degree of caution from some individuals as to whether it is 'right' to be openly viewed as a connoisseur of food or wine.

1.3 Major means by which gastronomic knowledge is disseminated

Gastronomers are arbiters of taste, making pronouncements on what might be regarded as gastronomic. The gastronomes are, and have been, figures like Egon Ronay, Jean Valby, Robert Baty, Dr Auguste Becart, Michel Genin, Raphael Anson, Marcel Boulestin, Curnonsky, Pierre Androuet, Jean Anthelme Brillat-Savarin, and Alexandre Balthazar Laurent Grimod de la Reynière.

The gourmet is someone who is an interested and learned participant, a connoisseur of table delicacies. However, there are many more gourmets and gourmet organizations than there are gastronomes, and the spread of gastronomy in society is carried on more by the gourmet and the epicurean organizations.

If the gourmet and epicurean organizations are one of the major media of transmission, their inclusion obviously implies exclusion, and there are many individuals who do not join gastronomic organizations, for a multiplicity of reasons, but who are genuinely interested in cuisine. Reasons vary. Two of the main reasons offered are the high cost, and geographical location. Often the gastronomic events take place in out of the way places, or in large metro cities, which imply additional costs in transportation and accommodation. This is where the importance of the gourmet and epicurean organizations lie, for they are often more regionalized. It is also possible to find organizations like La Confrerie de la Chaîne des Rôtisseurs, which operates in 118 countries but have regional centres of operation with regional members linked to a national body. In the main, however, gastronomic knowledge is disseminated, mainly to the middle and upper socioeconomic groups, by various forms of written and visual media.

Many of today's food and wine lovers do not really see the need for intellectualization and classicalism, and to a great degree they are right. Their role is the enjoyment of good food and good beverages in good company. However, there are also those with a great desire for intellectualization and knowledge of classical and other cuisines: these are the professional gastronomers. Michel Bourdin thinks, 'the profession is like a pyramid of excellence'. He suggests that excellence comes from the top, and so if the chef is very good and very mature then it will work well, but if the chef is not mature enough, or not good enough, it is then impossible to get people of a certain calibre to work with them. 'It could in fact lead to the blind leading the blind and gastronomic knowledge failing to be passed further down the pyramid and onward to guests.' He also suggests that stages can't be jumped. 'Very excellent chefs and lousy chefs can be forty years of age. Chefs can also go either way at age twenty or twenty-five. This is a vital age, for sometimes chefs feel they know everything at this age but later know that they do not.' He does not suggest to any chef that they should be a head chef before they have maturity. He defines a chef as 'someone who has people not working under them, but for them'.

He proposes three stages:

- Stage 1 others work under you.

- Stage 2 others work with you.

- Stage 3, the optimum, being a chef of a great place and the work is as much for you as for the place.

He suggests that it is in this last stage when gastronomic knowledge will be really effectively disseminated.

Anton Mosimann believes it to be important that major chefs should have an international outlook. He says,

> I personally do a lot of travelling, I do a lot of promotions, I do a lot of television work overseas, and it brings the world together. It is experience. I come back with ideas all the time, which then I can use in London, or Switzerland, use for my young people again, so everything becomes more international. If you stay in your own little home kitchen, then you get blinkered somehow, so I think international travel and experiences are vital. I would recommend any chef to travel internationally; it is another way in which gastronomy is disseminated.

The media

In the UK up until the mid 1980s television programmes about food and beverages were produced in static TV studios and were on the whole unimaginative. There was, however, to be an abrupt transformation in this type of programming: characters like Delia Smith, Anton Mosimann, Raymond Blanc, Antonnio Carluccio and Rick Stein (who took a degree in English from Oxford and clearly demonstrated the new place within the industry for individuals with improved educational/academic qualifications) made food more than a mere distraction. It became educational as well as entertaining and presented its relationship with the wider tourism industry. These groundbreaking individuals used enticing narration, energy and enthusiasm to sell their message. The programmes also tended to have a more professional look and feel to them and had skilled camera work, which has yet to be bettered in today's programming of food and beverage. Their work not only led to a dissemination of gastronomic sensibilities, it also led to the development of mass medium of gastronomic transmission.

Food writers and the press have also been responsible to a large extent for the transmission of popular gastronomic values in society with figures like Sir Clement Freud, Anne Willan,

Paul Levy, Claudia Roden, Madhur Jaffrey, Jancis Robinson, Sophie Grigson, the Scotto sisters, Craig Brown, and in the past, Elizabeth David and Jane Grigson.

Food journalism, food writing, food and beverage photography and food and beverage television have blossomed. In tandem, lexivisual food and beverage publications, food stylists and picture editors, food-related publishing and publishers are all seeking to devote sections or whole books, magazines, colour supplements and papers to the topic, in what has become an exciting new dimension in the modern life style.

Print media, and television are a major part of everyday life and keep people acquainted with new developments. As mass media of gastronomic influence and transmission they have been able to change the expectations of the dining public and hotel guests in both positive and negative ways.

Television has enhanced and revolutionized communications as much as writing and printing did in its day, and yet television has in point taken us right back to the earlier oral tradition, in which it is the spoken word that determines what is expressed. Some chefs have received so much attention that their names have become instantly recognizable in the home. The elevation of the chef has attracted gifted people to the industry, but it has also attracted individuals whose pre-eminence bears little or no resemblance to the art or science of professional cookery, but who can woo an audience by virtue of their skill as entertainers.

There is currently a wealth of gourmet, gastronomic and other multifarious food and beverage stimuli to be drawn from. Televisually, the gourmet and gastronome can have as passionate an interest in food and beverage away from the hospitality scene, muted by a detached involvement with some of them becoming, in effect, the armchair chef or gastronomic voyeur. In these cases the television chef might be identified as gastronomic pornographer, inspiring and inflaming passions, which are only satiated by a quick trip to the kitchen or delicatessen. Television programming it appears, offering a window onto gastronomic culture, has still to peak in the early part of the new century.

Most recently it has been considered by some that it is not so much the 'star chef' but kitchen envy, which draws the television audiences to food programmes. Here the star chef presides over generally oversized, uncluttered and glamorous kitchens, designed to inspire and cook in, even though a good percentage of viewers may never attempt to replicate the dishes on display.

Michel Bourdin suggests that

> media chefs appear to be part of the current evolution of the chef, but it's like getting a Michelin star. You don't work towards it, you just do your job properly and you are selected as a star Michelin. In the media you do your job and then if people like what you are doing you become a media chef. But you should not work to become a media chef, you are just a chef, and you should work for your guests. If chefs want to be media stars they should go into music or be a singer or into show business but not attempt to be a chef. All the great chefs I have known, the ones who are still alive are very modest people, very much hands-on, because they realize that the profession is stronger than the individual. In music it is easy because of all the help you get from impresarios and sound systems help you do one performance in a day, but we have five or more performances to do well in a day. It is difficult. I would not suggest that it was a help to be a media chef. If you become a media chef it is only after a certain time in your career but be a chef first and then hopefully if you have a possibility to become more of a media personality, take a chance but don't aim to be a media chef – just be a very good chef.

Bourdin feels that the whole TV cooks and chefs' bandwagon has become too much like a circus. He admits that it has helped the profession to become known but reckons that some housewives can do better than the TV chefs and, at the end of the day it could make a fool of the chef. Bourdin feels that it is entertainment: 'you can sit down and switch off, we don't really learn much about the profession of the chef from these programmes'. Cookery programmes could be treated differently. They could be, according to Bourdin, 'more inspirational'. Very few programmes show the chef as an artist and many more show circus acts. He doesn't see why the chef should not be a star, as long as he or she does not believe too much in it. Bourdin also believes that the media has changed the expectation of guests: 'It has pushed people to eat out more often and it has made people realize that you can have a good time out without the strain of having to do it yourself. It takes a lot to push people to eat out and this is the greatest thing that the star chefs have done.'

Guides

Guides to eating establishments fall into three basic categories:

1 Guides that provide factual information and classify establishments with reference to a set of criteria, for example how many bathrooms, when the restaurant is open etc. These include:

- The *Automobile Association Members' Handbook*
- The *Royal Automobile Club Guide*
- Hotels and Restaurants in Britain
- Tourist Board guides

All of these organizations also award stars or crowns. Generally, the more stars/crowns awarded, the more facilities there are. However, it should be remembered that many establishments are not included in these guides; lack of recognition does not mean that they are less good.

2 Guides that give some evaluative measure. These include:

- *The Egon Ronay Hotel and Restaurant Guide*
- The Good Food Guide
- The Michelin Guide
- A series of *Where to Eat In* ... publications, e.g. 'London', are available from Tourist Board offices
- A range of publications, including newspapers, magazines and the trade press.

3 Guides that are linked to some marketing initiative (although the rules governing entries in these guides ensure some measure of consistency among those included). These include:

- Prestige Hotels
- Relais and Château
- Les Routiers
- Derek Johansen's Guide.

Guides and recommendations may be of use in choosing where to eat, but there is nothing like *personal experience*. Today's diner is confronted with a wealth of choice; increased experience will lead to greater knowledge and to the ability to read the signs of a good or poor establishment. The latter will always be a personal distinction and depend as much on one's own experience as on the needs one has at the time.

Potentially the most important serious and accurate 'guide', especially for restaurants and chefs, and for the transmission of gastronomy, has been the Michelin. The Michelin guide had been the *vade mecum* of French travellers for over a century. The physical looks of the guide changed little since the first edition was given free at all French petrol stations in 1900. The new millennium however saw a crucial and incisive change: after using symbols for 100 years, the 'Red Guide' now adds concise narration to benefit its readers. The guide also presented a new cover consistent with Michelin's heritage to inaugurate the Red Guide brand. The Red Guide series includes twelve titles, nine of which are country guides: France, Italy, Germany, Spain/Portugal, Benelux, Switzerland, Great Britain/Ireland, Portugal, and Ireland. Two are city guides – Paris and London – and there is one guide for Europe.

The Michelin, which works for the run-of-the-mill diner, as well as the foodie, the gourmet and the gastronome, sells approximately 750,000 guides annually. This is no mean feat when you look at a 21st century middle class which has become highly sophisticated with the aid of modern chefs, gourmets and gastronomes, and the rise of assorted media.

The Michelin guide rarely gives interviews, and neither accepts advertising nor advertises; it has been this way for more than three-quarters of a century. Analogies at one point were made between Michelin's operations from 1900 onwards and medieval monks: Michelin guide inspectors travel throughout their area of responsibility incognito, paralleling the early monks. It was they who were most knowledgeable about food, beverages, including liqueurs, wines, beers and the provision of hospitality. In countless ways much of our history and understanding of food would have been lost without the monastic tradition. The need for journeying with business or pilgrimage as prime concern gave rise to the need for hospitality along the way, and the monasteries adequately provided this service.

A comparison between the Michelin stars in France in 1992, compared with the start of the new millennium is as follows:

FRANCE	1992	2000
★★★	19	22
★★	87	70
★	495	407
Total stars	601	499

This shows the fluidity of movement and is testament to the independence of the guide inspectors, who demand high standards of excellence. Integrity rests on this independence, as professional inspectors carry out their duties incognito and pay all of their bills. Guiding precepts for inspectors are: 'guidance not orders' and 'information not misrepresentation'. This allows for free and informed decisions based on the traveller/diner's own needs and desires. A cardinal rule of inspectors is to work anonymously and to draw their own conclusions, in this way they can embody the average traveller and assess free of influence, a hotel's or restaurant's service. The profession of Michelin guide inspector (keystone of the famous Michelin star rating system) emerged between the two world wars. They often have a background in the hotel and restaurant industry as well as unquestionable interest in board and lodging. In addition there is the necessary palate and highly developed sense of observation. Inspectors travel some 25,000–30,000 kilometres per annum. This is because the inspectors experience every property before adding or taking away a star. The inspector's report is analysed over possibly several in-house meetings, with perhaps further visits to a property. In essence a property can be visited from once to four or even five times in the year.

Table 1.2 Stars over Europe at the start of the new millennium

Country	★★★	★★	★	Total stars per country
France	22	70	407	499
Italy	3	17	197	217
Germany	4	16	181	201
Spain and Portugal	3	8	87	98
Benelux	3	23	124	150
Switzerland	2	9	87	98
Great Britain/Ireland	1	12	86	99
Main cities Europe				
Austria		2	8	10
Denmark		1	5	6
Greece			1	1
Norway		1	3	4
Sweden		1	8	9
Grand totals	38	160	1194	1392

Source: Michelin Red Guide

It can be expected that in one-star restaurants, guests will be served cuisine of high quality. Two-star restaurants are expected to possess well-researched dishes, a good wine selection, and an excellent standard of sophisticated service. The third star can to many seem an Olympian feat since restaurateurs do not really know what they are trying to beat, as there are no published standards. In general the restaurants wishing three-star status must serve truly exceptional cuisine, and be worthy of a special journey.

Bernard Naegellen, long-term Director of Red Guides, has in the past stated: 'there has to be a personality behind the food that you can feel'. For example, at Bocuse, that personality would come from Paul Bocuse himself, and would be tangible in the house style and presentation of the food. At Auberge de l'Ill at Illhausern it would be through father-and-son chefs Paul and Mark, and Paul's brother Jean Pierre, who heads the front of house operation. At Les Prés d'Eugénie it is discernible through Michel Guérard and his wife, Christine.

Problems face the guides, like any other organization. Taking the Michelin Red Guide as an example, although considered by many to be a travellers' bible, many others see it as being too conservative, an example being that Bernard Naegellen to this day does not acknowledge the existence of nouvelle cuisine.

The major independents among guides sold in France are the Michelin and the Gault Millau, *The Good Hotel Guide* and *Le Bottin Gourmand*. Le Bottin's problem is that it is only issued in French; it is however gaining ground within France. Bottin's listing with comments on hotels and restaurants is covered by Departement and uses a star rating system of one to four for restaurants and keys for hotels. *The Good Hotel Guide*'s section on France focuses understandably only on hotels, and therefore a second purchase would be necessitated to cover restaurants. It also uses the quotes of tourists and travellers but with no grading.

The *Guide Gault Millau* picks out rising stars and talent quicker than does Michelin, but in many ways this in itself can be viewed as a risky business since shooting stars can all too easily burn up before they reach their zenith. Gault Millau uses symbols like Michelin, one

Table 1.3 Generic listing of what may be looked for when assessing a restaurant

Aspect	Includes
Linguistic and non-linguistic evaluation	Reservation, welcome/reception demeanour, and body language
Interior design, and décor evaluation	Comfort, lighting, decorative accessories, colour, planning and layout, materials, furnishings, function, signage and graphics
Sensoric evaluation	Taste, colour, texture, mouth-feel, temperature and presentation of menu, wine and other beverages, freshness
Environmental performance evaluation	Interior environment, acoustics, ventilation, extraction, heating, toilet facilities
Impression management	First impressions/first 5 minutes, where the restaurant excels, if at all
The information and selling routine	Alternatives, empathetic merchandising, embellishments
Technical evaluation	Cooking, seasonality, ingredients, and quality, skill in purchasing, skill/dexterity, the wine and beverage lists, food service, time considerations, malpractices, service personnel performance, attention to detail
The bill and concluding routine	Accuracy, clarity, discretion, departure demeanour, and body language, holistic impression

to four toques (chefs hats), plus a grading of one to twenty for restaurants and one to five towers for hotels. Inclusion in this guide is generally favourable, it is interesting to read and is chatty in approach, and does have English translations.

Michelin having in many cases been perceived to be slow to award, has also been criticized for being slow to take away. Another problem facing all of the guides is that they can ill afford to alienate or create too great a breach between the restaurant fraternity and the guide's own judgements. The guides must also strive to maintain their credibility in the market place. In fairness to Michelin one should say that the inspectors are not visiting restaurants for chefs, gastronomes and beverage critics alone, for this group tend to receive specialist treatment. Michelin are reflecting what happens the rest of the time, with ordinary eaters, who are the bulk of the trade. Moreover, establishments cannot rely on the vagaries of Michelin or the other guides and the food critics to bring success, for in many cases it can do the opposite and instil in the public eye the idea of expense, formality, élitism, exaggerated expectation and unease.

Public relations

Some top chefs become media personalities and generate press attention. Those focused upon in this book certainly have followed this route. The reason for this is founded in their ultimate newsworthiness. Success can be determined in many ways but principally by the positive guest and public relations strategies they employ (in many cases these are contrived with the assistance of guest and public relations personnel). For the top chefs, public relations play an essential role. It is they who disseminate information to the specific media the chef wishes to reach in order to maintain a recognizable profile.

Issuing press releases, advertising, promotional trips, photo opportunities, lecture tours, publishing, in-store book signings, giving endorsements, television and radio appearances and courting a willing press, are catalysts for promoting a chef's businesses to a specific public, providing opportunities to promote, inspire, persuade, inform, educate and hopefully exceed expectations, but ultimately increasing revenue. This cannot be executed in a blinkered fashion, for chefs deal with a complex product, tied indispensably to the chefs themselves, and requiring the strategic positioning of information and the satisfying of positive communication goals.

Seducing domestic and international diners with alluring flavour combinations and sensations, and to an increasing extent, to identifiably inspired concept cuisines linked to specific individuals, has generated dedicated media interest. However, the chef who has enthusiasm for food, and has an ability to explain what they are aiming for and how to achieve it, can doubly milk the situation by writing a book dealing with the various aspects of their particular concept cuisine.

The idea of writing about food is an ancient one, which was revived by the French subscription to the view of eating and gastronomy as part of the social milieu. This view was strengthened by the works of people such as Brillat-Savarin, Grimod de la Reynière and Curnonsky, to the extent that there has been an unbroken practice of, and specialization in, dedicated food and wine journalism and publication to the present day.

Contemporary premier chefs are largely propagandist, much of which rests on the necessity to keep their restaurants in the spotlight. Although these restaurants can often appear to be the preserve of a dedicated élite, what these chefs do appear to have achieved is a democratization of gastronomy, or at least, of their own cuisines. This has been carried out by stripping to essentials their philosophies and recipes for distribution across various media, and social strata, to reach and influence as wide an audience as possible.

1.4 Determinants of European gastronomy

Modern day European gastronomy can be considered to be the result of a complex interplay between two key things. These are:

1 **Gastro-geography** – the location of the European continent and the specific location of the individual countries within it (see map in Figure 1.1).

2 **Gastro-history** – the history of Europe and the individual countries within it, the influences of the countries that surround it, and also those beyond with which Europe has been and is involved.

Thus the cuisine and eating habits and traditions of any area within the European continent are as much to do with the physical location of them as they are to do with the socio/cultural, economic, political, legal, ecological and technological influences, and developments over time, those that are current, and those that are on the horizon.

Gastro-geography

Geography concerns gourmets, gastronomes and chefs in many individual ways. It can be interpreted as the research medium describing the surface of the earth, involving study of

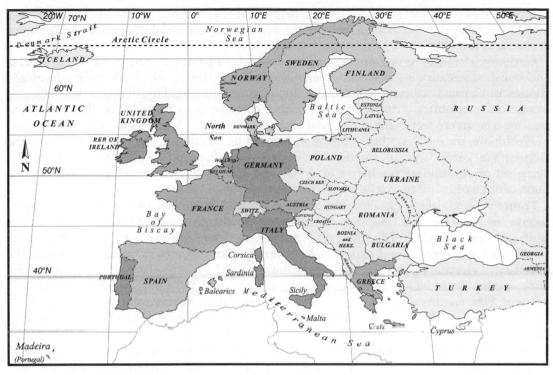

Figure 1.1 Map of Europe

the earth's physical features, vegetation, climate, products soils and peoples. The information used by the geographer is drawn from multiple fields such as biology, meteorology, astronomy, geology and anthropology.

Though geography is allied closely to the physical sciences of geology and biology, many consider it within the domain of the social sciences. Geography's foci are on the nature of place, the connection between the places and the association of individuals with their habitat. Geography like most other sciences can take subdivision with ease into numerous specialized fields (see Table 1.4). *Physical geography* involves a study of such things as oceans, climate and vegetation, land, water and the environment. With further division these can subdivide into climatology and oceanography.

Table 1.4 Gastro-geography

Physical geography	Climatic zones, temperature, geology, precipitation, natural vegetation, land and water
Human geography	Population migration, density and culture and tradition
Medical geography	Diet, nutrition and health and diseases
Economic geography	Agriculture, farming and food production

Environment, climate, the oceans and vegetation affect physical geography. These have all played a substantial role in all of the countries of Europe. Let us take for example Germany, France and the UK.

Germany's Hamburg has, in the main, daily hauls of fresh fish bound for the city's chic and polished restaurants, including sole, plaice, eels and turbot, which are the predominant species in German waters. Shellfish also abounds, with Heligoland lobsters, mussels and oysters as specialities. Fruitful and generative coastal plains provide for fine cattle and poultry. The rivers teem with carp, trout and pike, and those same rivers provide an ideal microclimate, on the steep banks of the Rhine and its tributaries, for great wines from the German vineyards. Culinary frontiers can be drawn on all maps with, in Germany, Frankfurt being set on its culinary borderline or divide and Hamburg, Baden and Munich being the main centres of culinary excellence in the country.

France's geographical position (see map in Figure 1.1) is such that it is well placed to receive the best from what is a great climatic variation. In the south, the Mediterranean gives fruit and vegetables a full flavour and lusciousness. There are many hidden riches in the south: cool sea breezes and substantial sunshine produce vines in profusion, whilst the diversity of climate and soil type produce character and variety, with 45 per cent of French wine coming from the south. In the north there are excellent shellfish, oysters, mussels and lobsters. Fine creams and butters like *Echire* are produced in this colder climate, as is the famed French onion. A substantial peasant diet with foodstuffs, which can be stored or preserved throughout the winter months, exists to the centre, east and southwest of the country. On these substructures the contrasting regions have evolved their astonishingly divergent identities. When considering this it might be worth remembering that the final boundaries were not laid down until the middle of the last century.

Britain has been important since the time of the Caesars, when their armies descended to plunder grain stores. Today Britain's importance lies in its ability to market and export the best of its produce, mainly Scottish beef, and the island's pork and lamb. With no part of Britain more than sixty miles from the sea, fishing is also important, with scallops, lobster, prawns and scampi being exported throughout the world. Venison, which has a major internal market, goes mainly to Germany and France.

Gastro-geography also includes anthropogeography (sometimes called *human geography*), which studies distribution of human communities on the earth in relation to geographical environments. *Medical geography*, also part of gastro-geography, deals with diets and nutritional diseases. Medical geography has been born out of an enthusiasm for knowledge, and the consuming desire to understand our environment and ourselves. As the centuries have advanced, information concerning health and disease has evolved, becoming more scientific, buttressed by evidence found to establish, address and focus on connections between diet and health.

Gastro-geography in extraction then is the geography of cooking and eating habits ordained by climate, soil, crops, history, tradition, psychology, commerce and national character. According to Dennis-Jones (1971), 'the world can be divided into culinary zones, which are as marked as those provided by political boundaries, altitudes, rain, religion, crops, skin colouring and many other geographical factors which are mapped in modern atlases'.

The world may be divided into areas with contrasting approaches to food and eating which have clearly defined frontiers. Evolutionary consideration becomes very relevant. It can be viewed that dividing the subject of gastronomy into separate areas is to derive a concoction of interesting subsets. There is much to find out about current eating and drinking habits and modes, and a great imbalance to rectify concerning the distribution of food across the nations of the world.

Gastro-history

Scientists, social scientists and historians are all engaged in different branches of the same study: the study of man and his environment, of the effects of man on his environment and of this environment on man. The object of the study is the same: to increase man's understanding of, and mastery over, the environment. 'History has assigned to it the task of judging the past, of instructing the present for the benefit of ages to come' (Von Ranke, 1952).

Gastro-history deals with the history of hospitality and gastronomy (which itself has an eminent history) under the umbrella heading 'gastro-history'. It can be visualized that this in itself is a massive area and just as gastro-geography has been subdivided into specialisms, so has the history of hospitality. Our history is collective memory, the store of experiences through which individuals can cultivate a sense of their social identity and their ultimate prospects. One of the finest bonds consolidating large social groupings is their members' awareness of a common history showing 'how group identity has prevailed through shifting circumstances' (Von Ranke, 1952).

Gastro-historical sources encompass every kind of evidence that individuals have left from their past activities: records from oral tradition passed down through the ages, the written word, technologies, material artefacts, the arts, photography, film and video as well as the shape of the landscape. Among the humanities and social sciences, history is unique in the great variety of its source materials. The historian frequently draws on other specialists like the archaeologist, anthropologist and art historian. From the High Middle Ages (*circa* AD 1000–1300) onwards, the written tradition took precedence over the oral tradition, and the written word survives in great abundance, much more so than for any other source for Western history.

The fifteenth and sixteenth centuries testify not only to a visible growth in the keeping of records by the state and other corporate bodies, but also the rapid spread of printing which encouraged literate production of many different kinds, especially writings; religious and alimentary in nature. Through the centuries since that time, written sources have tended to be precise as regards place, time and authorship, and thus can reveal the actions and thoughts, as no other source can do, of the men and women whose vitality gives the study an edge.

Gastro-history illustrates how food was once for all humankind a fundamental requisite for life; indeed for some even in the 21st century it remains so. But in Europe today food and beverages have been transported from the world of vital provisioning and nourishment into a much more intricately woven suite of elements ranging broadly across life style, status and citizenship. For today more is achievable, realized and accomplished with food and beverages. It commands our attention and it beguiles and intrigues many more individuals across the social spectrum than ever before. The lure of professional food preparation and presentation and service has stood the test of time. Indeed all over Europe there is reinvigoration in dining and a reinvigoration of the industry.

1.5 Approaches to the study of gastronomy

At the beginning of this chapter we identified four subdivisions of the subject of gastronomy, namely:

1 practical gastronomy

2 theoretical gastronomy

3 technical gastronomy

4 food gastronomy.

The subject can be approached from any or all of these perspectives and also from any combination of them. Additionally, we identified that the two key determinants of modern gastronomy are:

1 Gastro-geography
2 Gastro-history

Again, either or both of these, and/or the elements within them, can provide starting points for gastronomic explorations.

This book has been designed to support a range of combinations of approaches and perspectives. As we have already seen, this first chapter lays the foundations of the subject and the various approaches towards it. The essential skills of exploration are identified in section 1.6 below. Chapter 2 is concerned with the history of the development of gastronomy in Europe. Chapter 3 extends the foundations laid in this chapter and the historical perspectives summarized in Chapter 2 to the present day, with an identification of current trends. Considerations are given to a whole range of factors, which are now subsumed into the subject of gastronomy.

Chapter 4 leads from those who have laid the modern foundations of gastronomy to those who are laying the future ones. Profiles of some of the key contributors are detailed and conclusions are drawn about their distinguishing characteristics. Chapter 5 then takes the subject further by first considering the influence facing cuisine and gastronomy at the start of the 21st century. The status of the chef is examined together with the importance of vision, leadership and entrepreneurialism. The book ends by looking at the inter-relationship between gastronomy and philosophy. The individuals, who have observed, have thought and have had something to say about food and beverages, are those who have contributed the most to the development of European gastronomic culture. These are the gastrosophers, who epitomize and define gastrosophy as the new science.

To support the exploration further, there is also a bibliography and a glossary of terms, and two appendices. The people mentioned in the text are all listed in Appendix A and Appendix B provides a listing of trade, professional and gastronomic contacts. The bibliography contains both the sources of all the references given in the text, as well as a listing of other source material, which was consulted in the preparation of the text.

The sheer volume of information available might seem daunting. However, you do not have to read all of these texts. A guide to your initial reading is given in Table 1.5. This table gives an annotated listing of some key texts that you might want to consider as a starting point. In addition, you should also be reading articles from the professional, trade and academic press. Joining a professional association is also a valuable way of developing networks. In addition, especially for the exploration of gastro-geography and gastro-history, an interactive CD-Rom world atlas can be a worthwhile investment. Many of these allow for the in-depth examination of physical features and historic developments, through for instance being able to look at Europe at different points in history over the past thousands of years. A staggering amount of detail about specific locations is also available on these interactive atlases.

Study and achieving gastronomic living

Studying gastronomy as an amateur can be demanding, especially if you are attempting to do so on your own. It is, however, ultimately rewarding. You will need to develop a love of food and cooking; a desire to seek out the best possible ingredients and sources of supply. You will

Table 1.5 Key gastronomic texts

Ackerman D (1995) *A Natural History of the Senses*, Vintage Books, New York	Essential reading for students of gastronomy as it provides a highly accessible in-depth coverage of the senses
Cousins J, Foskett D and Gillespie C (2001) *Food and Beverage Management*, 2nd edn, Pearson Education, London	Designed for students and practitioners involved in a variety of levels in food and beverage (or foodservice) management. Presents a systematic approach to the design, planning and control of food and beverage operations, recognizing the necessity to manage operations as operating systems and a business framework
Durkan A and Cousins J (1995) *The Beverage Book*, Hodder and Stoughton, London	Comprehensive introduction to the study of alcoholic and non-alcoholic beverages. Also includes coverage of the professional sale and service of wine and other drinks
Fine GA (1996) *Kitchens: The Culture of Restaurant Work*, University of California Press, Berkeley	Combined interactional-structural approach to the study of restaurant work within the American industry. The occupational sociological background reveals insights into the work-culture of the industry, making it applicable beyond the book's US boundaries
Lashley C and Morrison A (2000) *In Search of Hospitality: Theoretical Perspectives and Debates*, Butterworth Heinemann, London	Provides a wide-screen view of hospitality from a number of disciplines: philosophy, sociology and social history, and concentrating on the study of hospitality across the range of human, social and economic settings
Lillicrap D, Cousins J and Smith R (1998) *Food and Beverage Service*, 5th edn, Hodder and Stoughton, London	Fundamental requisite for the study of food and beverage service. Provides a basis for study and acts as a reference source for both students and practitioners
Montagne P (1995) *Larousse Gastronomique*, Paul Hamlyn, London	Dedicated gastronomic reference providing an anthology of haute cuisine and other great classical traditions. Synthesizes the history of food and cookery in an approachable and well-illustrated fashion
Peynaud E (1996) (translated by Michael Schuster), *The Taste of Wine*, 2nd edn, Wiley, New York	More for the advanced student of gastronomy. It comprises a complete and scientific examination of the practice of wine tasting, the senses and their function. Comprehensive and not laden with unnecessary jargon
Robinson J (1999) *The Oxford Companion to Wine*, Oxford University Press, Oxford	Essential text for the lifelong study of wine and the vine. The most complete compendium of essential wine knowledge assembled in contemporary times. The book is easily accessible for amateur and professional usage
Simon J (1996) *Wine with Food*, Mitchell Beazley, London	Extensive coverage of the pairing of wine with food. Above all the book encourages experimentation, though this does not detract from the weight of valuable information available, taking experimentation out of the equation for busy amateurs and professionals
Telfer E (1996) *Food for Thought, Philosophy and Food*, Routledge, London	Offers a detailed approach to the importance of food, cooking, morality, gastronomy and philosophy in hospitality
Unwin T (1991) *Wine and the Vine: An Historical Geography of Viticulture and the Wine Trade*, Routledge, London	A cornerstone text in the historical geography of viticulture and the wine trade from prehistory to the present. The subject is discussed as both as unique expression of the interaction of people in particular environments, rich in symbol and meaning, and as commercial product of great economic importance

also through time demand quality and detail when dining away from home and will get to know the best restaurants for special dining and others for more regular dining.

The development of an attendant interest in all kinds of beverages is likely (and necessary) to follow your initial interest in food. It is not unusual however to develop an interest in beverages first and follow this with interest in food. Some organizations focus in on different aspects of gastronomy, for instance L'Ordre Mondiale des Gourmets Dégustateurs des Vins, Eaux-de-Vie, Liqueurs et Spiritueux, is quite naturally focused on the very best wines, spirits and liqueurs as its centre of activity, whereas the Confrerie de la Chaine des Rôtisseurs, which operates in 118 countries, is centred on food gastronomy. Both organizations unusually (but sensibly) accept professional and amateur members.

All of this will through time lead to personal knowledge, sophistication and expertise in social gastronomy and food and beverage culture. This book will go some way to improving your knowledge of gastronomy but it is worth remembering that there are many others with the same passion for food and beverage. Some like-minded individuals will join formalized organizations but others may prefer to keep their interest in food and wine amongst close friends and acquaintances. The main thing is enjoyment and health from your new-found way of living: for gourmets and gastronomes are not hobbyists seeking a fashionable and brief dalliance with the joys of the table, as their interest is most likely to become a health promoting and lifelong life style.

Professional study

The professional study of gastronomy is gaining momentum, and the people who make it into the culinary world's premier league need, as Anton Mosimann calls it, 'attitude':

> for me it has always been attitude, it is very important that somebody wants to work and is willing to work, willing to learn and study. They need to be able to give pleasure to other people. People on our waiting list know there is something to come, they are eager and that makes life much easier.

Those who want to get on have dedication and high aspirations. Paul Gaylor considers that 'young talent need to be totally committed, if not they might as well forget it'.

For those seeking a career in the hospitality industry, a thorough grounding in the basics is a prerequisite and logical step in anyone's hospitality career. You need cognisance of the language and skills of the trade and therefore formal training at an accredited institution is an excellent starting point. Eventually, having sought sound employment and built a solid foundation working with other professionals willing to share their knowledge, you will then be in a position to add super-structural elements to boost your industry credibility.

Some students of hospitality, however, want to move too quickly. They seek instant gratification (a feature of confidence exceeding experience) from money in possibly the wrong job, whereas what would in the medium term bring more benefits to their career (and in fiscal terms also) is the building of knowledge in depth by running with their training over a reasonable period to build confidence, credibility, relevance and communication.

A good hospitality education will also build in skills to deal with a dynamic and changing environment in employment. They will also ensure that you receive action centred learning and become a competent self-starter. All of which will help you become an ultimately more saleable individual. With recognized qualifications from a good institution, companies will want your intellectual and functional ability, woven with a strong client focus, maturity, enthusiasm and motivation.

Structure and appeal in gastronomy

Gastronomy is part of the experience economy. All of the chefs you will read about in this book have businesses that *don't* compete on the basis of price or a reliance on cost cutting to bring in their clientele. In today's competitive culture of mass tourism and media influenced tastes, the forms and manifestations of hotels and restaurants are determined not by marketing strategies and target group segmentation but by those who can add value to their businesses. Hoteliers and restaurateurs need to serve premium food and beverages as a means to build guest satisfaction and bolster revenue. This is not as simple as it initially appears, as crucial to this effort is the support of vendors in achieving the consistent quality discerning guests expect and will be prepared to pay a premium for. You also need a group of skilled personnel in food operations and food service, and a management layer whose work ethic is based on achieving the best possible end result.

In the period of the Belle Époque, a single stylistic norm prevailed; today, however, there is much more diversification and a subtly differentiated international clientele travelling either on business or for leisure. Today every business competing to extend their life cycle needs to become customer-centric, customer-driven and customer-focused. Recognizing experiences as a distinct economic offering can provide a key to economic growth and the extension of business life cycle. No one dines in a Michelin or other starred restaurant because they are primarily satisfying hunger. Therefore it is necessary to understand what is happening in these and other fine dining restaurants.

What is the appeal of fine dining and gastronomic settings? A range of gastronomic differentiators may shed some light on the complex and richly woven functional and sociopsychological needs that can be met.

- Appreciate the virtuosity of the chef

- Experience something new

- Experience the restaurant's positive reputation

- Place to be seen – 'aspirational'

- Celebrate in superior ambience

- Conspicuously do business

- Experience an élite life style

- As a statement of self-identity

- As a statement of preferred life style

- Experience uniqueness and theatricity

- Celebrate rights of passage – births, birthdays, anniversaries, business deals etc.

- Experience a series of designed sensations conveying a fine dining or gastronomic theme for which guests pay

- Experience the complex interplay of visual, aural, tactile, flavour and aromatic sensory impressions

- Combined social experience

- Creation of a positive psychological environment affecting all of the senses

- Making one feel good about oneself
- The offer of food for thought
- Potential to experience an overwhelming and memorable fine dining/gastronomic experience.

Understanding the need for satisfactions

The factors identified above may be summarized as the set of satisfactions (or potential dissatisfactions) that the customer receives from a meal experience. The satisfaction may be physiological, economic, social, psychological or convenience as follows:

- Physiological needs, for example to satisfy hunger and thirst, or to satisfy the need for special foods.
- Economic needs, for example staying within a certain budget, wanting good value, a convenient location or fast service.
- Social needs, for example being out with friends, business colleagues or attending special functions such as weddings.
- Psychological needs, for example responding to advertising, wanting to try something new, fulfilling life style needs or satisfying or fulfilling the need for self-esteem.
- Convenience needs, for example it may not be possible to return home or the desire may be there for someone else to prepare, serve and wash up.

Dissatisfaction can fall into two categories:

1 Controllable by the establishment, for example scruffy, unhelpful staff, cramped conditions.
2 Uncontrollable, for example behaviour of other customers, the weather, transport problems.

Customers may then want to satisfy all or some of the satisfaction needs, and be protected from the potential dissatisfactions. It is important to recognize that it is also the reasons behind wanting or having to eat out, as well as the food and drink themselves that will play an important part in determining the resulting satisfaction, or dissatisfaction, with the experience. It is quite possible that the motivation to eat out is not to satisfy basic physiological needs at all.

Although these satisfactions, and potential dissatisfactions, can exist in all dining experiences, there is a more heightened set of expectations in dining at the higher levels. The proprietor, and all other personnel in the business need to be aware of the complex interplay at this level of the industry. Whilst fine dining may be the focus of the experience, it is the higher order needs that may also be required to be met.

All of the businesses outlined in Chapter 4 (see page 119) have been established around experience-rich, defining objects, meaning and symbolism. Their branding includes critical assets to delivering and communicating the experience, such as the business/chef's name or both, the design, the advertising, the reputation of the business, its products and services, its projection of quality and the service expectation. Exceptional businesses will build loyalty by using functional, rational and emotional values to keep their clientele.

Considering experience

Notes prepared during a dinner at the Michelin three-starred Bocuse Restaurant in Lyons show the following as rich cognitive experience. The role of design and interior design played a strong part in the experience; the very much over-the-top exterior of Bocuse served not so much to entice as to stimulate mixed feelings, many of which were focused on the whimsical properties of the building and its colour palette. This was definitely not going to be an oppressively stuffy gastronomic and devotionally inspired event.

On entering what struck was the gracious and genuine welcome. The trail to the table led through one beautifully laid dining area after another, past the restaurant's shop and upstairs where other discrete dining rooms and fireplaces elicited a smart but homely effect. Virtually everything arriving at the tables was of general interest to all of the players in this unfolding drama. Madame Bocuse toured the tables, maintaining a weathered eye on detail and quality. Food arriving for parties became photo opportunities; of the dishes themselves, and of the eager participants of this ritualistic dining. Service staff were highly professional and eager to please, they also as requested, took pictures of guests behind dishes which had arrived from the kitchen. The experience-rich culture was infectious, and its fleeting nature appeared to require capturing for posterity. The Bocuse shop sold (amongst many other items including books) cameras pre-loaded with film so that although the event would be consigned to memory – a hard copy image could also exist to bolster the effect. No furtive fumbling into jackets or handbags was necessary to preserve the experience for posterity as guests quite openly photographed their companions and their dishes.

There appeared to be nothing hushed or religious in the experience, but there was the palpable impression of shared experience, of expectation, of quality, and the total dedication to the art of the table and a delight in experiencing such a meal. Rather than entering a holy of holies we had entered a venue for shared celebration, the goal of which appeared to be making you feel ultimately at home. [Figure 1.2 shows the likely path of expectation in a gastronomic meal.] This was an ultimate celebration, the enjoyment of which was infectious. Although dining alone on this occasion, there was a

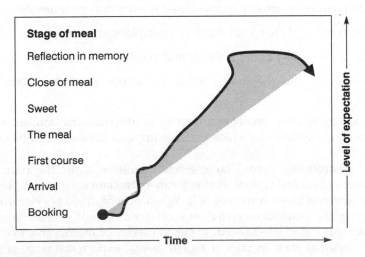

Figure 1.2 The path of expectation

definite desire to return with friends and colleagues. Although dining alone, you did not feel unaccompanied, as you were part of a unique and all too fleeting experience. Eight young and upwardly mobile Japanese stereotypically photographed themselves and the unfolding drama of a gastronomic meal. They appeared to be well aware of the status of Bocuse, who visits Japan regularly. A father and son dining together received a birthday cake with candles and were invited to join in with a rendition of happy birthday played on a barrel organ by a red liveried Bocuse doorman. The entire room celebrated that event by singing and clapping. Celebrating and respecting each other was just as important as celebrating the food.

Bocuse has a robust competitive edge, witnessed in the hallmarks that distinguish a brand as unique – commanding consumer loyalty. Quality and prized experience emerged at the head of our joint litany of expectations. Toward the cheese course and dessert the dining room became a virtual showroom of fragrant confections and aromatic cheeses, which were wheeled in on six trolleys causing our expectation to heighten still further. The meal lasted four hours but drifted along, as we were all part of an equally appreciative audience.

What can be learned from this experience? It was a cocooning adventure and one that was difficult to leave. A false preciousness existing in some grand hotel restaurants *vis-à-vis* dress codes and adherence to a hushed veneration of the chef was nowhere to be seen. At 'Bocuse' there were men in pullovers with dark trousers and white socks, enough to make a stuffy maître d'hôtel wince, yet all were celebrating equally the dining experience, each having no lesser regard for respecting the chef or the establishment. None of the near-surface preciousness and brittle nature of egos in callow youth was to be seen. Even the more usually absent salt and pepper was given prominence in the form of silver busts of the chef himself with the condiments within arm's length of the guest. There were also opportunities, as in retail, to follow the chef's proposals or to bespoke dishes from the Carte des Gastronomes.

The defining features of chefs like Bocuse are that they:

- are visionary leaders of their businesses and of gastronomy;
- have international if not global status in their industry;
- maintain creative culinary artistry in renowned destination restaurants;
- promote the profession of chef with them as exemplars at its apex;
- maintain the highest quality of ingredients and product;
- have a personality behind the image which is defined in their restaurants and their personnel; and they
- understand that key to their business longevity is individualization, diversification and experience-rich environments in which both leisure and business can be enacted.

The appeal of gastronomy is to a large extent cognitive; you take part in a designed experience that makes you feel special, that you can appreciate on many different levels. You are not part of a commoditized conveyor belt. When purchasing a service you purchase an amalgam of intangible activities carried out on your behalf. When you purchase an experience you are paying to be seduced, to enjoy a series of memorable events, which will engage you in a personal way. As part of a gastronomic experience what is staged for you should be a complete and holistic production, offering cultural cachet in an interweave of fantasy and reality. In this sense 'cultural cachet' implies that these restaurants and properties offer 'cultivation, sophistication and the opportunity for gastronomic and/or intellectual enrichment, from design and architecture in the restaurant to the sensory interaction with the food through, sights and sounds, aroma, tastes and textures to customised service and differentiation by experience' (Gillespie and Morrsion, 2000).

The meal experience concept

In examining dining experiences, in whatever context, it can be useful to apply concepts such as the meal experience. The study of gastronomy is not only about experiences at a high level, it is also about considering the development of cuisine and food and beverage traditions from a variety of perspectives. Applying conceptual frameworks provides for systematic examination of the development of gastronomy.

The meal experience concept takes account of a wide range of possible meal contexts. If people have decided to eat out then it follows that there has been a conscious choice to do this in preference to some other course of action (Cousins *et al.*, 2001). The reasons for eating out may be summarized under seven headings:

1 Convenience, for example being unable to return home, as in the case of shoppers or people at work or involved in some leisure activity.

2 Variety, for example trying new experiences or as a break from home cooking.

3 Labour, for example getting someone else to prepare, serve food and wash up or simply the physical impossibilities to house special events at home.

4 Status, for example business lunches or people eating out because others of their socioeconomic group do so.

5 Culture/tradition, for example special events or simply because it is a way of getting to know people.

6 Impulse, for example simply spur-of-the-moment buying.

7 No choice, for example those in welfare, hospitals or other forms of semi- or captive markets.

The decision to eat out may also be split into two parts: first, the decision to do so for the reasons given above and then the decision as to what type of experience is to be undertaken. It is generally agreed that there are a number of factors influencing this latter decision. The factors that affect the meal experience may be summarized under the following headings.

Food and drink on offer • • •

The food and drink are the core products of the food and beverage operation. Choices will be made about the range of foods and beverages on offer, the choice, availability, flexibility for special orders and the quality of the food and drink.

Level of service • • •

Depending on the needs people have at the time, the level of service sought should be appropriate to these needs. For example, a romantic night out may call for a quiet table in a top-end restaurant, whereas a group of young friends might be seeking more informal service. This factor also takes into account services such as booking and account facilities, acceptance of credit cards and also the reliability of the operation's product.

Level of cleanliness and hygiene • • •

This relates to the premises, equipment and staff. Over the past few years this factor has increased in importance in the customers' minds. The recent media focus on food production and the risks involved in buying food have heightened awareness of health and hygiene aspects. It is not only about being clean and hygienic but it is also about being perceived to be clean and hygienic.

Perceived value for money and price • • •

Customers have perceptions of the amount they are prepared to spend and relate these to differing types of establishments and operations. However, many people will spend more if the value gained is perceived as greater than that obtained by spending slightly less.

Atmosphere of the establishment • • •

This is difficult to quantify, as it is an intangible concept. However, it is composed of a number of factors such as: design, decor, lighting, heating, furnishings, acoustics and noise levels, the other customers, the staff and the attitude of the staff.

The meal experience factors essentially provide a way of summarizing all of the factors that might be taken into account in considering or evaluating meal experiences. Cousins *et al.* (2001) put forward the notion that all the factors are present in any experience; however, the importance attached to them can depend on two things.

First, the nature of the dining experience, and the needs the customer is wanting to satisfy at the time, will alter the importance attached to the factors. This can be demonstrated in Table 1.6, which identifies possible different rankings for different types of meal experiences.

The second change in importance is caused by the nature of the balance of the factors in an operation. For instance, in a limited menu, limited service operation, the level of service and menu range will be low and predetermined. This will cause the perception of the importance of the other factors to be heightened. Thus, for instance, in this example, there will be a greater expectation for a good price/value for money ratio, and an expectation of a higher level of cleanliness and hygiene.

The meal experience factors then can provide a useful tool for the systematic exploration of the nature of demand being met, and the extent to which this is being achieved. It also has the potential to be used as a tool for the systematic inter-comparisons of different operations, of the same type or of different types.

Price, cost, value and worth

Although values are attached to various products because of the perception of the needs a product can satisfy, the ability to realize those goals is dependent on the ability to pay. But when considering the meal experience specifically, payment or cost is not just about having the required amount of money (Cousins *et al.*, 2001). Choices are made by considering the relationship between price, cost, worth and value:

Table 1.6 Possible factor ranking for different meal experiences

Reason for meal experience	Possible factor ranking
Night out	Atmosphere Food and drink Service Price Cleanliness and hygiene
Gourmet event	Food and drink Service Atmosphere Cleanliness and hygiene Price
Cheap meal	Price Food and drink Cleanliness and hygiene Service Atmosphere
State banquet	Service Atmosphere Food and drink Cleanliness and hygiene Price

Source: Cousins *et al.*, 2001

- **Price** is the amount of money required to purchase the product.

- **Cost** includes, as well as price, the cost of not going somewhere else, the cost of transport and time, the cost of potential embarrassment, the cost of having to look and behave in a required manner and the cost in terms of effort at work to earn the money to pay the required price.

- **Worth** is a perception of the desirability of a particular product over another in order to satisfy a set of established goals.

- **Value** is not only the personal estimate of a product's capacity to satisfy a set of goals it is also a perception of the balance between worth and cost.

Good value for a food and beverage experience is where the **worth** is perceived as greater than the **costs**, and poor value is where the **costs** are perceived as greater than the **worth**. When examining why certain food and beverage operations are or are not successful, it is rarely price alone that is a determining factor. It is the cost to the customer or those involved in the experience (or deciding not to be involved) and the complex reasons surrounding this that will often be the cause. People with the capacity to pay may avoid various types of restaurant simply because the other costs involved are too great for them, such as the personal cost of being made to feel embarrassed.

The catering cycle as an analysis tool

When examining and inter-comparing similar or different types of food and beverage operation it is useful to adopt approaches that will allow for the application of a systematic approach. One approach is to use the catering cycle (Kracknell *et al.*, 2000) as an analysis tool. The catering cycle can be used as a dynamic model (Cousins *et al.*, 2001). Figure 1.3 gives the eight stages of the cycle and indicates the issues that could be considered under each stage.

There are two dimensions to using the catering cycle in this way:

1 By using the catering cycle to present the information that has been generated, it will help to organize what is known about an operation and its performance. More importantly though, it will also help to identify where there are gaps in the information and where additional information might be required to make the evaluation more complete.

2 Viewing the operation as a cycle will help to identify the operational strengths and weaknesses. Within the cycle any difficulties that are identified in one area of the cycle will

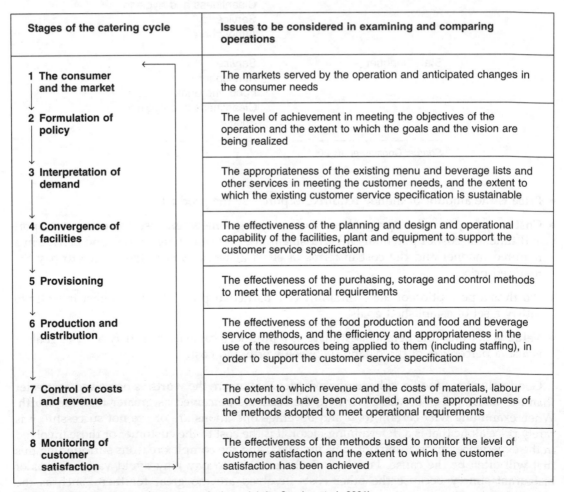

Stages of the catering cycle	Issues to be considered in examining and comparing operations
1 **The consumer and the market**	The markets served by the operation and anticipated changes in the consumer needs
2 **Formulation of policy**	The level of achievement in meeting the objectives of the operation and the extent to which the goals and the vision are being realized
3 **Interpretation of demand**	The appropriateness of the existing menu and beverage lists and other services in meeting the customer needs, and the extent to which the existing customer service specification is sustainable
4 **Convergence of facilities**	The effectiveness of the planning and design and operational capability of the facilities, plant and equipment to support the customer service specification
5 **Provisioning**	The effectiveness of the purchasing, storage and control methods to meet the operational requirements
6 **Production and distribution**	The effectiveness of the food production and food and beverage service methods, and the efficiency and appropriateness in the use of the resources being applied to them (including staffing), in order to support the customer service specification
7 **Control of costs and revenue**	The extent to which revenue and the costs of materials, labour and overheads have been controlled, and the appropriateness of the methods adopted to meet operational requirements
8 **Monitoring of customer satisfaction**	The effectiveness of the methods used to monitor the level of customer satisfaction and the extent to which the customer satisfaction has been achieved

Figure 1.3 The catering cycle as an analysis tool (*after* Cousins *et al.*, 2001)

cause difficulties in the elements of the cycle that follow. For instance, difficulties with purchasing will then have had effects on production and service, and control. Similarly the difficulties experienced under one stage of the cycle will often have their causes in the stages that precede it.

The application of the catering cycle helps in considering the operation as a whole, i.e. as an operating system. Approaching the analysis and evaluation of a food and beverage operation using the catering cycle will help to determine the limitations of the information that is known, which will then lead to a more objective evaluation of the operation and its performance.

When analysing operations, the true causes of difficulties in any of the eight stages and the implications of them are also more easily and accurately identified. Being able to identify and understand these various interrelationships will mean that the evaluation of an operation, and inter-comparisons with other operations, will be systematically approached and thus better informed.

1.6 Developing the skills of gastronomic exploration

Gastronomy is a source of pleasure and of lasting interest. Learning about gastronomy is as much about gaining experience as it is about gaining knowledge. Indeed the learning is the experience. It is also a never-ending source of fascination. For the exploration of gastronomy there are some essential skills to master and there is some knowledge to gain. This will help to provide you with a framework to which you can relate your existing and future gastronomic experiences.

Leaning about gastronomy requires a combination of the experience gained through the use of the senses and the use of the brain, which records the sensation. The skills necessary for the exploration of gastronomy can be divided into two broad categories. These are:

1 Essential skills

2 Organoleptic skills.

Essential skills

These skills are the range of skills that are necessary in order to enhance the learning experience through knowledge and competence. For some people these skills will have already been mastered; for others they are at present aspirational but will be developed over time.

Table 1.7 identifies the 13 essential skills[1] and describes the abilities that would be expected in those who have mastered them. The first three skills are about perspective and autonomy. The next four (4–7) are the core cognitive skills that are normally applied in any serious study endeavour. The remaining six (8–13) are those that are not necessarily relevant to all subjects or disciplines but are very relevant to the study of gastronomy.

---

[1] This identification of essential skills is based on the South East England Consortia (SEEC) generic level descriptors 1999. (SEEC comprised 50 higher education institutions.) The level of the description of the skills presented here is at undergraduate honours degree, and is also appropriate for NVQ/SVQ level 4.

Table 1.7 Essential skills for gastronomic exploration (Based on the SEEC generic level descriptors of essential skills 1999)

Essential skills	Description
Operational and study contexts	
1 Context	Be able to study and work within complex and unpredictable contexts demanding selection and application from a wide range of innovative or standard techniques
2 Responsibility	Be autonomous in planning and managing resources and processes within broad guidelines
3 Ethical understanding	Demonstrate awareness of personal responsibility and professional codes of conduct, and have the ability to incorporate a critical ethical dimension into studies and work
Core cognitive skills	
4 Knowledge	Have comprehensive/detailed knowledge of major discipline(s), with a depth of knowledge in areas of specialization, and an awareness of the provisional nature of the state of knowledge
5 Analysis	Be able to analyse new and/or abstract data and situations without guidance, using a wide range of techniques appropriate to the subject
6 Synthesis/creativity	With minimum guidance, be able to transform abstract data and concepts towards a given purpose, and be able to design novel solutions
7 Evaluation	Be able to critically review the evidence supporting conclusions/recommendations including its reliability, validity and significance, and can investigate contradictory information and identify reasons for contradictions
Other transferable skills	
8 Psychomotor	Be able to perform complex skills consistently, with confidence and a degree of co-ordination and fluidity, and be able to choose an appropriate response from a repertoire of actions, and undertake the critical evaluation of your own and others' performance
9 Self-appraisal, reflection on practice	Demonstrate confidence in the identification and application of own judgement criteria, and in the challenge of received opinion, and can reflect on actions undertaken, including the actions of others
10 Planning and management of learning	With minimum guidance, be able to manage own learning, using a full range of resources, and can seek, and make use of, feedback
11 Problem solving	Demonstrate confidence and flexibility in identifying and defining complex problems, and the application of appropriate knowledge, techniques and skills to their solution
12 Communication and presentation	Be able to engage effectively in debate in a professional manner and produce detailed and coherent project reports
13 Interactive and group skills	Be able to interact effectively within a learning or professional group, recognize or support leadership or be proactive in leadership, demonstrate the ability to negotiate in a learning/professional context, and be able to manage conflict

Source: Based on the SEEC generic level descriptors of essential skills, 1999

Organoleptic skills and the five senses

Underpinning the essential skills, identified in Table 1.7, is the ability to undertake and be disciplined in organoleptic evaluation. Organoleptic skills are the sensory evaluation skills, utilized in the evaluation of all types of food and beverages in an analytical context, using the senses of sight, sound, smell, taste, and tactile or viscous perceptions.

We have conventionally been thought to possess five senses: sight, hearing, touch, smell and taste. However, touch comprises all sensations from the body surface including a pressure sense, the joints' position sense and muscle and movement sense, viscera, pain, thermal sensitivity senses and a position sense. Stimulation of the five senses has a direct effect on both our physical and mental health. The senses act on three important body systems: the autonomous nervous system, the immune system and the hormonal system.

Our five senses give us the ability to communicate with the world in the most simplistic and also the most complex and precise way. Our understanding is informed by the senses, which work together to provide the mind with accurate descriptions of the food we eat, the beverages we consume and much more. Sensory systems can be envisaged in simple terms as continually making assumptions about events in the world. The brain makes informed guesses, based on messages sent to it in tandem with some simple assumptions. Urgent messages and questions are constantly flashing through nerve cells along cross-linked pathways and feedback loops in the brain for answer; is there a colour imbalance in the menu? How will this salad taste with a vinegar and oil dressing? Is this Thai green curry going to be too hot to eat?

Each of the senses should be treasured for they are virtually irreplaceable. Out of the millions of people who own a computer, only a fraction will use it to its fullest potential. Similarly, only a minute part of our sensory potential is used to our advantage. This in itself should not overly concern the student of gastronomy because many individuals have all but lost the ability in modern times to determine more. There has been deterioration in our ability to sense more efficiently. This is especially the case with the sense of odour and flavour perception, though all of our other senses are also affected. What abruptly elicits our attention is change. The senses are finely attuned to change and receptor cells transform this stimulus into electrical signals – the language of the brain. For example, in a classically inspired dish the sauce should always be the same; any change should instantly be detected. Stale food or a wine fault will also be quickly determined, and poisonous foods may be quickly ejected from the body. Part of our gastronomic evolution and progression is to train ourselves to do more as sensing and sentient beings.

The French novelist Marcel Proust, in his book *A la recherche du temps perdu* (Remembrance of Things Past), had an instinctive curiosity which excited and stirred feelings and conjured up memories from his past. In describing what happened to him after consuming a spoonful of tea in which he had soaked a piece of *madeleine* (a type of cake), he accurately alluded to both taste and smell because most of the flavour of food comes from its aroma, which is transported up the nostrils to cells in the nose, which can also be accessed through a passage in the back of the mouth.

There are distinctive dangers ahead for gastronomy and the art of good living in the 21st century as more and more people become less discerning and fail to adequately use and fully appreciate their senses. If we do not hone our senses our sensitivity diminishes, as does the opportunity for inspiration and gustative reminiscences. Lethargy in the honing of the senses can be easily detected in certain quarters of the hospitality industry as clear acceptance of mediocrity, the standard, unchanging, uninspired and uninteresting, the bland and the flavourless. This cuts across everything from the food manufacturer to the vinifier, the simplest café or cafeteria to the restaurateur and hotelier, who, understanding that they do not need to put a great deal of effort into providing the very best, do exactly that.

Provision of the least uninviting and least unpalatable can lead to general acceptance of everything from irresponsible policy and decision making at government level, to unsavoury and unhealthy animal and crop husbandry. Flavourless meat, poultry, game, bread and cheese, naming but a few foods, and mass production of uniformly uninteresting foods, banality in the service encounter and stagnation in hotel provision, design and management. It is generally held that everyone should have an interest in eating the best that they can afford. It is however the duty of the gourmet and gastronome to expect the best they can afford and to seek out real quality in everything from food, beverage, service and accommodation. It is also a duty to inform those not meeting these exacting needs of their deficiency.

The relationship between taste and odour perception • • •

Taste is detected in different parts of the mouth but mostly on the tongue. Sweetness is detected at the tip and centre of the tongue, acidity on the upper edges, saltiness on the sides and tip, and bitterness at the back. This is illustrated in Figure 1.4.

- Sweetness and dryness will be immediately obvious.

- Acidity will be recognized by its gum-drying sensation, but in correct quantities acidity provides crispness and liveliness, especially to beverages.

- Astringency or tannin content (usually associated with drinks like tea and some red wines), will give a dry coating or furring effect, especially on the teeth and gums.

- Body is the weight or feel of the food or beverage in the mouth.

- Flavour is the essence of the food or beverage, and the longer tasting the flavour, especially for wines, the better.

- Aftertaste is the finish of the food or beverage on your palate.

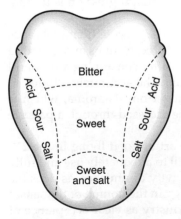

Figure 1.4 The tongue and the taste perceptors

Overall balance is determined by the evaluation of all the above elements, which hopefully are in correct proportions.

Much of what we think of as our sense of taste, however, is in fact about 80 per cent smell. The human nose can detect up to 10,000 different odours at minute concentrations. Taste would be meaningless without the sense of smell. It is smell that provides a wealth of pleasure in the process of tasting. For the student of gastronomy the sense of smell is vitally important as it is used to judge, interpret and fully appreciate food and beverage. Diane Ackerman, in her book a *Natural History of the Senses* (1995), elegantly explained the nature and significance of this sense in statements like, 'nothing is more memorable than a smell'. 'Smells detonate softly in our memory like poignant land mines.' 'Hit a trip wire of smell, and memories explode all at once.' Our smell sense can be incredibly precise especially if it is used efficiently. Training is vital and will allow you to successfully analyse your impressions and ultimately supply you with an olfactory repository of accurate vocabulary to describe your findings. This vocabulary will be the foundation on which your taste is established. Your final analysis and impressions will generally be formed by multiple senses – those of sight, smell and taste. By feeding the brain with additional information from a variety of the senses, the better our memory will be at decoding the pleasure encountered.

Without molecules there could be no sense of smell. Aromas are perceived in two ways: first, directly through the nose (direct olfaction) and secondly when aromas reach the nose after passing through the mouth (retro-olfaction). We either accept or reject them, like or dislike them. We employ our sense of smell, first to check out, and then to enjoy our food. In odour hedonics aroma and enjoyment are commonly linked to foods and beverages but also to freshly cut flowers. Connoisseurs of fine wine understand the importance of smell or 'bouquet', indeed what we think of as our sense of taste is about 80 per cent smell, for only four elements: sweet, salty, sour and bitter, can be tasted, and so reliance on the subtle sensitivities of our noses imparts the rich nuances of 'flavour'.

Our brains are almost completely divided into hemispheres – left and right. There is now general acceptance that the left hemisphere is more concerned with logical thought processes and verbalization, and the right with intuitive, creative thought. It is a curious fact that smell messages from the left nostril travel, via the left olfactory nerve, to the left logical side of the brain. Smells picked up by the right nostril mainly affect the right, intuitive side. The right side of the brain can react to odour more emotionally. Pleasant odours gain a deeper access to our nervous systems, because we do not block them. The right hemisphere it is suggested is more involved than the left in the feeling known as euphoria, and in the functions of imagination and pleasure. We have what could be determined a layered response to odours. The two hemispheres respond separately – the left intellectually and the right creatively. Aesthetic appreciation of odours is also tied in with instinctive reactions, which rarely reach our conscious mind, and with emotional reaction, which we sometimes cannot identify or explain.

It is also worth considering the purity of smell and taste. Sight and hearing in tasting sessions can be valuable but can also be a distraction. Hearing others enthuse or describe can confuse the brain into realizing what is not there. Seeing can distort the impression of a wine for instance, through the label being attractive or the name of it triggering memories of past experience and potentially introducing prejudice. Relying on smell and taste alone (with the brain making sense of it all and recording the experience) can be a more sure way of tasting what is actually there.

Healthy eating and drinking

Gastronomy is not about excess. In gastronomy moderation and appreciation go hand in hand. Nowadays there is a greater awareness of the need to consider health when eating and drinking. More choice and availability, whilst being the mark of a developed society, leads to a necessity for greater care when selecting food and drink.

Food • • •

Much has been published recently about food and its link with health. Moves towards better balanced diets containing fewer animal fats and less salt and sugar and more roughage are having a positive effect on health. However there is a need for some sense here. *Balance* in the diet is more important than slavish adherence to healthy eating rules. Foods such as butter and cream are not intrinsically *bad* foods; it is *excess* which is the problem, not the food itself.

Alcohol • • •

The great majority of the population who drink alcohol do so for many reasons: to quench a thirst, as a relaxant or simply because it is enjoyable. A *small amount* of alcohol does no harm and can even be beneficial. However, the more you drink and the more frequently you drink, the greater the health risks. Alcohol depresses the brain and nerve function thereby affecting one's judgement, self-control and skills.

Most of the alcohol you drink passes into the bloodstream from where it is rapidly absorbed. (This absorption may be slowed down somewhat if drink is accompanied by food.) Almost all the alcohol must then be burnt up by the liver, with the remainder being disposed of in urine or perspiration. The liver is like a car with just one gear. It can only burn up one unit of alcohol in an hour so, if it has to deal with too much alcohol over the years, it will inevitably suffer damage.

So what are the *sensible* limits we can go to if we wish to avoid damaging our health? Of course, if you stop drinking alcohol you cut out any risk. However, medical expert opinion from the Royal College of Physicians sets the limit at *27 units* a week (spread throughout the week) for men and *21 units* a week (spread throughout the week) for women.

> 1 unit = $\frac{1}{2}$ pint of ordinary beer or lager
> or a glass of sherry (50 ml)
> or a glass of wine (125 ml)
> or a measure of vermouth or other aperitif (50 ml)
> or one measure of spirits (25 ml)

But take note of the following points:

- In Scotland, an ordinary spirit measure is 30 ml – $1\frac{1}{5}$ units. Also some extra strength lagers and beer have sometimes two or three times the strength of ordinary beers. Remember too that many low calorie drinks contain more alcohol than their ordinary equivalents.

- Some alcohol remains in the bloodstream for up to 18 hours after consumption. This should be considered in relation to the legal limits for alcohol in the blood when driving.

- The number of units required to reach the maximum permitted levels for driving varies between individuals but it can be as little as three units.

- There are about 100 calories in a single unit of alcohol. The amount of calories adds up quickly and can increase weight. However, replacing food with alcohol as a source of calories denies the body essential nutrients and vitamins.

From these guidelines we can see that if a man drinks 36 units or more of alcohol throughout the week (e.g. 18 pints of beer or $1\frac{1}{4}$ bottles of whisky) then he is likely to be damaging his health. Similarly if a woman goes beyond 22 units (say $1\frac{1}{2}$ bottles of sherry) throughout the week, then a risk to her health is likely.

George Bernard Shaw once said 'eat at leisure, drink by measure'. This is good advice. However, if you do go too far then remember every pleasure has a price; overindulgence in alcohol leads to hangovers. A hangover is a headache resulting from (a) dehydration of the body caused by the alcohol, (b) the presence of congeners (additives etc.) in the drink, and (c) lack of real sleep. This is why we suffer after drinking to excess. A hangover is an unpleasant experience and people are constantly searching for effective cures. However, as in so many things, *prevention* is always better than cure:

- It is always advisable to drink less and to eat well before an evening of drinking. Food lines the stomach and acts as a buffer against the war that alcohol wages.

- Avoid mixing drinks if possible.

- Be wary of concoctions such as laced drinks, dubious punches, wine cups and foul, cheap wine.

- Drink lots of water before you go and after you come back from a heavy drinking party.

If, however, you have failed to heed this advice and you feel absolutely rotten in the morning, try one of the following remedies:

1 Taking one of the many proprietary brand bitters will help, or at least shock the system in the attempt. Underberg and Fernet Branca are particular favourites.

2 Take a brisk walk to the chemist, inhaling deeply on your way, and ask for a dose of kaolin and morphine. This is a rather drastic solution but it works.

3 The 'hair of the dog' – well why not, if you believe it will do you good!

And finally

It is worth remembering that we are all different, particularly in our ability to taste. The palate is not fixed; it develops with age and all of us are somewhere on that journey. This is one of the reasons why our tastes change. When we are young we tend to prefer sweeter things, but as we mature we begin to move towards more savoury and drier tastes, then we learn to appreciate more subtle or sophisticated flavours. But there is no guarantee that any of us will be at a particular point at a certain time. Some people will always prefer milder and less dry taste sensations; others will find that their tastes change at different times. Therefore, always be confident in buying and enjoying the foods and beverages *you* like and always trust your own judgement.

Above all, gastronomy should be approached with a certain amount of adventure and fun; perhaps with a sense of humour and the realization that the experience may not always be perfect; may not meet your particular taste; or may not be what you might regularly eat or drink. But sometimes the experience will be exquisite. This is the fun and joy of discovery, and of enduring fascination. Above all, enjoy the journey.

1.7 Summary

This chapter has provided an introduction to European gastronomy and has demonstrated the breadth of gastronomy as a subject. It has identified the amateur and the professional approaches to gastronomy. At its simplest expression, amateur gastronomy has as its focus the enjoyment of good food and good beverages, in good company. These individuals will also be careful to eat the best food they can afford and will become through time more and more discerning. Professional gastronomes have the highly responsible role of interpreting from a range of stylistic norms the food that they will prepare and present. They also have to creatively develop and execute with daily precision and consistency dishes that set the tone of their establishments. To remain successful, they must also be acutely aware of the vagaries of a sophisticated clientele, the changing nature of dining, and the operation of a complex business. This should never be undertaken in a creative vacuum, for the best gastronomes will consider the work of other equally important specialists dealing with management of the facility, wine and food service and purchasing specialists who all have their input to ensure a holistic experience. Various approaches to the exploration of gastronomy have been identified together with details of the essential skills necessary to realize learning and achievement. Both amateur and professional gastronomes should be in lifelong exploration for personal knowledge, sophistication, expertise and fulfilment, in the culture of good living.

The development
of gastronomy
in Europe

Aim

This chapter summarizes the historical factors that have influenced the development of gastronomy in Europe.

Objectives

This chapter is intended to help you to:

- explore the origins of the European gastronomic tradition

- gain knowledge of the various historic influences on gastronomic development within Europe

- identify the nature and contribution of the founding fathers of gastronomy

- view, from a number of standpoints, the complex developments which have contributed to the establishment of European gastronomy

- identify trends in gastronomy to the 20th century.

2.1 A brief history of early European gastronomy

The Greeks

In European society it was the advent of Greek civilization that brought into public record the preferential eating habits of ancient societies. Greater variety was introduced in foods, not simply through diversity, as in a greater abundance of fish and seafood, which was plentiful, or new crops, but in the forms basic commodities took. By 500 BC Greeks had also become dependent upon the importation of wheat for their bread (Leeming, 1991). The Greeks in fact produced a great variety of bread products, some historians numbering seventy types, with barley bread being given to the poor.

Regrettably there are no intact copies of Greek cookbooks that survive to this day. However, fragments of Archestrate's writings remain with most of his recipes dealing with roasting and frying. Much of what is known of Greek gastronomy is based on the writing of Archestrate, who was a Greek poet and gastronome of the 4th century BC (Peterson, 1991). When the ancient Greeks began to enjoy the pleasures of the table they were gourmands rather than refined gourmets, that is, they ate heartily but fed very badly, consuming all kinds of combinations of foods. Gastronomy and the connoisseur were outclassed by gluttony and gourmandism.

Through time the Greeks became more discriminating in their choice of food and eventually they allowed their cooks to use the skills and knowledge they had acquired in deciding what were the most appropriate food combinations able to keep their masters in better health and also save them money. Historians have variously speculated that the system, linked with Greek medicine, powerfully influenced both Middle Eastern and Western European cuisines (Peterson, 1991).

The sybarites of the trading city of Syberius became recognized for their cuisine to the extent that the city was the centre to which more famous Greek cooks directed themselves for education in the art. Cooks were allowed to exert full authority over the organization of their kitchen. At that time many of the cooks working in Greece had been brought from Sicily. The flair and innovatory skills of the Sicilian cooks were such that they had made a reputation for themselves in the culinary arts, through their ability to prepare eye-catching displays of foods from the simplest of ingredients. They created many new dishes, and with each new dish invented, the creator had complete copyright on it for twelve months before any other cook was allowed to feature it. This led to abandon, as each master urged his cook to produce even more sumptuous dishes for the feasts to which he invited his guests. These functions set an increasingly high standard of production skills, by making ever more demands on the creativity of the cooks. Gradually the rich transformed their gluttonous habits and, through the influence of their Sicilian cooks, developed as gourmets. The Greeks came to regard cookery as an art form, with eating and drinking as its expression.

The Romans

A great deal of what we know about Roman cooking originates from before the first century AD in the writings of Marcus Gavius Apicius who described the art of the table in a collation of recipes dating from circa 42 BC to 37 AD and outlined cookery and its processes and dining in Imperial Rome. However, much more can be pieced together of earlier happenings. Ancient Romans were developers of gastronomy, their intentness at pilfering new food stuffs and new methods of doing things during their many conquests adding greatly to their own culinary customs and practices. After Rome had been rebuilt in 390 BC the very rich vied with one another for the high quality of the dishes they offered at their dinner parties.

The conquering of other lands has also been one of the most powerful influences in the development and growth of gastronomy. We can still view the Romans' mark today in our food, with the sauerkraut or sauerbraten of contemporary Germany, Ricotta cheese tart, gnocchi and the sweet-sour sauces of Italy. New ingredients brought back from each new conquered land invariably increased the range of food products.

Lucullus (110–57 BC) was one of the conquerors, and he brought back so many rare and unusual foodstuffs that his fame spread and surpassed his reputation as a general, to infamy as the greatest gourmet of all times. Lucullus spent his wealth on giving sumptuous feasts and banquets, for which these choice and unfailing commodities were cooked by the most intricate methods, and ornamented in the most elaborate style. Today we speak of a 'Lucullan feast' as meaning an Epicurean occasion at which the standard of the food, wine, cookery and service are of the highest order, and a restaurant named after Lucullus would obviously have to be sybaritic because of this visible link with holistic exoticism. Lucullan wine tastings accompanied by food to complement the wine was provided at different times of the year in Germany by the 28th generation Count Erwin Graf Matuschka Greiffenclau of the Schloss Vollrads, until his death in 1998. The family Greiffenclau has 775 years of experience of viticulture and have estimably the longest winegrowing tradition in the world, according to lengthy research carried on in France, Spain and Italy.

The Romans ate their feasts from a reclining position rather than seated at the table and plenty of space was allowed for the entertainment that became an integral part of the feast. As recumbent dining became unfashionable and sitting upright at table became normalized, dishes founded upon finely diced chopped or minced food components were succeeded by joints of beef, game, poultry and pork. The main reason for the transition was the necessity to use both hands while eating, which had then come into fashion with the eating of larger joints. Carving then became an art form entrusted to the carving officer, who was placed well up the household hierarchy in noble dwellings. Meat at table was identified with status, and would hold this significant position until the later period of the 20th century. Affluent Romans ate large quantities of meat. Pork especially was considered to be a delicacy.

Other prominent figures from the Roman world include Trimalcion, renowned for his lavish feasting and entertainment; Petronius, Emperor Nero's immortalized 'arbiter of elegance', and Atheneus, the Greek author. Lucullus and other notables liked to offer guests such performances as dancers, clowns, singers, musicians, magicians and raconteurs to amuse, excite and titillate in order to generate an atmosphere that would cause the event to end in an orgy, thus satisfying all the senses. These events were obviously confined to the very wealthy.

In the works of Petronius, and other noteworthy Romans, one might quite easily conceive Rome to be a city of eternal banquets and sumptuous feasting. However, if one looks deeper into Roman history these gatherings were in fact the exception and not the rule. Latin cooking had originated from a humble and quite meagre custom. Also the Romans mainly drank water; dispelling another myth that they constantly, and in great numbers, consumed vats of wine.

The Romans reared livestock in large numbers and had interests in agriculture, but it was with the commercialism of the salt trade that greater links with the Etruscan and Greek communities were established (Montagne, 1938). The salt was produced by evaporation of sea water at river mouths. The pay cheque, which we enthusiastically wait for each month, derives its name from salt. The Latin 'salarium', from which we obtain the word salary, was the Roman legionnaire's salt ration. Salt was identified with the good life and with wealth. We speak of people even today of being the 'salt of the earth' or being 'worth their salt'. The silver saltcellar was also a central ornament on the tables of the rich, marking off the close friends of the family from those who were 'below the salt' and therefore less worthy.

The development of gourmandism became well reported in Roman manuscripts with the lavish banquets in Imperial Rome of Tiberius, Lucullus (who adopted the refinements of the Greek courts in the East), Cicero and Pompey. The excesses of the affluent are well reported in history, and they were sufficient to warrant laws such as that passed by Fannius in 204 BC to eliminate orgies and gluttonous behaviour in households. By now customs and rules of etiquette had become well established, both in the eating at table and attendance by slaves allocated to specific aspects of service. Cooks, once regarded as toiling slaves, became culinary artists, and demanded high wages to match their new-found position. Aesthetics gradually had central importance, and colour was stressed with saffron commonly used to obtain yellow, spinach or leek juices to obtain green, and shades of red were gained from sandalwood and sunflowers.

To Britain, the Romans brought with them discernment for food, and were enlightened concerning its preparation, embracing centuries of experience. Among the first plants they brought were the cultivated varieties of various fruits and vegetables, such as pears and apples, cabbages and onions. They also brought herbs and spices. Pepper was the colonizing Roman cook's favourite seasoning, closely followed by ginger and cinnamon. Cooking-soda and olive oil were also used. The Romans had also brought with them pheasants, rabbits and guinea fowl. However the last two species died out after the Romans left and were not re-introduced until several centuries later. The colonizing Romans favoured wheat and they urged the Gauls to grow it as opposed to rye and barley. Bread was held in high esteem and was often flavoured with fennel, poppy or cumin seeds. It was the Romans who brought the vine and wine with them on their travels. Beer, cider and perry (made from pears) were also available (Johnson, 1990). The Romans also brought 'garum',[1] made from the brine of fermented and salted fish, and asafoetida, which smelled strongly of garlic. These all came to be used in Britain and Gallo-Roman territories just as much as in Rome itself.

As in Greece, where principal proponents of the gastronomic arts had not been cooks, but gourmands, so too in Roman society the pursuit of the subject depended on the gourmand. Apicius who lived in the reign of Tiberius and whose prodigality in cuisine was mentioned by Pliny the Elder, collated recipes (from the Latin *recipe*, 'take') and the methods used by leading cooks and published them in the first known cookery book. Etymologically, it also is interesting to note the role in Greek and Roman large households of the 'archimagirus' or 'chief imaginer' or creator – who was responsible for drawing up the list of fare, and so presaging the first menu composer.

In the first century AD the Romans were in Scotland and Germany as well as many other countries. The foodstuffs they brought with them were more than food for survival alone. Wherever the Roman Legions marched, they brought Roman civilization as well. The Romans also carried away to Rome the alimentary specialities of the lands they had conquered. This caused a certain amount of culinary homogeneity. During the period of invasions following the decline of the Roman Empire, Gallo-Roman traditions intermingled with offerings from the barbarian invaders whether Goths, Franks or Vandals, and were by degree remodelled into what is commonly termed today medieval cuisine.

---

[1] The Greeks gave semantical meaning to foodstuffs. If the concept of good eating is semantically conjoined with the indulgence permitted by affluence, then possibly 'garum' might qualify as one of the first exponents of gastronomy. Garum was a salty fish relish whose main esculent commodity is hazy and contested by historians and others alike.

Wine and other alcoholic beverages

Enough has been written to indicate that the consumption of drinks containing alcohol is widespread and has a venerable and honourable history. Feasting, often religious in origin, has been a feature of all the great civilizations dating from at least 6000 BC and it is more than probable that alcohol, in some form or other, played an important part in these celebrations.

The grapevine is as old as history itself. The earliest evidence is found in the fossils of some sixty million years ago, though it is improbable that this grape could have been used for making wine. However a vine found in the relics of the later quaternary period of the Upper Palaeolithic Age (about 100,000 years ago) was one whose fruit was capable of producing wine and is probably the original source of the many species of vines and varieties of wine which successive civilizations have developed all over the world.

The vine had grown wild in both Europe and the East. The art of cultivating the vine (viticulture) and wine making (vinification) had, according to mythology, been taught to the Greeks by Dionysus. However, it is certain that viticulture and wine drinking had already started by 4000 BC. The first developments were in the Middle or Near East, around the Caspian Sea and in Mesopotamia about 6000–4000 BC, in Asia Minor and Phoenicia about 3000 BC. Texts from the tombs of the 5th, 6th and 7th dynasties of Egypt show that wine was in general use throughout Egypt in 2750–2500 BC. It had also been the Egyptians who had first spread the art throughout the Mediterranean, particularly in Sicily and southern Italy. There had then been further development of wine making and drinking in Europe accompanied by the spread of Greek civilisation, first in the Aegean and then on the mainland in about the 16th century BC.

However the substantial and widespread establishment and development of viticulture throughout Europe is predominantly due to the ever-widening influence of the Roman Empire after the decline of Greece. Wine production had taken root so firmly and grown so rapidly that wine was being exported to other countries in the Western Mediterranean and to Spain and Gaul, the last two of which were to develop their own vineyards over the next few centuries to such an extent that they eventually surpassed their Roman tutors.

Although it is likely that the Gauls were familiar with the vine well before the Roman conquest (first century BC), the quality of the Roman wines and new methods introduced by the conquerors gave considerable impetus to viticulture. The foundations of French, German and Spanish wine production were to be well and truly laid by the Romans.

The Romans also brought the vine to Britain but for climatic reasons[2] its cultivation did not become widespread. There were certainly vineyards in Anglo-Saxon times but it was probably the Normans who later stimulated the planting of vines in England, a development which was to be extended by the Church until the dissolution of the monasteries in the first half of the 16th century. There are vineyards today, which produce some interesting wines, but the British have relied almost entirely on imports.

Wines are not the only drinks that have a long history behind them. There were various beers produced by the fermentation of different grains, or beer-like drinks such as mead, made from honey and grain. Such drinks spread most rapidly in the countries where the soil and climate were not really suitable for viticulture. The spread of brewing throughout Europe had, like viticulture, also been largely due to the rising tides of Greek and Roman

---

[2] The vine flourishes well within the latitudes of about 30° and 50° north (and south) of the equator. This means that all of southern Europe is within the northern band and the band itself extends at its most northerly limit, up to the south of England – and across Europe at around that latitude.

civilizations. It is likely though that brewing had probably originated in Babylon and beer from malted barley was certainly available from about 6000 BC, coming to Egypt around 2000 BC.

There are also the distilled drinks such as brandy and whisky, although these were to appear in Europe much later during the later part of the medieval period. Brandy for example was to become widespread in Europe by the middle of the 17th century, and whisky distillation was a feature of Scottish life from the 15th century. Again, however, distillation was known in the East long before it was introduced into Europe.

2.2 Medieval and Renaissance cuisine, and the rise of France

After the fall of the Roman Empire, gastronomy took sanctuary in the monasteries until the 15th century, when the Renaissance revival in the arts, and the pursuit of good living, were predominantly promoted by the Vatican. It is with the royal and religious courts from the 5th to the 10th century that we find bountiful resources and aliments becoming readily attainable. The monastic orders lived off the land, produced wines, spirits and herbal liqueurs, and manufactured their own breads, cheeses and honey. It can be reasoned that the cooking of the monasteries and other religious orders, to a great extent, shaped regional gastronomy and with the royal households developed the features of a culinary art.

Apicius' book was placed in print and gastronomy kept alive during the Dark Ages. The most eminent and distinguished approaches to eating at this time came from the Borgias of Rome, a Spanish-Italian family who were at the height of their power during the late 15th to 16th centuries. Alfonso (1378–1458) was the founder of the family fortunes and became Pope Calixtus III from 1455 to 1458; Rodrigo Borgia became Pope Alexander VI in 1475/6–1507. Other Italian families also contributed, such as the Medicis of Florence, beginning with Giovanni de Medici who became Pope Leo X, and who was a well-known theatrical epicure.

During the 11th century rôtisseurs and cuisiniers in general were part of lordly households residing within the castle. In lordly, princely or royal kitchens, there were appreciable numbers of staff. The kitchen was divided up between various services, which continued quite separately through the offices of well-regarded functionaries. The maître queux, (administrative chef) was solely responsible for the entrées. The rôtisseurs took sole responsibility for roasting and spit roasting, and they were called 'hateurs', a word depicting its roots to *hatier* – andirons or firedogs which were adorned with hooks for supporting spits (Valby, 1993).

Hateurs had to choose the meat and lard it, then supervise the roasting process, and were also charged with the task of basting the meat and poultry during cooking. Old people who were of no use for general kitchen work and children were titled happpelapins (galopins) or spit turners. Happelapins translate as small gophers or general dogsbodies. Customarily royal and lordly kitchens employed more rôtisseurs alone than the total cuisiniers employed in today's largest kitchens (*Larousse Gastronomique*, 1971).

We can hypothesize how these élite rôtisseurs in lordly households later become public rôtisseurs. This can be gleaned with the help of historians from the Middle Ages, such as Funk-Brentano, who expressly tells us that many castles flourished and became genuine villages. Through time the skilled workmen and women living and labouring for their lord or royal personages (the armourers, smiths, saddlers, weavers, tailors, lacemakers and embroiderers etc.) increased in number day by day until in the end they assembled themselves into what could be termed self-help associations, and who paid subscriptions and called themselves 'fraternities' (Valby, 1993).

It was mainly the accumulation of a number of abbeys, monasteries and lordships that then fashioned the embryo of cities. Evidence can still be found today of such evolution in some large towns, e.g. Abbeyes de St Georges, Rennes and de St Melaine. As these towns developed assorted trades bodies swiftly viewed that it was both advantageous and essential to band together in order to make their work easier and accomplish more by learning from each other.

These were associations for perfecting techniques and mutual assistance. They now had the approval of their lords to work for the rest of the castle, and also for any other customers requiring their assistance. Their masters gained also in that they retained the services of these individuals and also received fees and dues. Workshops were now to be found external to the castle yard, spreading themselves into the forming city, and displaying their wares in order to gain sales. These, through the passage of time, were the origins of shops available to the passer-by (Valby, 1993). Those who lived in the newly formed cities were by convention meat and bread eaters. The guilds and fraternities of butchers, rôtisseurs and bakers were very powerful organizations in the earliest cities partly because individuals' fortunes could be quantified by the amounts of these aliments that they were able to purchase.

The fraternities later mainly assembled themselves by professional alliance in streets in specific areas; arising from the grouping of these craftsmen, many streets and areas have kept their name down the centuries to this day. The fraternities imposed guidelines and regulations on their membership, establishing themselves into brotherhoods; possibly religious brotherhoods in the first instance followed by trade corporations thereafter.

We can hypothesize that these customs and rules subsequently became professional laws, which would have become obsolete if it were not for (in the time of Saint Louis), Etienne Boileau (or Boyleaux), a provost of Paris, who had the idea of assembling all of the regulations together in a commendable compilation by the name of 'Book of Trades' in 1258. Workers' associations were given the name of 'corporation' or 'guild'. Many guilds that were around at this time are still alive today and many others have been formed since. A substantial number of them were also related to food and beverage guilds.

The first really professional master chef who springs to mind is Taillevent (or sometimes spelled Taillevant), who worked for a striking group of French royal households (Willan, 1992). Born Guillaume Tirel in Pont-Audemer, Normandy, round about 1310 (he died in Pont-Audemer circa 1395 and is buried in Hennenbont in the priory of Notre Dame), the boy who would become the first prominent French chef to make his mark on gastronomic history became in 1326 a kitchen aid (happelapin) for Queen Jeanne (Jeanne d'Evreux), wife of King Charles IV (Page and Kingsford, 1971).

Taillevent was entrusted to turn the roasting spits in front of the open fires. Some accounts say he was known as Taillevent because of his dexterity and speed, while others state that it was because of the length of his nose. In 1346 he entered the service of Philippe de Valois (King Philip IV), as (keu) cook. In 1349 he was given a house in Saint-Germain-en-Laye as reward for the standard of service the King had received. He also soon became an ecuyer (squire) and shortly after joined the household of the Dauphin in that position, becoming cook in 1355. He held the same position in other famous houses, for the Duke of Normandy (1359–61), Charles V (1368–73) and later, in 1381, for Charles VI, who honoured him and, in 1392, elevated him to master of the King's kitchen provisions (*Larousse Gastronomique*, 1971).

He is best known for *Le Viandier*, thought to be the first professional treatise written in France, and upon which all French cooking was founded until, in 1472, J.B. Platina's *De Honesta Voluptate* eclipsed it. *Le Viandier* was commissioned by King Charles V, and

Le Viandier is thought to have been prepared prior to 1380, with some authors implying that it was commenced as early as 1373 (Page and Kingsford, 1971). The principal feature of *Le Viandier* is that it learnedly and expressly documents the foodstuffs of the 14th century, something that the King wished various masters and specialists of the time to do in their own fields. The complete translation of the title into English follows:

> Hereafter follows *The Viandier* describing the preparation of all manner of foods, as cooked by Taillevent, the cook of our noble king, and also the dressing and preparation of boiled meat, roasts, sea and freshwater fish, sauces, spices and other suitable and necessary things as described hereafter

(As can be surmised, 'viande' in original French implies all foodstuffs, not just meat.)

The work particularly details a complete synthesis of all aspects of cookery, and the various aliments eaten in the 14th century. Many copies of *Le Viandier* spread among the haute monde and chefs prior to the printing press. The main offering of *Le Viandier* lay in its emphasis on soups, spicy sauces, mainly saffron, pepper, ginger, cinnamon, and ragouts including, not only meat, game and poultry, but also fish. The principal cooking methods mentioned were roasting and boiling. An aspect of the importance of this text is that it upholds and confirms all that we know about medieval cuisine, and shows the influence of the Greeks and Romans to great effect, as well as the integration of the aliments they brought with them into the indigenous food patterning of a nation.

Many copies of *Le Viandier* were in circulation among chefs and noblemen prior to the printing press and showed the then popularity of sweet and sour dishes in Europe as a whole. An example of this is German gruel with onions, almonds and lards of bacon (*Larousse Gastronomique*, 1971). Parallels can be drawn between Roman and medieval cooking and many writers have made this distinction drawing from Taillevent's book and the work of Apicius (Willan, 1992).

Naturally there had been very good cooking before Taillevent but it is from the medieval age onwards, and Taillevent's book *Le Viandier*, that haute cuisine as we understand it today became important. It developed into an expression of power and splendour reflecting human spirituality.

Without doubt between 1341 and 1626 a new world had emerged. Renaissance means 'new birth', the transition from the Middle Ages to the modern world. The 'Renaissance Man' typified the Renaissance ideal of wide-ranging culture and learning. In arts and science, the Renaissance in France confirmed vital advances, but not however in the art of cuisine. There was not so much a decline but more of stagnation in technique and taste, which was slow to change. In fact the pace of change for the peasantry in Britain and France specifically and in the rest of Europe generally was virtually imperceptible. However all this would change in the following century.

At the time *Le Viandier* was still a great classic medieval work. However, in food and eating there was a switch of focus to literary endeavours in cuisine, a situation that has blossomed ever since. The initial focus of attention in writing was towards healthier eating; combating of obesity and health matters in general. Interest in dietary and health matters greatly interested the doctors, scholars and intellectuals of the day.

Traces of culinary creation, individuality of taste and personal achievement, can however be recognized as rooted in the Renaissance period. The exploration of the New World now introduced ingredients such as chocolate and potatoes. Coffee from the Middle East also appeared at this time. As a result of the long wars between France and Italy, diplomatic reciprocity and sovereign marriages, trade between the two nations increased; vegetables and fruits arrived from Italy, sugar was also popularized, having once been used only for its perceived therapeutic value.

Tableware such as forks appeared and it was frowned upon to pick up food in one's fingers. Crockery and glassware was popularized, ousting pewter, and plates now appeared instead of the trencher (individual wooden two sided platter). Kitchen equipment was also to gradually change, there was an increased variety of dishes appearing, and the meal itself became more cultured. The three basic courses of a meal remained as in medieval times; for example a banquet's first course would spotlight more often than not a hot liquid concoction like a potage, fricassé or hash. The second course would be a roast and or boiled meat, poultry or game, and for dessert, small cakes, dried fruits etc. would be served followed by dairy produce, fresh fruit and sweet items served in a separate room.

2.3 The fount of gastronomy

French cuisine has an international image of authority and esteem. The cuisine has been instrumental in affecting all Western cuisines, especially European. France has often been described as the birthplace of gastronomy, but how did it take on this mantle? Most definitely, France is a country of moderate climates and amazing varieties of produce can be culled from its many regions, but this super abundance of fresh quality produce alone does not explain why France became one of the world's greatest gastronomies. Gastronomy needs its professionals, as well as eager patrons and novices who spur on the professionals to greater sophistication and presentation.

Many groups and individuals in history have brought about gradual change in cooking and eating habits. The difference, which can be viewed in our time, is that transitional phases in cooking and eating habit can be as fleeting as a decade. Just how far back we have to go to locate the origins of the gastronomic activity has already been discussed. Distinct French cuisine is easily traced back to the 1500s (whereas distinctive and distinguished British cuisine dates only from the 1700s). In France we look in the direction of two very dissimilar communities, the Gauls and the Romans.

Right back through the centuries each age could be identified not only by its artefacts but also by the distinctive aliments enjoyed by the wealthy. The Romans brought with them a highly sophisticated cuisine, and Roman epicureanism became embedded and blossomed in the French diet over hundreds of years. The earliest French writing on culinary matters dates from the beginning of the 14th century and records more of what the élite ate than what peasants could access. The haute monde were provisioned from their lands and held absolute hunting rights.

The effect of *Le Viandier* had lasted up until the rise of the Florentine chefs under Catherine de Medici and publication of *Le Cuisinier français* (1651) by the founder of French classical cuisine, François Pierre de la Varenne (1618–1678). This publication introduced a new appreciation of the culinary art and was produced in 30 editions in some 75 years. The book has variously been praised and undervalued, however there were few other contemporary works in the field of cookery appearing in France throughout the 16th century. No matter what was said of *Le Cuisinier français*, it was certainly the first book with any major and surviving influence since *Le Viandier*.

The reason for this work's runaway success appears to be that it was the first to chronicle the enormous development and progress that French values and royal court cooking had undergone during the enlightening influence of the Renaissance. Major changes arrived as a result of the marriage of Catherine de Medici of Florence to Henry II of France in 1553. Catherine was in fact chosen to marry Henry by his father, François I (1515–47), for he was well aware of Italy's power in the arts and politics. It would also not have escaped his notice that Lyons, the banking capital of Europe at that time, had a burgeoning Italian population (Willan, 1992).

Catherine was only 14 years old when she married Henry II, but her influence should not be underestimated. She controlled France for over 50 years and her dominance was partly attributed to the fact that she was the wife of one French king, and the mother of another three. Catherine brought her own cooks, pastry cooks (considered to be individuals of influence in the larger households) and domestic staff to the French court in 1553. They reproduced their own Florentine specialities and other Italian practices stemming from the Medici court. This assisted in refining and improving the then standards of French hospitality and cuisine. It is from here that can be seen a subtlety, delicacy, care and love moving into French cuisine (Page and Kingsford, 1971).

The French also readily raised this new cuisine to new heights of courtliness, and through this process, seized for themselves the culinary leadership of Europe. Catherine was also responsible for introducing the Florentine art of table decoration to the court. This included the finest silverware, glasses, table linens, earthenware and the fork (*Larousse Gastronomique*, 1971). Catherine, a Tuscan, was also acknowledged as having introduced the artichoke to France, which caused considerable scandal at the time for her fondness of the vegetable was considered sinful since it was generally considered to be an aphrodisiac and unsuitable for consumption by a young woman (Willan, 1992).

Catherine's consumption was considerable. Chroniclers at Louis XIV's court, in their graphic accounts of the Sun King's own colossal consumption, recall her ability to match it. She was also known to have frequent indigestion. This entire period was known as one of excess. Gradually France overtook Italy as the foremost country in the art of cooking and began to lead the world in matters of gastronomic excellence (Mennell, 1985). Michael de Montaigne, a French essayist summarizing the spirit of the new cuisine, affirmed that it was literally this emergence of a great attention to detail, harmony and balance, which made the Renaissance arts so momentous. A later French Medici queen, Marie de Medici, wife of Henry IV, was also to be credited with similar achievements to Catherine's, at the beginning of the 17th century.

The close of the Middle Ages had coincided with a cultural watershed – the creation of the printing press. St John states, 'in the beginning was the word', and right up until the 14th century the oral tradition was the only real way in which cooks and chefs could learn their craft. The printed word appeared in the 15th century (1475), when Johannes Gutenberg developed the principle of movable type (Mennell, 1985).

Individual national tastes emerged from the prevailing European tradition and the implications for gastronomy from the written word were immense. Alimentary subjects featured significantly amongst the earliest printed material. The very first cookery book appears to have been the much-acclaimed *Kuchenmeisterey*, which was published in Nurnberg in 1485, and was to be republished in a total of 56 editions. By *circa* 1650, cookery books had been printed in all of the major Western European languages, and from here onwards the growth in printed matter concerning all aspects of eating, foods, and cookery grew until today, where there are more books about food and beverages published than any other subject.

Tastes in food, particularly for the haute monde, markedly developed in the first 100 years of printed texts being available. The written word on culinary matters was picked up on much more quickly in France than in England, where changes were much more gradual. We are given the hint that a lot of these early works were written for practitioners by practitioners; the reason forwarded is that the books were printed in what was classed as native or vulgar languages, and not the more élite and scholarly Latin. One can of course only hypothesize whether this was indeed the case, for very little direct evidence exists, and there is scarcely any data collected by governments on the literacy of their communities before the 19th century.

Rates of literacy are thought to have increased considerably in France between the Renaissance and the French Revolution. In England a revolution in literacy is spoken of having taken place between 1540 and 1640, and Italy followed place. The written recipes and books on food topics and the beaux-arts broke the absolute dependency on oral tradition within circles of professional and literate cooks. Dishes and their ingredients were now more readily fixed in the mind, and the entire exercise heightened giving recipes a prescriptive character.

Later on as recipes became more distinctive, and measurements more precise (necessary for perfecting results), printed recipe collections may have brought into play pressures toward conservatism and conformity, versus change and innovation. There was also a pressure toward literacy for the men and women operating in craft fields. With all of these pressures there came about amongst practitioners, who now shared a common *répertoire* of recipes and production methods, a shared social prestige, technical cohesion and professionalism, which has stood the test of time and is much in evidence in today's professionals.

2.4 The genesis of a grand cuisine: the 17th and early 18th centuries

From the 16th century, it had taken the maîtres de cuisine and maîtres de table of France less than a hundred years to build the culinary reputation that has lasted into modern times. From then, the transformation to new classic cuisine really appeared in the 17th and 18th centuries, demanding the skills of a literate, trained group of professional cooks who operated in the homes of the noble élite and the wealthy, and in hotels. In ordinary homes, the regional cuisine and bourgeois cuisine was influenced by non-professional cooks, who were in the main women (Hubert-Bare, 1991). Grande cuisine was by degree casting off countless former distinguishing aspects, and was now stimulated by everyday peasant and bourgeois kitchen essentials, like lentils, pumpkins, asparagus and root vegetables. Peasant fare slowly became acceptable to the haute monde, for during that period it was voguish. Truffles were withdrawn from peasant cookery and became uniquely for aristocratic consumption; a similar fate would befall morels and other aliments (Brears, 1985).

Yet another appreciable distinction in cooking references of the Middle Ages and those of the 17th century concern the substitution of butter for lard. In *Le Viandier* lard was most prominently used, but in the 17th century butter was now allowed on fast days and also during Lent, and like the morel and truffle, butter was to become one of the central aliments in the new classic cuisine. The roux appeared in the 17th century, based on flour and butter, and was a requisite as a thickening agent. The roux was first mentioned in *Le Cuisine français* written in 1651 by François Pierre de La Varenne, kitchen steward (ecuyer de cuisine) to the Marquis d'Uxelles

The dominant fluid flavouring agents in medieval sauce making were vinegar and verjuice, which were very acidic. Vestiges of these sauces can still be seen in simple sauces like the English mint sauce, the French vinaigrettes, and in relishes and salsas. Some more modern versions have been refined and a diminished acid content remains, as in the classical Sauce Robert. Other far-reaching departures comprised the procedure of reduction, which would lend sauces a good consistency. Gravy (jus) resulted from deglazing the pan in which meat had roasted (Peterson, 1991).

These were the forbears of the fonds de cuisine, the central preparations upon which cooks in the 1800s would subsequently build an entire thesis of cuisine. The last prominent cook of the 1600s, François Massialot, provided 23 recipes for coulis or cullis, which was based on reduced meat stock, scented with herbs and thickened with bread (Hubert-Bare, 1991). The age of sauces and saucing had begun, and a new aesthetic evolved with criteria that are not unlike those of today. Other sophistications included mousses, quenelles, boudins and godiveau. These preparations are simple today utilizing current technology (like food processors), but at the time they emerged, they were incredibly complex and involved for the cook.

The aristocracy set standards of estimable taste in their kitchens. Keeping up with the new taste of the nobility became a vital and marketable area for new authors of cookbooks and was in demand by the rising bourgeoisie, some of whom were investing in country estates. Many books were marketed towards country and landed gentry. In 1654 two important volumes were published, *Les Delices de la campagne* and *Le Jardinier français*, written by Nicholas de Bonnefons, an ardent contemporist and valet to King Louis XIV. One volume addressed food preservation and horticulture, the other focused on cuisine. One of Bonnefons' primary maxims was that 'aliments should taste as nature intended, with the ability to keep possession of their full flavour' (Hubert-Bare, 1991).

2.5 The enlightened 18th century

Haute cuisine had been developing and flourishing in France at least from the mid 1600s, and continued to do so during the Rococo age in the period before the French Revolution of 1789, which is a massive landmark in the history of French eating. Louis XIV had enjoyed very formal table service. His maître d'hotel staged theatrical dining occasions once or twice a week at Versailles, where the king was literally on show for everyone to see. However, with the succession of the Regent Philippe d'Orleans from 1715, some far-reaching transformations were brought about. The Regent, a man, who also liked to eat well, differed from Louis XIV in that his idea of good taste was commensurate with closeness and fellowship.

Disagreement amongst cuisiniers continued in this century as in the last, with some striving towards modernity and lightness in cuisine and others wishing to stick to the ancient methods. The nouvelle cuisine of the time was well established by the 1740s but it was very labour intensive and presented dishes that were complex and extravagant. There had been a great deal of conjecture and hypothesizing about food. François Marin wrote in 1739: 'modern cuisine is a kind of chemistry' (Willan, 1992). Marin was amongst the 18th century's greatest cooks, who dignified sauces, placing them in a classification of their own; he also stated that stock was 'the soul of sauces' and was imperative to the emergent nouvelle cuisine.

Another prolific writer was Menon, although not much is known about his life (Willan 1992); even his first name remains a mystery! However, Menon was one of the most widely read authors of his day. More than 100 years separated him from *La Varenne*, when cookery was still rooted in Italy and the medieval ways. Menon is remembered because of his publication *Souper de la cour*, which provided abstract and technical guidance to professional cooks. *Cuisinière bourgeoise* was an astute and level headed work which became a bestseller and was pitched for women readers, with its recipes based on market produce and foods from the garden (Willan, 1992).

In *La-Science du maîtres d'hôtel cuisinier*, Menon stated, 'Cookery refines the coarse elements of foodstuffs, strips the tiniest pieces to take advantage of the earthy extracts they contain.

It brings them to perfection, purifies them and, in a way, transforms them.' This could be viewed as the parlance of the alchemist. Analogies would be drawn between the chemist and the cook, both being intent on the pursuit of excellence through the development of techniques to form a distillation founded on the basic elements adaptable to a multiplicity of conditions and circumstances. Vincent de la Chapelle, whose sauce Espagnole is recognized as a classic sauce and still produced, put together *Le Cuisine moderne* (1735) and, like Marin, set out the cardinal criteria of grande cuisine.

As modernist theories progressed and flourished so too did philosophy, and the slow fuse was lighted for the explosion that was the French Revolution. During this period cuisine burgeoned and the haute monde spent ever-larger sums on entertaining. The bourgeois could not follow aristocratic trends and so for them adjustments had to be made. Regional dishes sprouted and became important. Less complicated production caught the eye of some aristocrats, although it was more of a flirting with native specialities, on occasion for reasons of health and girth, and to a lesser extent by virtue of concern for egalitarianism (*La Nouvelle Maison rustique*, 1740).

Most of the top cooks wished to work in Paris, and the first Parisian cafés were created, in which intense political discussions took place. In France the auberges (or inns) had existed as long ago as Roman times and the abbeys welcomed travellers right up to the time of the French Revolution in 1789. The numbers of post-houses (where stagecoaches stopped overnight or waited whilst horses were changed) increased until the arrival of the railway age, and the inns played a social as well as a political role (Leeming, 1991).

2.6 The founding fathers of European gastronomy

During the late 18th and early 19th centuries French gastronomy prospered. In this period two men considered to be amongst the founding fathers of modern gastronomy are most historically noteworthy. These individuals are Jean Anthelme Brillat-Savarin and Alexandre Balthasar Laurent Grimod de la Reynière.

Jean Anthelme Brillat-Savarin

Born on 2 May 1755, in Belley, in the Ain district, the son of Marc Anthelme Brillat,[3] he spent his youth in Bugey, an area famed for its source of rich local produce. He gained his interest in cookery from Aurore Brillat, his mother, who was an accomplished cordon bleu cook.

Having studied law at Dijon, and joined the bar at Belley, Brillat-Savarin later became a French magistrate and gastronome, having also studied chemistry and medicine (Tannahill, 1975).

Following the fall of the Girondins in 1793, not long after Brillat-Savarin was elected Mayor of Belley, and at the commencement of the Terror, he was denounced by the revolutionary tribunal, arrested and sentenced to be shot. He escaped from prison and went into exile in Switzerland. He then moved to Holland, from where he set out for the United States of America, staying there for three years. During his time in exile he lost all of his possessions, including a vineyard. He made a living in America on the income from giving French lessons, and also from his earnings as a violinist with the orchestra of the John Street Theatre in New York.

---

[3] He adopted the name Brillat-Savarin later in life after an aunt left him a fortune on the strictest condition that he took her name (*Larousse Gastronomique*, 1971).

Brillat-Savarin enjoyed many culinary excursions in America until 1797, when he was granted approval to return to France. After a period he was appointed councillor to the Supreme Court of Appeal, a post that he continued to hold until his death. Brillat-Savarin was to remain unmarried; his leisure time spent formulating treatises of varying kinds on history and economics, his writings also including a work on the duel. In 1808 he was made a 'Chevalier de l' Empire'.

His interests were many and varied, his spare time taken up by archaeology, astronomy, chemistry and gastronomy, appreciating good restaurants, especially Véry, Grand Vefour, Tortoni and Beauvilliers. He frequently had company at his home in the Rue de Richelieu in Paris, where he hosted assorted meals and cooked himself, specialities like tuna omelette, fillet of beef with truffles and stuffed pheasant (Drayton, 1975).

The Physiology of Taste • • •

Two months prior to his death, the book that would eventually establish him a legendary figure had been published and arrived in the bookshops. It was a turning point in gastronomic literature, recognized as having been created by a cultivated and highly developed gastronome. Its full title was *Physiologie de gout ou Méditations de gastronomie transcendante, ouvrage théorique, historique et à l'ordre du jour, dédié aux gastronomes parisiens par un professeur, membre de plusieurs sociétés littéraires et savantes*,[4] although the book is also known by its shorter title as *La Physiologie du gout* (*The Physiology of Taste*, 1826).

The book was an instant best-seller, arousing Balzac's excitement and the envy of Carême. Some complained of the book's omissions, one of which was a chapter on wines. Brillat-Savarin's aspiration lay in his desire to fashion the culinary art as a true science, calling on medicine, physics, chemistry and anatomy, which gave the text an appearance of pedantry. This is an unfairness to Brillat-Savarin, for he was a tremendous scholar, and storyteller, who could be anecdotal with an elegant humour. His work was, after all, didactical (fitted to teach an art or science), tracing cause from effect scientifically. Having kept body and soul together through all regimes from the Revolution, through the Empire to the Restoration, he finally died after contracting a cold whilst attending a Mass being offered for Louis XVI in the basilica of Saint-Denis on 8 September 1826. He was buried in the Père Lachaise cemetery in Paris (*Larousse Gastronomique*, 1971; Leeming, 1991).

Physiologie de gout remains for many individuals to this day an instructive, informed and pleasant read, for the amateur and the professional alike. Brillat-Savarin was, in spite of those who would snipe at his success, an erudite, scholarly individual, gastronome and master. His work came at precisely the right time for the edification and education of the rich and informed bourgeoisie, who had a great respect for the past but also admired progress and the good life they were living at the time (Drayton, 1975; Mennell, 1985).

Alexandre Balthasar Laurent Grimod de la Reynière

Born in Paris in 1758, the son of a wealthy *fermier-général* (tax collector), Grimod de la Reynière was handicapped by a genetic malformation of the hands; one hand was shaped

---

[4] The full translation of this title is 'Physiology of taste or meditations on transcendent gastronomy, a theoretical work, historical and current, dedicated to Parisian gastronomes by a professor, member of several literary and research societies'. Brillat-Savarin was using the word physiology here to mean 'the scientific analysis of the workings of living beings'.

like a claw and the other like a goose's foot. He was rejected by his aristocratic mother, and he ultimately became estranged from his entire family. Grimod would appear to have compensated for his physical handicap with his utter passion for food.

While striving for his law degree, he developed a taste for scandal and his extravagant behaviour made him quite infamous. He published *Reflexions philosophiques sur le plaisir par un celibataire* while working to become a qualified barrister. Shortly after he qualified he arranged an extraordinary dinner at the end of January 1783, sending the invitation cards to his guests with the following text 'You are invited to attend the funeral procession and burial of a feast that shall be given by Master Alexandre Balthasar Laurent Grimod de la Reynière Esquire, barrister to the high court, drama correspondent of the journal Neuchâtel, at his residence in the Champs-Élysées. You are invited to attend at nine o'clock in the evening and the meal will be served at ten' (*Larousse Gastronomique*, 1971).

He was one of the best drama critics of his day, and had a passion for literature. But his indiscretions continued, and after one especially disquieting embarrassment, the nature of which was never disclosed, his family secured an order against him under the King's private seal, sending him on retreat for three years (from April 1786 to 1789) to a Bernardine monastery close to Nancy. At the table of the Abbot he encountered the art of good eating, which still existed in monastic settings. Grimod set about improving his knowledge in his further retreats, in Lyons and Beziers (Montaigne, 1958).

To earn an income during this period he started in business in Lyons as a grocer, selling also perfumery and hardware. During this time he travelled the length and breadth of the various fairs in the south of France. On hearing of his father's death in 1792 he returned to Paris. At his father's mansion in the Champs-Élysées he re-established his lavish dinner parties, and once more returned to his work as a drama critic, but was later banned from doing so and he then turned to writing about restaurants. This resulted in his series *Almanach des gourmands* (1804–1812). This covered Grimod's reminiscences of Paris, including a very successful food guide. In 1808 he issued his *Manuel des amphitryons*, which equipped the nouveau-riche of the period with an insight into what Grimod believed should be the customs, etiquette and the rules of conduct by which they should abide.

Grimod also stamped his authority on gastronomic affairs by setting up a 'jury of tasters' who would award a gastronomic certificate, entitled '*legitimation*', to foods or dishes presented to them. The jury met periodically at Grimod's mansion in the Champs-Élysées, where in sober fashion they tasted and consumed that which was brought by tradesmen who were basically seeking publicity from the '*legitimation*', pronounced 'always usually favourable' by the gastronomic court.

Grimod's most influential jury members comprised the Marquis de Cussy, Cambacérès and Gastaldy (a doctor and gastronome who expired at table when he was almost a centenarian!). Once again Grimod after a while fell foul of complaints and had to give up his jury. Placed in jeopardy by the prospect of lawsuits, Grimod discontinued the issue of the *Almanach*. By now his mother had also died and he inherited the last of her extensive wealth. He married the woman he had been living with for the past twenty years and went to live in rural countryside among his enduring friends, Doctor Roques and the Marquis de Cussy. Grimod de la Reynière died on Christmas Eve 1837 in Villiers-sur-Orge, during the midnight feast (*Larousse Gastronomique*, 1971).

Amphitryons • • •

Grimod popularized the word 'amphitryon' in his published work *Manuel des amphitryons* in 1808. He was one of the first to lay out what he thought to be correct behaviour at the table.

As maintained by Grimod, consideration and diplomacy was necessary, as well as generosity, good management, the employment of a good chef, and the critique and acknowledgement of good food. Despite the fact that the word is infrequently used today outside gastronomic circles, one rule, ordained by Brillat-Savarin, continues unaltered: 'To invite someone to be your guest is to undertake responsibility for his happiness all the time that he is under our roof'.

The amphitryon therefore is an individual who entertains guests at their table. The origins of the word are sketchy. According to mythology Zeus, wishing to tempt the mortal Alcmene, took on the form of her husband – Amphitryon – and gave her a son, Heracles. In Molière's comedy inspired by this story, the servant Sosoe, uncomfortable for having to serve two masters and resolving ultimately to serve the one who guarantees him board and lodging, says, 'the real Amphitryon is the host who supplies dinner', insufficient in itself, since one also is required to know how to do it and execute it successfully.

2.7 The genesis, multiplication and acculturation of the restaurant

The celebrated chefs of this period now had to harmonize their labour with respect to public, as opposed to private, dining, and in doing so they quickly refined French cuisine (Leeming, 1991). The new patrons perused the penmanship of the founding fathers, Brillat-Savarin and Grimod de la Reynière, as well as *eminence grise* (influential individuals behind the scenes) authors on gastronomic themes. In so doing the patrons gained a rounder comprehension of the worth of their cuisine and grew to evaluate it by dint of frank critiques themselves.

Contrasted against the aristocrats and beau monde, the new bourgeois and nouveau riche preserved their country roots and a comprehension of the source of their food. It is interesting to note that the 'virgin model' of eating place open to the public, which came to be known as a 'restaurant', made its appearance in Paris some two decades before the Revolution. Their emergence was a great stimulus to the rapid development of more refined and elaborate food in the hands of the famous chefs of the Napoleonic and Restoration periods, among whom the most famous would be Carême.

Marie Antoine Carême (1784–1833) became the most sought after French chef and gastronomer of his age, and lived in a time where independence of thought and action was commonplace. Carême's success is extraordinary, for he was totally self-educated; he taught himself to read and draw (talents in which he later became very accomplished) whilst working for Bailly, a famed patissier. The publication of his first two books came in 1815, *Le Pâtissier royal* and *Le Pâtissier pittoresque*. He would later become the doyen of his profession through his further publications.

The great era of the noble households was all but coming to a close and the staff in these households became greatly decreased. Carême was one of the last great chefs to work in private service. He was employed by some of the most noted households in Europe, and became chef to Talleyrand, worked for the Prince Regent (later to become King George IV), for Baron Rothschild, Czar Alexander I, and others.

Carême was an impatient man, often chiding his peers for their lack of innovation and vision. Aesthetics and the elaborate presentation of food was one of his greatest passions. He was a master of adding visual value and impact to his work, he believed in the total experience of dining, and he set about producing the architectural *pièce montée* (set piece), which he learnt about from Bailly. He spent a great deal of time investigating and copying classical architecture. It took such a hold on him that he used it in his cooking generally. Dishes were presented on elaborate *socles* (bases). He also produced ornate carvings and statuary in lard and in spun sugar, which became essential, though inedible, aspects expected from Carême's lavish dinners. Carême's answer to the various detractors of his work was that he was also creating for the mind and heart, and that he was pleasurably filling the gastronome's leisure time.

Carême also revolutionized the chef's dress. He favoured white as it denoted cleanliness and he and his staff wore double-breasted jackets; the breast of which could be changed over if the front got splashed or marked. He also determined that chefs' hats be different in height, thus distinguishing the cooks from the chefs. The chefs wore tall hats and the cooks smaller versions, more akin to skullcaps. Carême himself wore a hat reputedly 18 inches tall. These have been worn for a long time since by other head chefs, and are known as king crowns.

This was the period of not just haute cuisine, but a grande cuisine was developing and a conclusive *coup de grace* was given to cuisines of former times. The division between domestic and professional cookery expanded, as did the related division between female and male cooks. Aligned to the advent of a cookery profession (catering to a dining public), there also surfaced the 'bourgeois gastronome', not a cook or professional in the hospitality field, but one knowledgeable in the art of eating, and a leader of public opinion in matters relating to taste.

The restaurant could trace its ancestry back to several different kinds of institution, though none of them had quite matched the restaurant's combination of style, and type of food. Nor could they match the social milieu and social function of the restaurant (in the 1700s you could only eat at inns, which served at fixed times an equally fixed menu). Earliest forerunners of the restaurant, were, conceivably, the cookshops, characterized in accounts of medieval cities around the early 1100s, where individuals could send their own meat to be cooked, or where they might also buy a hot dish ready cooked, and be able to choose from joints, pies and puddings. This was important to the lower citizenry, but also frequented by all ranks. The larger houses were the only places with adequate means of cooking. The cookshops gradually, in England and elsewhere, evolved into the more sociable coffee houses of the late 1600s and, in London these became the hub of political machinations and pecuniary knowledge (Mennell, 1985).

Closest to the later restaurants in the mid to late 1700s, in terms of their social functions and the foods they served, were the English taverns (the word 'tavern' signifies originally a place where men went to drink wine, as contrasted with the ale-house where beer was sold). The socially superior client might be expected to frequent the tavern on a regular basis. Indeed, these venues became, in the later 1700s, centres of social life. In France, to attract and retain valuable business the aubergistes fed their customers well, keeping the inns open all day. The inns were haunts of the working classes, and drink with a table d'hôte menu was available daily.

The taverns' reputation for quality grew. However, in Paris there was little equivalent. The first restaurants opened there in the last years of the ancienne régime. A restaurant is an establishment where food and beverage is prepared, served and consumed, between set hours, either from an à la carte, or fixed price menu, i.e. table d'hôte. Restrictions by the guilds over the preparation of certain foods (some establishments having the ability to sell potages or broths but not pies, others ragoûts and not roasts) meant that a restaurant, in the form recognizable to us today, was a laboured and gradual development. The word restaurant first appears in the 1500s, meaning a food which restores (from *restaurer*), used more specifically for a rich soup capable of restoring one's strength. Very gradually, the word began to mean an eating-house. In 1765 a man named Boulanger, who sold soup in the Rue Poulies, christened his soups 'restaurants' and wrote on a sign, 'Boulanger sells magical restoratives', adding to the sign a joke in culinary Latin:

Venite ad me omnes qui stomacho laboretis, et ego restaurabo vos.
(Come to me all you whose stomachs labour, and I will restore you)

With a desire to build up his menus and unable to serve ragoûts, or sauces, because he was not a member of the corporation of traiteurs, he had the idea of serving his customers sheep's feet in white wine sauce. The traiteurs brought a lawsuit against him, which publicized both Boulanger and the sheep's feet! Eventually Boulanger won the case and a parliamentary decree that his dish was not a ragoût was a triumph, for everyone rushed to try it. Even Louis XV had the dish at Versailles, although the King, who was a real gourmand, did not share the general enthusiasm.

The restoratives were laid out on small marble tables, and eventually inspired other 'restaurateurs' to start up establishments in a similar manner. Later on in the 18th century, restaurants as distinct and separate places from inns and hotels started to emerge in Paris and around 1770 they became so popular that they spread across France and on to other European countries.

In France, with the initial rumblings of the Revolution, the clasp of the guilds eventually broke and privileges and monopolies were eliminated. The restaurateur was now given freedom to serve full meals from a repertoire, which included all classifications of dishes. The restaurant, as Brillat-Savarin tells us, enabled everyone 'to make, according to his purse or according to his appetite, copious or delicate meals, which formerly were the prerequisite of the very rich'.

A few restaurateurs became national celebrities after Boulanger. Antoine Beauvilliers (1752–1820), a chef who would lead the classical school of thought of his time, left the employ of the Comte de Provence (later Louis XVIII), to gain prominence as a restaurateur, and the first recorded chef proprietor. He often welcomed his guests in the regalia of an officier de bouche de reserve, wearing his dress sword (Kracknell and Nobis, 1985).

As France drew towards the Revolution, in the 1780s (various dates for this have been recorded – 1782, 1783, 1786), Beauvilliers established at no. 26 rue de Richelieu the first restaurant deserving of the name (Hubert-Bare, 1991). This establishment, known as La Grande Taverne de Londres, became the first successful enterprise at a high level and was the initial legitimate restaurant, as we know it, in Paris. Beauvilliers introduced the innovation of writing his dishes on a menu and producing them at small individual tables. He was also, as Brillat-Savarin records, the first to issue an 'inflated bill' (Willan, 1992: 144).

Beauvilliers had to close this restaurant because of revolutionary activity – his previous favour with the aristocracy during this period cost him 10 months in prison. However, upon his release he moved premises and opened a second restaurant, in his own name, and this time the embodiment of gastronomy in its period.

In 1814 Beauvilliers wrote *L'Art de cuisine*, in which he treated food service, food management and cooking as an exacting science. This was to be the first creditable book to succeed Menon's *La Cuisinière bourgeoise* in seventy years (Willan, 1992). He also joined forces with the man considered to lead the romantic school of thought of the period – Carême, the last great chef in private service – to write *La Cuisine ordinaire*, although both men were considered to be rivals during their lifetime. Beauvilliers' reputation lasted throughout the Empire and Restoration, with the doors of his business not closing until 1825, five years after his death, and before competition between himself and Carême could become bitter (Mennell, 1985).

Now was a time in which restaurants could flourish more out of necessity, as aristocrats fled the country in fear, and enterprising chefs left without jobs sought employment in the new restaurants or opened businesses of their own. There is no doubt as to where the supply of personnel came from: restaurateurs had, in general, learnt their trade in noble households (Mennell, 1985).

During the Revolution even condemned people enjoyed their food, for restaurateurs had contracts to provide rich prisoners with quality meals prior to being guillotined. Indeed the ringleaders of the Revolution were frequently gourmands: Danton, Mirabeau and Saint-Just all dined in restaurants of note like the Frères Provencaux and Meot, where they relished epic dinners. Whether the Revolution caused the rise of the restaurant, or whether, as is more believable, it merely accelerated a trend already under way, there is no doubt that the advent of the restaurant marked a new stage for the cookery profession, and for cookery itself (Hubert-Bare, 1991).

The gastronome equalled money with influence (they led opinion) and the chef had knowledge, aestheticism and patronage. The customer also now had a wider choice within a better atmosphere, and they could decide what they wanted to pay and so eat accordingly. By this time coffee, chocolate and tea had become daily beverages and ice cream, an earlier gem of the nobility, was popularized. In the region of Normandy, Marie Harel from the village of Camembert, made a cheese that was later to be treasured worldwide, and pâté de foie gras (goose liver pate), the Alsatian speciality, had become much prized (Montagne, 1938; Hubert-Bare, 1991).

One effect of the Revolution was the abolition of the guilds and their privileges. This made it easier for people to open a restaurant. Those who mainly took advantage of this were then the cooks and servants from the large houses, whose owners had fled or died. After the worst excesses of the Revolution were over a general feeling of well-being existed, and this, coupled with the chance of enjoying what was after all, usually only available to the aristocrat and the rich, i.e. the chance of enjoying the fruits of the table, created an atmosphere in which restaurants became an established institution.

2.8 Demand to be self-consciously modern and avant garde

The Deputies of the revolutionary period helped to establish, securely, the fashion for eating in restaurants. One much respected Parisian restaurant in the post-revolutionary period was Aux Trois Frères Provencaux, at the Palais Royal. This pioneering establishment was run by Barthelemy, Maneille and Simon, who, interestingly, were not 'frères' (blood brothers) but brothers-in-law, and were not, as one might also think from the restaurant's title, from Provence! The restaurant closed in 1869, but it was in this place that great chefs and cuisiniers of the likes of Dugléré, Casimir and Moisson carried out their initial campaigns (*Larousse Gastronomique*, 1971).

Eating out in the late 1700s was much more considered a part of the life of rich gentlemen in London than in Paris. (And respectable modern gentlewomen did not eat out anywhere until well into the 1800s.) Within the developing social figuration in France, modes of individual behaviour and cultural tastes were looking to be innovative and avant garde. Innovation did not rest solely on gastronomy, however, for this was a period of great change. In music the Baroque period (1600–1750) had come to a close and the Classical period (1750–1840) was under way and would be followed by the Romantic era. Modern expressiveness was revealed, and this also took the form of a new type of writer on gastronomic matters, the gastronomic critic. These people put food history and gastronomic gossip high on the list of reading matter for those on the fashionable scene after the Revolution. This was also the period that saw the proliferation of gastronomic dining clubs.

Hayward (1956) hints at other ways in which social and political changes of the Revolution increased public demand for restaurants, though these are purely speculative: 'Very tentatively the nouveaux riches preferred to eat in restaurants because the patriotic millionaires who had enriched themselves by the plunder of the church and nobility, were fearful in those troubled times, of declaring the full extent of their opulence, and thus, instead of setting up an establishment, preferred gratifying their epicurean inclinations at an eating house.'

It is not just changes in wealth that affected the balance between eating at home or eating out, but also changes in the food that was wanted, especially below the ranks of the very wealthiest. The leading chefs of the post-revolutionary era evolved a much more complex and ornate cuisine, from the remnants of courtly food which had already implanted its authority as a model to be imitated further down the social scale, and to a much greater measure than in England. Only the richest could produce a resemblance of this food in their homes – for it called for costly ingredients and a large kitchen staff, as can be viewed by the model examples in 'The stratification and division of labour in the kitchen' (see Chapter 4, Table 4.1, page 116).

Grimod de la Reynière (1806) argued that 'a full time specialist rôtisseur was essential if the highest standards were to be attained in roasting, for it required his full attention, and a cook (whose casseroles, marmites and ovens require complete attention) could not conceivably roast as well'. Thus the road to highly stratified systems was under way. Though restaurants with these types of operations were very expensive to frequent, it was still much cheaper to visit them than to attempt to attain the economically preclusive standards of hospitality in the home. Eventually there came about restaurants to suit all pockets in Paris.

None of the speculation about the growing demand for restaurants is as concrete as the effects of the Revolution on the supply side. The revolutionaries wished to displace conventional aspects, and multiple viewpoints, radically setting aside the guilds and closing the aristocratic kitchens, sending their cooks out to seek alternative employment. Supply need not be seen purely in a response to existing demand; it can be viewed through the workings of fashion, which can create its own demand (Mennell, 1985; Willan 1992). There was more equality now between chef restaurateur and diner than there ever could have been with the cook and his noble patron.

At the start of the 1800s, the fawning and grovelling emphasis of the prefaces with which the chefs of the 1600s and 1700s, who were author-cooks, devoted their recipe books would have been unthinkable. Newer routes to the summit of the culinary profession were now possible. Rather than go through the process of humbling themselves and seeking favour with one of a trifling number of rich patrons, aspiring cooks could now gladly challenge each other for the custom of a greater body of diners-out. Mary Berry, writing in post-Revolutionary France, penned the following. Though not especially with cooks in mind, it is quite apt: 'The fashionable tradespeople and professors of the arts of luxury, now feeling independent of all protection from their superiors, trusted entirely to the superiority of their talent, or their taste, for success' (1828, cited in Mennell, 1985).

Under the Directorate from 1795 to 1799 until the beginning of the First Empire in 1804, when revolutionary activity had at last diminished, and the French were still in a period of conspicuous excess and gourmandism, a resurgence of interest in gastronomy was noticeable. Chefs everywhere put pens to paper and wrote about the pleasures and love of eating, in an intellectual and erudite fashion. It is now, at this point in the history of gastronomy, that we see the emergence of authoritative figures whose influence through time has seen them classified as the masters of gastronomy.

2.9 The 19th century: the Golden Age

It is during the 19th century that the great master chefs start to materialize, chefs who have left us dishes that are still international classics to this day. It is now that we can observe massive changes in these grand kitchens, with the evolution of the 'partie'[5] system with its specialist chefs, the introduction of cast iron stoves and the supplanting of the spit and accompanying fires by ovens. It is now also that we see the emergence of the 'chef' proper, who manages his/her brigade with consummate skill. And at this time basic preparations were classified and catalogued.

An example of the chefs appearing in this time and contributing to developments is Alexis Benoist Soyer. Born in 1809 at Maux-en-Brie near Paris, he followed his elder brother, Phillipe, into training as a chef. Phillipe had gone to London as the cook to the Duke of Cambridge and invited Alexis to join him for a while before encouraging him to gain experience in the kitchens of a number of the big houses of the time. He is most remembered as the Chef of the Reform Club, in London's Pall Mall, a post that he held for twelve years.

However, through an interest in providing good food to large numbers of the poor, he became involved in the soup kitchens set up at the time of the corn harvest failure in 1845. As a result of this experience, the British Government invited him to go to Dublin to advise during the potato famine. It was there that he designed and had made a model kitchen, which could feed 1,000 people an hour. On his return to London he also created a feeding kitchen for the impoverished silk-weavers of Spitalfields. By now he had also written and published a number of books on cooking and had invented various pieces of kitchen equipment.

When he heard of the appalling conditions being experienced by the troops at the Crimean War, Alexis volunteered to go to the war front, at his own expense, to help and advise. This he did, supported by the many influential contacts he had made during his time at the Reform Club. In the hospitals and barracks he found that the food that the men received was adequate in quantity but uneatable, mainly because of the way it was being prepared. He centralized the food production and taught people how to undertake this. To ensure that fuel and heat were used economically, he modified the design of the cooking stoves he had designed for the Dublin kitchen and had a large number of them made in Britain and shipped out to the Crimea. The resulting design, 'The Soyer Field Stove', was so successful that, with minor modifications, they were still in use within the British army until 1980. Also, to improve bulk tea making he designed the 'Scutari Tea-pot', a container with a removable, perforated, interior cylinder.

He worked closely with Florence Nightingale, and did much to make improvements to the conditions of the army in the field. Eventually, like her, he succumbed to Crimea Fever. On return to Britain at the end of the war, although still suffering from the effects of his illness, he undertook the responsibility of redesigning the kitchens for the Wellington Barracks. It was to be his last creative effort. He died on 5 August 1858 (aged 49 years), one month after the kitchens were formally opened.

Alexis Benoist Soyer was a man of France, who gave such a lot for other people, particularly the poor of Britain and Ireland and, more especially, generations of officers and men of the British Army. He not only improved the lot of the British Army at the Crimea but also paved the way for the improvement of army and other forces catering generally. His

---

[5] The 'partie' system according to Escoffier is detailed, as part of considering the legacy of Escoffier, at the start of Chapter 4, page 116.

cookery books had sold in their hundreds of thousands, and his three major works were, *The Gastronomic Regenerator* (1846), *The Modern Housewife* (1849), a book aimed at the middle classes, and *Shilling Cookery for the People* (1854), a highly successful and influential book aimed at instructing the poor in good and frugal cooking. He also wrote a history of food and cooking, *The Pantropheon* (1853), a much respected and unrivalled book to this day.

In France the grande cuisine was at the height of its powers. France now considered itself a culinary rocket; indeed it classified itself as the capital and principal exponent of good taste in everything esculent. Major culinary events were staged and executed by the premier chefs of the time – namely Carême and Talleyrand. Aliments arrived in Paris from the four corners of the globe and were much appreciated by Parisiens. Grimod de la Reynière wrote in 1806, 'It is the place where respective qualities of everything that man uses for food are best appreciated and where the ways of transforming them for the benefit of our senses are best understood.'

In this century the gratification of the palate became paramount, and the confidential and intimate dinners, suppers and sexual manoeuvring seen around table in the last century has disappeared or gone underground. Gourmands are unashamedly male and egoistic. They now attend dinners which are male only assemblies and, as lone misanthropes, frequent the very best restaurants. France was in a state of flux at this time, with much diplomatic and political machinations and rebuilding to organize and undertake.

This century also saw the formation of the cardinal culinary principles and techniques, which were to later form the genesis of an international gastronomy, a *cuisine sans frontières*. Pot roasting (*poêle*) and braising (*braise*) appeared as two contemporary methods of cooking in this century. Certain meats and fowls could be slowly cooked in lidded pots, and by taking the basic kitchen *fonds* as their basis, they too were recorded and included in the classic culinary *répertoire*. The use of butter and other fats increased and sauces became thicker and were used to mask the dishes.

The service of food was also to receive some remodelling. Along with the gradual building of the classical French cuisine since the 16th century, had been the changes and development

Table 2.1 Menu structure of French service (19th century)

Service 1
Potages (soups)
Hors-d'oeuvres chauds ou entrées volantes (hot, small entrées)
Relevés (large joints)
Entrées chaudes (small cuts)
Grosses pièces sur socle (centre courses)
Rôtis et salades (roasts with salad)
Entremets de légumes (vegetable courses)
Entremets sucrés chauds (hot sweets)

Service 2
Rôtis et salades (second different roast and salad)
Entremets de legumes (second different vegetable course)
Entremets sucrés chauds (second different hot sweet course)

Service 3
Entremets sucrés froids (cold sweets)
Grosses pièces sur socle (highly decorated mounted sweet course)
Fruits, compôtes, desserts (fruits and stewed fruits of all types)

of menu construction and sequencing, which had led to the development of the service à la français. This consisted of three types of service with several courses within each service, as shown in Table 2.1. Each course also contained several choices, and for special occasions, all the dishes in each service and in each course could be increased in number. The service of the food commenced with the dishes within each service being presented and displayed together. The dishes were then removed for carving, dissection and portioning, and they would then be served. The hot dishes were kept warm, according to their type, on red-hot charcoal trays, or bains-marie (hot water baths), often built into the design of bowls and dishes on which the foods were presented. At the end of each service all the tables and service area would be cleared ready for the next service, and then the process would be repeated.

From about 1880, the service à la français was to lose favour and be replaced over time by the service à la russe (although the service à la français survived to some extent with the bourgeois, for they saw it as a sign of their success and wealth). This new form of service was introduced into Paris high society by Prince Alexander Borisivitch Kourakine, the tsar's ambassador to Paris during the Second Empire (*Larousse Gastronomique*, 1971). In the service à la russe the various dishes were presented and served to the guest at the table one after the other in a prescribed sequence (see Table 2.2). This form of service aided the timing of courses and the flavour of them, and also this style of service displayed the chefs' endeavours to a much better advantage. The development of the service à la russe was also

Table 2.2 Menu sequence of Russian service (from about 1880 onwards)

1 Hors-d'oeuvre froid	cold appetiser
2 Potage	soup
3 Hors-d'oeuvres chauds ou entrées volantes	hot appetisers or small entrées
4 Oeuf et farineux	egg or rice and pasta (farinaceous) dishes
5 Poisson	fish course
6 Entrée chaud	hot entrée, garnished
7 Relevé ou pièce de résistance ou grosses pièces	main course, joint of meat or poultry with garnish of vegetables and potatoes
8 Entrée froide	cold entrée
9 Sorbet	water ice flavours
10 Rôtis et salades	roast course with salad, usually poultry and game, sometimes other meats
11 Entremet de legumes	hot or cold vegetable course
12 Entremet chaud	hot sweet course
13 Entremet froid	cold sweet course
14 Entremet de fromage	cheese savouries, hot or cold, cheese selection
15 Dessert	selection of fresh fruit
16 Café	coffee, filter, mocha, Turkish, etc.

to provide the foundation for the European menu construction and sequencing, which became well established at the beginning of the 20th century. It has also, with some further development, become the basis of the modern European menu construction that is still used to this day (see Chapter 3, page 70).

At the close of the 19th century, with increasing tourism and the prosperous traveller visiting the elegant spots in Europe in pursuit of the best fare and top hotels, French chefs were in a prime position to influence and contribute to the art of providing great hospitality. Culinary style and table manners had evolved from the cookhouses, taverns and restaurants and had now fanned out all over Europe and beyond.

2.10 The 20th century

By this point grande cuisine had peaked and the only options open to it were stagnation or decline, which could lead in theory to a new culinary renaissance. The masters' works it would appear, could not be surpassed, they could only be recast. However a number of men had already appeared on the scene who were to have a lasting impact on the development of cuisine and gastronomy. These included the chefs Georges Auguste Escoffier (1846–1935), Édouard Nignon, (1865–c.1934) and Fernand Point (1897–1955), and the gastronome Maurice Edmond Sailland, known as Curnonsky (1872–1956).

Escoffier was to be the one who handed over the doctrines of the classical cuisines of Europe into the 20th century, with the publishing of *Le Guide culinaire* at the height of his powers in 1903, which ironically came at a time when he was working in London. *Le Guide culinaire* became the definitive text and it was not until the 1970s that its potency was seriously threatened amongst the leading hotel kitchens, displaced by nouvelle cuisine. The historical and cyclical characteristic of cookery since the French Revolution had been one of seeding, codification, desensitization and renewal, which seems to be allied to and develops from intervals of a transitional nature in the social circumstances of the catering profession. Escoffier's systematized codifications were founded upon a series of stock-based sauces, which permitted his cooking to travel well beyond France and so become truly international. Such is the importance of Escoffier that we return to consider his legacy in more detail at the start of Chapter 4 (page 114).

Édouard Nignon, who was born in Nantes (1865–c.1934), would be judged to be one of the paramount masters of French cuisine. He trained in the most prestigious restaurants (in France, Maison Dorée; Bignon; Potel et Chalbot; Magny; Noel Peter's; Laperouse; Paillard; Claridges in London and L'Ermitage in Moscow) and he was also head chef to the Tsar, President Woodrow Wilson and to the Emperor of Austria. In 1918 he managed the restaurant Larue, exchanging his white toque and chef's jacket for the black uniform of a maître d'hôtel. He was also the author of three books: *L'Heptameron de gourmets ou Les Delices de la cuisine française* (1919), *Le Plaisirs de la table* (1926) and *Eloges de la cuisine française* (1933). Nignon was renowned as a lover of literature and was accredited, although he was much less well known than other masters, for his contribution to revolutionizing cuisine in his lifetime. Theirs was an inflexible stereotypical regimentation, which had formed over the years in international gastronomy and which had to be broken down. This was to be effected by the onslaught of the First World War (*Larousse Gastronomique*, 1971).

Also instrumental in this process was 'Pampille', the pseudonym for Marthe Allard, who produced *Le Bons Plats de France*, which featured regional specialities highlighting chicken (poule-au-pot) and boiled beef (pot-au-feu). These simple appetizing dishes directly differentiated themselves from the expensive creations of grande cuisine. The next step on the push for transition in cuisine, and a breakdown of the monopoly of standardization, was the eight-day fair for regional gastronomy held in Paris in 1923. Here the French themselves could light upon the treasure store of neglected dishes from all over the country, something for which the National Council of Culinary Arts (CNAC) was founded in 1989.

If Escoffier has now been generally considered to be king of the cuisine ancienne, it was Fernand Point who was to be considered the father of modern gastronomy. To a greater extent than any other chef, Fernand Point characterized the representation to the world of the high-class French restaurant, which endures to this day. Figure 2.1 now summarizes the succession from the medieval masters through the masters of cuisine ancienne, to Fernand Point as the father of modern gastronomy. He had a profound and enduring influence on gastronomy in his time and on aspiring chefs who have followed. Again, such is this man's importance in the development of modern cuisine that we also return, in Chapter 4 (page 118), to consider his contribution further, and as a precursor to considering the contribution of some of his direct and indirect beneficiaries.

Maurice Edmond Sailland, born in Angers in 1872, was a culinary heavyweight and literary giant, and one of the greatest gastronomic writers and crusaders. Sailland, known as Curnonsky, transformed classical cuisine by way of his writing. He was an eminent conversationalist, and successful journalist and novelist, and it was he who proffered a well-informed and erudite analysis of prevailing and regional dishes to a now eager populace. This alone may have accorded him only fleeting influence as a gastronomic arbiter had he not accomplished something else. Between 1921 and 1928 he produced, in collaboration with Marcel Rouff, the 28 volumes of *La France gastronomique*; with Austin De Croze, *Le Tresorier gastronomique de France* in 1933; with P. Andrieu, *Le Fines Gueules de France* in 1935; and, without a collaborator, *Cuisine et vins de France* in 1953, and in 1940 he founded the significant and influential journal of that name. Sailland also was a rival to Michelin in that he edited a *Guide des touristes gastronomes*, with maps of each Departement of France, and listed restaurants, the dishes served and their ingredients. The focus and direction was now clear, and culminated in the 1970s and 1980s in a form of culinary reformation which would make French cuisine one of the most absorbing and attractive in the world, while also laying the ground for other national gastronomies to feature their own regionally distinguishing

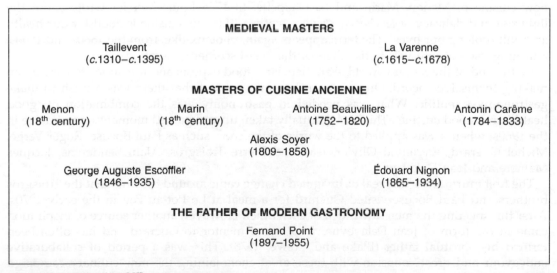

MEDIEVAL MASTERS

Taillevent	La Varenne
(*c*.1310–*c*.1395)	(*c*.1615–*c*.1678)

MASTERS OF CUISINE ANCIENNE

Menon	Marin	Antoine Beauvilliers	Antonin Carême
(18th century)	(18th century)	(1752–1820)	(1784–1833)

Alexis Soyer
(1809–1858)

George Auguste Escoffier	Édouard Nignon
(1846–1935)	(1865–1934)

THE FATHER OF MODERN GASTRONOMY

Fernand Point
(1897–1955)

Figure 2.1 Medieval to 20th century masters

aliments. Curnonsky had ensured the perpetuation of regional French cooking and had made the regional recipes freely available to everyone.

Once more dietetics was also to come to the fore, as it had done in the early days after Gutenberg. This time it had a still wider audience and became intricately entwined with gastronomy. This coupling was also advanced by the French gastronome and nutritionist Dr Édouard Pozerski de Pomiane (1875–1964). Pomiane was head of the food physiology department at the Pasteur Institute, and it was here that he spent his whole working life in the investigation of digestion and dietetics. His writings were lively and humorous and he is to this day still admired as one of modern France's most popular gastronomic writers, along with Curnonsky.

At no time before in the annals of food history has there been such a multitude of consumers so acquainted and informed about that which they consume as in the latter part of the 20th century. Once again, a fusion of diet and health has taken centre stage. In the Western world we now seldom regard our food in the context of staving off pangs of hunger, nor do we approach it along the lines of eating and drinking for pleasure alone.

By eating the correct food and of course taking moderate exercise we can now expect to improve our quality of life. The health-giving diet can be viewed as a route to a long and active life (Leeming, 1991). We have been assisted along this route by our oral and well documented history, from the medico-gastronomy of the Greeks with later assistance by the Arabs, and up through the centuries with concern over gluttony and poor diet to current medical and nutritional advice. Great chefs have worked tirelessly to refine the foods we eat until in the latter part of the last century we arrived at cuisine nouvelle – the latest in a long line of refinements in our food with the new cuisines of today, and a greater body of professionals than ever before to express it.

2.11 Cuisines nouvelles

New cuisines are not necessarily contemporary cuisines – new cuisines having been present in Greek and Roman times (Apicius spoke of nouvelle cuisine in the first century AD) and in every age since. However the term's probable first recorded usage was in the 1740s for the new cuisine of Menon, Marin and La Chapelle. In 1755 Louis Mercier wrote about the lightness and delicacy of *La Cuisine changée*, stating, 'the new cuisine is good for our health and will prolong our lives'. The term appears again, phoenix-like, from the 1880s and 1890s, attaching itself at intervals to the chefs of the post-Escoffier generation.

By the end of the Second World War, dieticians, food experts and nutritionists were again making themselves heard. Once again it becomes evident that there was a push to make gastronomy scientific. What was needed in gastronomy was the combination of 'good health' and 'good cuisine'. This was gradually taken up and gained momentum in France in the 1960s, when it was applied to the works of the chefs such as Paul Bocuse, Roger Vergé, Michel Guérard, Raymond Olivier, Jean and Pierre Troisgros, Alain Senderens, Jacques Maniere and Jean Delaveyne.

The first murmurs of any real or imagined change came around the time that the Troisgros brothers and Paul Bocuse visited Guérard for a meal at Le Pot-au-Feu in the early 1970s. After this meeting the men saw much of each other. However, another source of inspiration came in the form of Jean Delaveyne, who was a mentor to Guérard and has often been termed his spiritual father (Blake and Crewe, 1978). This was a period of collaborative endeavour and great collusion with these great chefs joining the new culinary campaign (Lazareff, 1992).

Guérard joined with the food critics and journalists Henri Gault and Christian Millau in 1972 to advance uncomplicated natural presentations in food. A publicity campaign ensued with a contemporary ethic and novel recipes. In doing so the 'nouveaux cuisiniers' launched 'another' Nouvelle Cuisine, which was at this point in time no more than the generation of journalistic technospeak, recreated to explain this particular culinary movement. It was no more than a distillation of the individual and diversified cuisines formulated and coined by Gault and Millau.

Nouvelle cuisine was in essence a manifestation of a defection from the Escoffier orthodoxy, which did not simply take place in France but also elsewhere in Europe. It was an acknowledgement without an agenda (part of the problem of nouvelle cuisine) that change was necessary, a response from the desire to question and innovate by a melting pot of young and inspired talent more than a co-ordinated action against dogma. Guérard, Bocuse and others still had a lot of respect for Escoffier but needed the freedom to evolve without being harnessed to strict classical codification.

With the theories that Guérard put forward, and the recipes provided in *La Grande Cuisine minceur*, Guérard amalgamated dietetics, aesthetics, health, ethics and gastronomy. Stereotypic dishes from the times between Carême and Escoffier went out, rejected as over-rich and over-complex, indigestible, with preparations that had become tired and associated with a previous age. In came the canon of respect for flavours and textures of individual aliments. Mousses were again the fashion, though now the hard work had been taken out and replaced by the ease of electric food processors. Cooking methods like steaming, poaching and the use of microwave ovens were in vogue and lighter more elegant saucing appeared. The roux was discarded and yoghurt, vegetable purées, reduced fat creams and butters were in favour (see Table 2.3).

The nouveaux cuisiniers embraced and advocated authenticity, natural production and simplicity. Principles guiding this new movement were total freshness of ingredients, lightness and harmony in all components and accompaniments, use of the basic and simplest cooking methods and types of presentations. The blueprint was made visible and championed by Gault and Millau in their magazine and in gastronomic guides.

Paul Bocuse was viewed as the originator of one of the most recent styles with his *Nouvelle cuisine française* in 1975. Bocuse was also one of the strongest critics of some of those culinary pirates who sought to emulate his efforts, stating 'I thought a barge-load of kiwi fruit, had hit one loaded with broccoli spears, and the salvage operation had flung these rediscovered items widespread throughout the restaurants of Paris' (Kracknell and Nobis, 1985: 185–6). To balance the view, Bocuse is not considered to be without sin, for he has often been accused in France as being piratical himself.

Bocuse has also stated that too many chefs were operating confidence tricks on their customers, by serving very small portions, which were supposed to provide a lighter diet with the accent on freshness of produce and new combinations of ingredients. He was amongst the first of a majority who felt exactly the same thing was happening to them. Some felt that the new system opened itself to abuse from pretenders, motivated solely by economics and caring little for the health and well being of their customers. Nouvelle came to signify small portions, fromage blanc instead of cream, no sugar and few carbohydrates. Sadly it was all too easy for the exquisite to become the ridiculous.

In a counter action many chefs, foodies, gourmets, gastronomes and their public became avid followers of the hypothesis that it was a system of cookery that demanded more thought and feeling involved in its execution and prescription than blind adherence to the classical repertoire. With balance, nutrition and health as counterpoints, it was a cuisine that could evolve to the benefit of the customer and the industry as a whole.

Table 2.3 Prescription for nouvelle cuisine

1 A rejection of unnecessary complication in the production of foods. The phasing out of elaborate dishes, and of rigid formulae and the introduction of simplicity in cooking methods.

2 A reduction of cooking times, to bring out true and some would argue forgotten flavours. Rapid cooking was now the order of the day, since the cooked food would be more likely to retain its maximum nutritional value by this method. Steaming and cooking en papillote also gained ground. Dry methods were applied, where foods were cooked in non-stick pans where oils could be lightly sprayed over the pan instead of being poured in. Other dry cooking methods were employed like grilling, true roasting and dry frying.

3 An insistence on the purchase of the freshest possible ingredients, across a full range of aliments, supported by daily purchasing.

4 A visible reduction in the volume of dishes available on the menu.

5 A reduction in the use of strong marinades, with game served fresher and not high. Light sauces were in, usually based on meat juices, or wine, essences, or light stocks that could be reduced.

6 A turning towards regional dishes for inspiration, and away from Parisien classicism in haute cuisine.

7 An elimination of rich and creamy sauces, Béchamel and Espagnole, with the roux now frowned upon. There was an increase in the use of good unsalted butter, lemon juice, vinegar, and fresh herbs. Natural harmony of the accompaniments was also a prerequisite. Flour, anything disguised or denatured, liaisons, fats that were saturated, and indigestible mixtures were frowned upon.

8 Equipment used in the kitchen changed, and new techniques were employed. Elizabeth David, who died in May 1992, suggested that cuisine nouvelle could not have developed the way it did had it not been for the intervention of the modern food processor, which appeared at much the same time as the new cuisine. In general, equipment was ultra modern, and microwave ovens were used professionally. There was also less distrust of frozen food, using it intelligently.

9 Dietetic implications were important and some senior chefs employed the services of nutritionists. The consumption of salt, sugar and fats was to be reduced.

10 Inventiveness and experimentation was in evidence, as was the economic benefits that could follow such a concept.

11 Normally, plated service of food requiring an increased hands-on approach, which was also labour intensive, evolved and a new aesthetic appeal proved this point.

Source: Mennell, 1985 from *Nouveaux cuisines: guide gourmand de France* (1970)

Words with rich meaning were descriptively fashionable among gourmets of this new cuisine. Terms such as light, airy, delicate, succulent etc. prevailed, and some misuse of the principles occurred from inexperienced and over-zealous chefs. This was caused by overcompensation, too much decoration, under-use of foods on the plates (tiny portions) and over-charging. Curious combinations also took much of the goodness away from what was and is a marvellous concept in cuisine.

The following shows a somewhat tongue-in-cheek attempt at the chef's new freedom in menu description where the chef wishes to explain every element comprising the dish:

'A luxuriant conglomeration of periodical fruits, moored in a framboise d'Ecosse arena, under a delicate quilt of crème anglaise and a mountainous piste of whipped cream, gathered in a corral of precariously arranged genoise fingers, inspired and scented with the Jerez's peerless nectar, from the indomitable house of Herederos de Argüeso, and ultimately sprinkled with a heavenly cosmos of diminutive candies endowed with brilliance.'

Rather than simply state 'Sherry Trifle' and exceed the guest's expectation by its visual appeal and taste, this chef has waxed lyrical to the detriment of the dish. Claude Fischler in an article for *Le Monde* titled the 'Socrates of the Nouvelle Cuisine' wrote:

The artist in this field is no longer characterised by his overpowering authority, but rather by the opinionated modesty of an exponent of the majestic art. In place of the cook as mercenary of the kitchen stove, we now have Socratic cook, midwife at the birth of culinary truth. (*Larousse Gastronomique*, 1971)

Nouvelle cuisine had emerged in an uprising against the Escoffier orthodoxy, markedly as stultified in international hotel cuisine. Like the ideas of Carême and Escoffier, the influence of nouvelle cuisine spread around the world. It can now be seen that this model will undergo seeding, codification, desensitization and renewal. The seed was sown in the students of Fernand Point of the Pyramide in Vienne. Codification came in the 1970s through the work of initially Roger Vérge *et al.*, and the publicity from Gault and Millau, it then spread throughout the world, in Britain through the work of chefs like Mosimann, Blanc and the Roux Brothers.

We can now quite clearly see that with its routinization and uptake, with less than experienced practitioners, and those who have gone more for the economic kill, these new and diverse cuisines under the most recent banner of nouvelle themselves will experience desensitization and become a doctrine to be replaced. Mennell and Levy, and Barr and Levy (quoted in Wood, 1991) have stated, 'nouvelle cuisine is simply the latest stage in the development of French haute cuisine'.

The cyclic revolution, in synopsis, has amongst other things always sought simplicity with more discrimination, and a move towards enhancing natural flavours from the principal and accompanying ingredients and, generally, a lightening of saucing. What has always happened is not an overthrowing of history and the past, but rather, a moving forward in the long-term process of development, utilizing the very best from each evolution, where tastes are refined continuously and cooking refined in tandem to satisfy them.

There has been, as Escoffier described it, 'civilizing of taste'. Each new development has involved the very best chefs not merely in an overthrow of the last, but also a renewal of recognizably the self-same pursuits of simplicity, refinement, restraint and, increasingly, a conscious calculation of precisely how each new seed will be received by a captive audience.

If one really ponders the subject, it was not feasible to expect practitioners to emancipate cuisine from well over a century of repetition, albeit reverential to the old masters, without some problems occurring. Gladly, it would seem that the over-zealous analytical period appears to have come and gone. With the establishment internationally of institutions reconstructed by looking to their national heritage, like France and the work of the CNAC, and a subtle blending of the rusticity of certain cuisines with enlightened approaches to nouvelle cuisine, European gastronomy has never looked in greater shape.

2.12 Summary

This chapter has described chronologically the various influences on the development of European gastronomy. It has traced the origins of European gastronomy from the ancient Greeks, the Romans with their creation of empire and the beginnings of fusion in cuisine, through the Dark and Middle Ages, and has identified the role of the higher levels of society in advancing gastronomic thinking and practice. The status of those involved in the culinary pursuit has increased over time and the contributions of those who were more than chefs, bringing a combination of philosophy and gastronomy together, has brought into the literature a way of thinking about gastronomy and cuisine. Health, diet and cuisine have become linked and the modern new cuisine has responded to this, as well as being a reaction against the potential strait jacketing of cuisine which had begun to appear in the post-Escoffier era. The scene was set for modern gastronomy to develop.

CHAPTER 3

Modern European gastronomy

This chapter reviews development in modern European gastronomy.

This chapter is intended to help you to:

- identify and explore a range of diverse developments in operations, service and menu provision

- consider influences on, and the technical considerations for the development of menus

- reflect on contemporary culinary refinement

- examine the reasons for the development of concept cuisines

- consider the effects of concept cuisines, including fusion cuisine, on the market

- explore the changes in, and the development of beverage lists

- identify the principles of achieving the balance between food and wine and other beverages

- reflect on the changing nature of dining

- consider philosophical meaning and symbolism in gastronomy

- review the profile of the apex of the hospitality industry and management at that level.

3.1 Diversity and development

Diversification in food and beverage operations

From about the middle of the 20th century, developments were to take place in cuisine, gastronomy and food and beverage operations, which were to be more seismic than any of those that had gone before. A diversification of food and beverage operations took place. A range of food and beverage operations was to be designed and developed for specific purposes, rather than being adaptations or scaled down versions of previously existing models and concepts. Demand for food and beverages was increasing, and with this specific customer requirements were diversifying and needed detailed examination. These new demands, together with the staggering developments in food technology, kitchen and production design and the application of operations management techniques, were creating new possibilities and alternatives.

Food and restaurant styles in Europe have diversified to meet the challenge of the range of demands that were being made. Examples of the food and restaurant styles that are now available are given in Table 3.1.

Service and menu sequencing interlinked

The original formality in European menu sequencing and service had become well established by the middle of the 18th century. Towards the end of the 19th century, the service à la françaised been replaced by the service à la russe (see Chapter 2, page 59). This Russian style of service improved the timing of meals and the flavour of the food for guests, as courses were served one after the other instead of a collection of courses being presented and served at one time. This style of service and its formal sequencing of the courses had also laid the foundations for the sequencing of courses that is still used today.

Within the service à la russe the basic elements of the classic (European) menu and its service were already present (the original structure and sequence is shown in Table 2.2, page 59). During the course of the 20th century there were some changes to the order and flow of the courses, the nature of some of the courses, and some amalgamation. The sequence also took in, for instance, the English savouries, and also some changes to the order of courses, where for instance cheese is now commonly offered following a main course. Lillicrap *et al.* (1998), for example, show a version of the menu sequence in which they include the alternative approaches of a sweet course being offered before or after a cheese course.

From the various origins and sources, a modern menu sequence can be constructed, and this is given in Table 3.2. This version of the sequence, or something very close to it, is used when European menus are compiled. However a number of courses are often grouped together. At its most simple this might comprise:

- starters – courses 1 to 4

- main courses – courses 5, 6 and 8 to 12

- afters – courses 13 to 16

- beverages.

Table 3.1 Typology of restaurants and cuisine

Bistro	Often a smaller establishment, with check tablecloths, bentwood chairs, cluttered décor, and friendly informal staff. Honest, basic and robust cooking, possibly including coarse pâtés, thick soups, casseroles served in large portions
Brasserie	(French for 'brewery') Family operated eating-houses in Alsace, which then spread throughout France and into the rest of Europe. This is often a largish, styled room with long bar, normally serving one-plate items rather than formal meals (though some offer both). Often it is possible to just have a drink, or coffee, or just a small amount to eat. Traditional dishes include charcuterie, moules marinières, steak frites. Service often by waiters in traditional style of long aprons and black waistcoats
New wave brasserie (Gastrodome)	Slick contemporary interior design, lighting and food, beverage and service. Rising stars in the kitchen producing innovative, contemporary cuisine often across culinary frontiers but not distinctly fusion. Definitely the places to be seen out and about. Just for a drink, a light snack or an impressive meal. Busy, bustling, often large and multi-levelled with a distinct buzz
Farmhouse cooking	Simply cooked and generous portions of basic, home-produced fare using good, local ingredients
Country house hotel cooking	Varies from establishment to establishment, but food is often modern style with some influence from classic or even farmhouse style. Often the home of top end restaurants
Classic/haute cuisine	Classical style of cooking evolved through many centuries, best chronicled by Escoffier. Greater depth of flavour. Style does not necessarily mean the most expensive ingredients – can include simply poached and boiled dishes such as chicken and offal. Classical presentation of food with table (silver, guéridon or plated) service
Ethnic	Indian, Oriental, Asian, Greek, Italian, Japanese, Creole and Cajun are just some of the many types of ethnic cuisine available, with establishments tending to reflect their origin. Many of the standard dishes are also now appearing within a range of other menu types
Health food and vegetarian	Increasing specialization of operations into vegetarianism and/or health foods (though vegetarian food is not necessarily healthy) meeting the needs of life style as well as dietary requirements
Popular catering and fast-foods	Developed from teashops and cafés through to steakhouses, and then incorporating takeaways and cafeterias, onto modern-day burger, chicken and fish concepts, sandwich bars, pub food, wine bars and with ethnic foods also being incorporated. Meeting the needs of all-day meal-taking (grazing) and especially meeting, leisure, industrial and travelling market requirements
Themed restaurants	Often international in theme but with a twist, e.g. Mongolian barbecue restaurant where customers choose their own aliments for main dishes and it is prepared in situ on a hot plate; Icelandic 'hot rock cooking' again prepared at the table; party themed restaurant with distinctive focus on cocktails or some other element, with talented waiting staff who can for example perform magic tricks; also themed by way of interior and architectural design, e.g. rainforest, catwalk, cooking theatre etc.
New/modern British/ French	Cuisine drawn from the classical style but with new style saucing and the better aspects of nouvelle presentation. Plated in the kitchen, allowing the chef the final responsibility for presentation
Fusion/eclectic cuisine	Modern development in cuisine using a variety of ingredients from all over the world. Intermixing of cuisine cultures, for example particularly western and eastern styles
International destination restaurants	Often Michelin rated, offering distinctive personality, cuisine, ambience, beverages and service. The home of gastronomy at the height of its expression. Expensive but value laden

Source: after Cousins *et al.*, 2001

Table 3.2 Modern European classic menu sequence

1	Hors-d'oeuvres	Traditionally a variety of salads but now includes items such as pâtés, mousses, fruit, charcuterie and smoked fish
2	Soups (potages)	Includes all soups, both hot and cold
3	Egg dishes (oeufs)	Variety of egg dishes
4	Pasta and rice (farineux)	Includes all pasta and rice dishes. Can be referred to as farinaceous dishes
5	Fish (poisson)	Fish dishes, both hot and cold. Fish dishes such as smoked salmon or prawn salad are mainly considered to be hors-d'oeuvres
6	Entrée	Generally small, well garnished dishes, usually with rich sauce or gravy. Potatoes and vegetables are not usually served with this course if it is to be followed by a main course. If this is to be the main meat course then it is usual for potatoes and vegetables to also be offered. Examples of this type of dish are tournedos, noisettes, sweetbreads, garnished cutlets or filled vol-au-vent cases
7	Sorbet	Lightly frozen water ices, and variations, often based on un-sweetened fruit juice and may be served with a spirit, liqueur or Champagne poured over
8	Relevé	Main roasts or other larger joints of meat
9	Roast (rôti)	Roasted game or poultry dishes
10	Vegetables (legumes)	Certain vegetables (for example asparagus and artichokes) may be served as a separate course, although these types of dishes are now more commonly served as starters
11	Salad (salade)	Often a small plate of salad that is taken after the main course (or courses), and is quite often a simple green salad and dressing
12	Cold buffet (buffet froid)	Includes a variety of cold meats, fish, cheese and egg items together with a range of salads and dressings
13	Cheese (fromage)	Includes the range of cheeses and accompaniments, including fruit, and also cheese based dishes such as soufflés
14	Sweets (entremets)	Both hot and cold puddings
15	Savoury (savoureaux)	Including simple savouries, such as items on toast, or in pastry, or savoury soufflés
16	Fruit (dessert)	Fresh fruit, nuts and perhaps candied fruits
17	Beverages	Traditionally coffee but now including a much wider range of beverages such as tea, tisanes, chocolate and proprietary beverages. (Although listed here to show the sequence, beverages are not usually counted as a course. Thus if a meal is quoted as having four courses, this must mean that there are four food courses and that the beverages are in addition to these)

Source: *after* Lillicrap *et al.*, 1998

This classic menu sequence[1] is used to determine the layout of menus as well as to indicate the order of the various courses. Although the actual number of courses offered on a menu, and the number of dishes within each course, will depend on the size and class of the establishment, most will follow the classic sequence.

The sequence itself was and is based on a logical process of taste sensations. This classic sequence provides the guide for the compilation and the determination of the order of the courses for function and special party menus. Additionally, it is common for both à la carte and table d'hôte menus (see below for definitions) to be constructed within this format, as is evident in many examples of modern menus.

Food and beverage service

The development of a diverse range of operations to meet the increasing diversity in demand also necessitated developments in approaches to food and beverage service. In all, some fifteen service methods were to be developed. Service processes and procedures based on systematic operations management considerations had led to service being considered both from the customer point of view as well as from the operations (or delivery) point of view.

Cousins *et al.* (2001) identify that food and beverage service actually consists of two separate systems, which are being managed albeit at the same time. These are:

1 the service sequence – which is primarily concerned with the delivery of food and beverages to the customer;

2 the customer process – which is primarily concerned with managing the experience of the customer.

Separating the service process into these two systems provides for a better understanding of the processes as well as some indication of potential options in the organization of food and beverage service in different types of operation.

The **service sequence** is essentially the bridge between the food production system, beverage provision and the customer experience (or process). The choices on how the service sequence is designed, planned and controlled are made taking account of the requirements of the operation.

Identifying the **customer process** endeavours to ensure that food and beverage service is *not* viewed as primarily a delivery process, with the customer being seen as a passive recipient of the service. The customers' involvement in the process is taken seriously and as a result it is properly considered in the design of the operation.

Essentially there are four different customer processes, based on what the customer has to undertake when they are in a food and beverage operation. These are:

(A) Service at a laid cover
(B) Assisted service – part service at a laid cover and part self-service
(C) Self-service
(D) Service at a single point (ordering, receipt of order and payment).

---

[1] The modern classic menu sequence given here is derived from traditional European (mainly Franco-Russian and Swiss and English) cuisine influences. The menu structure and menu sequence change considerably within the various world cuisines. Additionally, menu terms also vary, for instance in the USA a main course is commonly called an entrée and sweets commonly called dessert. The term dessert is also becoming more commonly used to denote sweets generally.

In these four service processes, the customer comes to where the food and beverage service is offered and the service is provided in areas primarily designed for the purpose. There is then a need for a fifth process where the customer receives the service in another location and where the area is not primarily designed for the purpose. This can be called:

(E) Specialized service or service *in situ*.

A summary of the five customer processes is shown in Table 3.3.

Within this categorization, all fifteen food and beverage service methods can be shown as in Table 3.4. (A more detailed explanation can be found in Lillicrap *et al.*, *Food and Beverage Service*, 1998.)

Classes of menu

Although the content of menus has been changing, menus can still be seen as being divided into two main classes, traditionally called à la carte (from the card) and table d'hôte (table of the host). The key difference between these two is that the à la carte menu has dishes separately priced, whereas the table d'hôte menu has an inclusive price either for the whole meal or for a specified number of courses, for example any two or any four courses. There are, however, usually choices within each course.

Table 3.3 Simple categorization of the customer processes in food and beverage service

Service method	Service area	Ordering/ selection	Service	Dining/ consumption	Clearing
(A) **Table service**	Customer enters and is seated	From menu	By staff to customer	At laid cover	By staff
(B) **Assisted service**	Customer enters and is usually seated	From menu, buffet or passed trays	Combination of both staff and customers	Usually at laid cover	By staff
(C) **Self-service**	Customer enters	Customer selects own tray	Customer carries	Dining area or take away	Various
(D) **Single point service**	Customer enters	Orders at single point	Customer carries	Dining area or take away	Various
(E) **Specialized or in situ service**	In situ	From menu or predetermined	Brought to customer	Where served	By staff or customer clearing

Source: Lillicrap *et al.*, 1998

Table 3.4 Food and beverage service methods grouped according to the customer process requirements

Service method group	Methods included

Group A: Table service
Service to customers at a laid cover
	1 Waiter:
	  (a) silver/English
	  (b) family
	  (c) plate/American
	  (d) butler/French
	  (e) Russian
	  (f) guéridon
	
	2 Bar counter

Group B: Assisted service Combination of table service and self-service	3 Assisted service ('carvery' type operations and buffets)

Group C: Self-service
Self-service of customers
	4 Cafeteria:
	  (a) counter
	  (b) free flow
	  (c) echelon
	  (d) supermarket
	
	(*Note:* some 'call order' production may be included in cafeterias)

Group D: Single-point service Service of customers at a single point – consumed on premises or taken away	5 Take away 6 Vending 7 Kiosks 8 Food court 9 Bar
Group E: Specialized (or *in situ*) Service to customers in areas not primarily designed for service	10 Tray 11 Trolley 12 Home delivery 13 Lounge 14 Room 15 Drive-in

Note:

Banquet/function is a term used to describe food and beverage operations that are providing for specific numbers of people at specific times in a variety of dining layouts. Service methods also vary. In these cases banquet/function catering refers to the organization of service rather than a specific service method.

Source: after Lillicrap *et al.,* 1998

Other menu terms used are carte du jour (literally 'card of the day') – which is usually a fixed meal with one or more courses for a set price. A prix fixe ('fixed price') menu is similar. Sometimes the price of the meal also includes wine or other drinks.

The key characteristics of the table d'hôte menu are:

- the menu has a fixed number of courses

- there is a limited choice within each course

- the selling price is fixed

- the food is usually available at a set time.

The key features of the à la carte menu are:

- the choice is generally more extensive

- each dish is priced separately

- there may be longer waiting times as some dishes are cooked or finished to order.

Fine dining restaurants tend to have both types of menus complementary to each other. Other types of operations such as brasseries, coffee shops, popular catering and fast food restaurants have menus based on these two concepts. These may often be seen to be limited forms of à la carte menus with all the dishes listed and priced separately, and where meal packages, or prix fixe menus run alongside them. These allow, for instance, guests to have a snack with a beverage, a full meal or just a beverage.

Developing menus

Developing menus for particular establishments tends to be the outcome of the consideration of a number of factors. These include:

- the nature of the customer demand being met

- suitability of a particular establishment to a particular area

- competition in the locality

- local food traditions

- access to the establishment

- the spending power of the customer

- likely volume of demand

- space and equipment in the kitchen and service areas

- production processes to be used (see Table 3.5 for a summary of modern food production methods)

- amount, availability and capability of labour

- availability of supplies and storage capabilities

- local legislative controls (such as licensing, and those governing trading standards).

Table 3.5 Methods of food production

Method	Description
Conventional	Term used to describe production using mainly fresh foods and traditional cooking methods
Convenience	Method of food production utilizing mainly convenience foods
Call order	Method where food is cooked to order either from customer (as in cafeterias) or from waiter
Continuous flow	Method involving production line approach where different parts of the production process may be separated (e.g. fast food)
Centralized	Production not directly linked to service. Foods are 'held' and distributed to separate service areas
Cook–chill	Food production, storage and regeneration method utilizing principle of low temperature control to preserve qualities of processed foods
Cook–freeze	Food production, storage and regeneration method utilizing principle of freezing to control and preserve qualities of processed foods. Requires special processes to assist freezing
Sous-vide	Method of food production, storage and regeneration method utilizing principle of sealed vacuum to control and preserve qualities of processed foods. Requires special processes to assist freezing
Assembly kitchen	A system based on accepting and incorporating the latest technological developments in manufacturing and conservation of food products

Source: Cousins *et al.*, 2001

Influences on menu dish content

Menu content, traditionally based on classic cuisine, is also continually being influenced by:

- food trends, fads and fashions
- the relationship between health and eating
- special diets
- cultural and religious influences
- vegetarianism.

Table 3.6 gives a summary of the issues included under these headings. A consequence of many of these influences is the need for a greater emphasis in offering alternatives such as low fat milks, e.g. skimmed or semi-skimmed, non dairy creamers for beverages, alternatives to sugar as sweeteners, sorbets alongside ice creams and polyunsaturated fat and non-animal fats as alternatives to butter. There has also been a great influence on cooking ingredients and methods, the development of lower fat dishes, lighter cuisine and attractive and decent alternatives for non-meat eaters with greater use of animal protein substitutes such as Quorn and tofu.

Table 3.6 Examples of influences on menu dish content

Food trends, fads and fashions

Like any other product, menus are subject to trends, fads and fashions. The various cuisines (such as nouvelle and fusion) are examples of lasting trends. Fads and fashions have included things like: everything with a coulis; kiwi fruit; food being set on a bed of wet potato purée: being on a bed of a variety of other things; a rosti of potato and various other ingredients, shaved vegetables; everything with a jus (juice or gravy); balsamic vinegar in dressings and in sauces, and roasted vegetables

The relationship between health and eating

Customers are increasingly looking for the availability of choices, and are requiring specific information on methods of cooking, e.g. frying, low fat, low salt etc., which will enable them to achieve a balanced diet. General consensus suggests that the regular diet should be made up of at least one-third based on a range of bread, cereals and potatoes, one-third based on a variety of fruit and vegetables, and the balance based on dairy foods, including low fat milk, low fat meats and fish and small amounts of fatty and sugary food

Customers are also becoming increasingly interested in food hygiene and food safety generally. There are also particular reactions to developments in food technology such as irradiation and genetically modified organisms and how these technologies are being used. Some customers are seeking to avoid these foods and some operations are already using the avoidance of these foods as a marketing feature. Additionally the use of organic foods is being promoted in a similar way

Special diets

There are a variety of medical conditions, including allergies, which affect customer choices, and which are more common than was generally understood. Special diets for customers may be as a result of:

- **Allergies** to food items such as gluten in wheat, rye and barley (known as coeliac), peanuts and their derivatives, sesame seeds and other nuts such as cashew, pecan, brazil and walnuts, as well as milk, fish, shellfish and eggs
  Diabetes (inability of the body to control the level of glucose within the blood), where the customer may be looking for low cholesterol food and the avoidance of high sugar dishes
- **Low cholesterol diets**, where the customer will be looking for dishes that include polyunsaturated fats or limited quantities of animal fats. Dishes might include lean poached or grilled meats and fish, fruit and vegetables and low fat milk, cheese and yoghurt
- **Low sodium/salt diets** where the customer is seeking dishes that include low sodium/salt foods and cooking with very limited or no use of salt

Cultural and religious influences

Various cultures and faiths have differing requirements with regard to the dishes/ingredients that may be consumed and often these requirements also cover preparation methods, cooking procedures and the equipment used. Examples of these are:

- **Hindus**, who do not eat beef and rarely pork, with some not eating any other meats, fish or eggs, and may be seeking cheese, milk and vegetarian dishes
- **Jews**, who seek to consume only 'clean' (kosher) animals and therefore will not accept dishes of pork or pork products, shellfish or animal fats and gelatine from beasts considered to be unclean or not slaughtered according to the prescribed manner. There are also restrictions placed on methods of preparation and cookery and also the preparation and eating of meat and dairy products at the same meal is not allowed

Table 3.6 continued

Cultural and religious influences *continued*

- **Muslims**, who will not eat meat offal or animal fat unless it is 'halal' (lawful, as required under Islamic Dietary Law) meat
- **Sikhs**, who will not eat beef or pork with some keeping to a vegetarian diet. Others may eat fish, mutton, cheese and eggs. Sikhs will not eat 'halal' meat
- **Roman Catholics**, where, although restrictions on diet are now very limited, many will not eat meats on Ash Wednesday or Good Friday, and some will not eat meat on Fridays

Vegetarianism

Vegetarianism may derive from cultural, religious, moral or physiological considerations. The various forms of vegetarianism may be summarized as:

- **Vegetarians: semi (or demi)**, who will not eat red meats, or all meats other than poultry, or all meats. These customers will be looking for dishes that include fish and may include dairy produce and other animal products
- **Vegetarians: lacto-ovo**, who will not eat all meat, fish, poultry but may eat milk, milk products and eggs
- **Vegetarians: lacto**, who will not eat all meat, fish, and poultry and eggs, but may eat milk and milk products
- **Vegans**, who will not eat any foods of animal origin. These customers will be looking for dishes mainly consisting of vegetables, vegetable oils, cereals, nuts, fruits and seeds.
- **Frutarians**, a more restricted form of vegetarianism, and these customers will not eat foods of animal origin or any pulses and cereals. These customers may be seeking dishes consisting of mainly raw and dried fruit, nuts, honey and olive oil (after Lillicrap *et al.*, 1998)

Technical considerations in menu construction

In addition to taking account of the factors identified above, there are also some technical factors that have to be considered. These include:

- **Variation in the colours of food:** this applies to individual courses as well as within courses.

- **Variation in the textures:** again between courses and within courses.

- **Avoiding repeating ingredients in different dishes:** e.g. avoid combinations like mushroom soup followed by chicken with a mushroom sauce. One exception to this is fruit, where, for instance, melon might be served at the start of the meal and strawberries at the end.

- **Mixing hot and cold dishes**: this not only makes the meal interesting but also helps in terms of preparation and service of dishes.

- **Variation in the cooking processes:** apart from avoiding, for instance, a meal where all the foods are fried, variations in cooking methods help in the kitchen organization where some foods are cooked in the ovens and others on the range, and some prepared in advance for reheating or service cold.

- **Planning of a logical menu sequence:** normally based on the classic menu sequence (see page 70 above). This sequence assists in the planning of courses so that they follow logically, in order that they can form a complete and balanced meal. This is clearly important for function menus but it is equally important to take into account when creating menus where the customer is choosing from a range of courses. The possible choices the customer makes should be able to be constructed into a classic sequence, even though a customer might want to make any other choice they like.

- **Consideration for the ease of eating:** this is particularly important if the meal is to be a buffet where people are standing up or resting their plates on their laps, rather than able to sit at a table. Buffets can be: (a) finger buffets, where the customers select and consume the food with their fingers; (b) fork buffets, where the customer selects foods which are then eaten with only a fork; or (c) a display buffet from which the guests select their food and then eat at a table.

- **Consideration of accompanying beverages:** taking account of the accompanying wines and other beverages in order to provide opportunities for harmony and balance between the two (see Section 3.5, page 87).

- **Consideration of service requirements:** this is as much about the technical requirements of serving the food and beverages to the customer as it is about the logistics of service sequence. In considering the service sequence it can be helpful to consider what the customer, as well as the staff, are having to experience. The five basic customer processes can be used to classify all the service methods (as in Table 3.3) but can also be used to indicate the appropriateness of particular methods to what the customer is expected, and willing to undertake during the meal service.

Menus as artistic representations of the age

Menu covers exhibit the evolution of the decorative arts as they mirror the colour palette and layouts adopted by designers at various moments in history. Menus have through time become highly collectable artefacts, explicitly those having connection with royalty, nobility and distinguished guests, visiting dignitaries etc. The most rare can easily become museum pieces, most especially if signed by the distinguished individuals who attended the meal. The Musée Escoffier at Villeneuve-Loubet, the Bodleian Library at Oxford and the Mosimann Academy in London, all have extensive menu collections.

Food is a cultural product like any other, and every era has had its own food ethics and aesthetics. Aesthetics sketch the way in which historical periods, and the values they incorporate, take shape. Menu design has played a decisive role in giving form to restaurant modernity. To give form here implies operating within a more common cultural context. The menu is a central management document. Figure 3.1 attempts to indicate the importance of the menu. The menu has the capacity to influence the type and style of service, the interior design of the restaurant, the character and style of service, the professional expertise and volume of staff, and the nature of the customers the business is likely to attract.

If menu design is inadequately handled it can severely impair a business, causing a downturn in revenue, which can haemorrhage cash flow. The design process is difficult to define for it invokes creativity and entrepreneurship, it seeks to optimize profitability and client well-being, and it is ubiquitous in a corporate environment comprising elements of

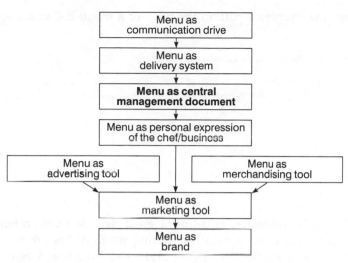

Figure 3.1 The menu and its importance to an operation

performance quality, durability image-creation and costs. Menu design must also allow for changes (total or partial) which may be daily, weekly, monthly or perceived as possible in the mid-term usage.

As food is a cultural product then menu language should be designed for the cultural individual, appealing to the mind as well as the palate. The language used in the menu must therefore give rise to appetite. Language is more than vocabulary, it is an enabling mechanism, explaining why and how individuals behave; it is more than the sum of what is written on the menu – it is how it is said and the elegant simplicity of its expression that has the maximum impact.

3.2 The birth of a menu collection: the paradigm of contemporary culinary refinement

Considering everything that took place during the 20th century, it is inconceivable to think that cuisine and gastronomy can remain stationary. Individuals can now cultivate their palates just as they might cultivate their intellect, for it is only prudent to have intelligent regard for the foodstuffs with which one intends to stoke the human furnace.

Menus can become fashionable if they follow the prevailing pattern of what is considered to be in vogue. The validity of a fashionable menu, or what makes it voguish, or culturally accepted, tends to be determined by those who lead in these matters. Some concept cuisines, for instance, have stood the test of time and entered the language.

The creative process in dish and menu development is fraught with pitfalls at all stages. The process is both cognitive and practical, requiring sensoric and economic evaluation, but the chef at this level of operation will benefit also from the concept that food is part of the environment that we consume and that foods and dishes are defined culturally. Thus, the chef has to address external factors like the psychological, social and cultural needs of individuals which food, dishes and the menu and wine list must meet, and also the economic status of the customer.

The progressive developmental path in the birth of a menu collection is:

1 Conception

2 Orientation

3 Decision

4 Purchasing

5 Production

6 Sampling

7 Endorsement.

Compiling a collection is intensive, entailing a great deal of work, often punctuated by doubt, some near certainties and periods of waiting while dishes are woven into a menu format. Menu design is a subtle alchemy of style and time-tested technical refinement. Successful compilation for fashionable restaurants is not immediate, but stems from a laborious process of professional evolution.

The intrinsic value of dishes to the modern chef is that they form part of what is considered to be a contemporary cuisine. In the past a collection of dishes forming a menu would be conceived in the way an item of clothing is – following pre-set rules, which respect proportions and volumes of ingredients. A codified repertoire of classically conceived dishes exists in the form of Saulnier's *Le Répertoire de la cuisine* (1991). This book has and does help to ensure:

- accuracy and clarity – through an international language of cuisine offering continuity in product, production, saucing and garnishing;

- standardized culinary appellations and vocabulary offering precise international inter- pretation by the chef, gourmet, gastronome and cognoscenti; and

- documentation of the sociocultural, gastro-historical and gastro-geographical origin of the dishes.

Menu development and transition

Menu writing, menu planning and the use of menus have undergone tremendous changes over the centuries, making it difficult to gauge explanations for certain things that we do unless we know something about our own history. Menus show the history and the development of gastronomy, they also reveal the conventions of the period, outline when dish appellations came into use and whether they had particular prominence through time. They also display the changing economy of the period and how menus represent the establishments for which they were designed.

The practice and ritual of naming dishes was widespread from the middle of the 18th century until the first two decades of the 20th century. Restaurants, chefs, gourmets and gastronomes of the time all had dishes named after them (Table 3.7 gives some examples). The classical menus containing these dishes communicate by the use of the culinary meta- language that is used in the kitchen and in menu design. These menus feature dish appellations that can be accurately deciphered by chefs, gourmets and gastronomes around the world. Today, the modern equivalent could be the individual chefs' signature dishes, which although existing in individual menus and in chefs' publications, have yet to be codified and recorded for inclusion into the European *répertoire*.

In recent times there has been some polarizing of position. Most haute gastronomie has moved towards taking on some aspects of nouvelle. However there are those who take a more traditionalist stance, where the *Le Répertoire* is viewed as the enduring classical theoretical model, supported by neo-classical cuisine.

The compilation of new dishes, giving rise to new menu collections, requires both specialist and ensemble skills. To use a musical analogy, the kitchen brigade are similar to the orchestral players, the premier chefs are the principal players, while the conductors, those who concentrate on the ensemble, are the pioneer, visionary innovators, whose 'collections' are personal expressions of their taste orchestrated through professional consultative processes. This in no way negates the skill of leading traditional practitioners, who ensure the survival of codified dishes from the classical *répertoire*.

Food fashion is transitory, and customers now anticipate new and distinctive dishes composed from carefully selected ingredients. This season's fashionable menus have a limited life span, akin to the cycle of the fashion world. Fashionable restaurant habitués can tire easily of predictability and uniformity. As chefs have attempted tirelessly to attract and encourage custom through transforming their menus with regularity, they may also have locked themselves into the endless cycle of menu changes to keep pace with customer expectation and demand.

Today's innovative visual hospitality features an unprecedented alliance with other hospitality specialists. Whatever a chef's contemporary prominence, he or she must collaborate effectively, and by necessity, with service personnel, purchasing specialists (to ensure quality), wine and spirit merchants, public relations and marketing personnel, graphic design consultants, business advisers and bankers. Today fashion-conscious chefs are increasingly concentrating on the holistic harmony of dishes on their menus, and presentational and aesthetic codes have been raised to new levels of importance.

Some of today's chefs have become synonymous with impressive design and seemingly impeccable craftsmanship. None of this though would have been possible if contemporary exponents of the craft had continued blindly to follow an existing *répertoire*. However, the *répertoire* is still the benchmark for determining the classical progression in cuisine, for it offers a comprehensive and systematic presentation of culinary theory. Like many other chefs before them, those who responded to the nouvelle cuisine and were either amongst the founding fathers of the movement or its major exponents, or the inventors of concept cuisines, had eventually to design a cuisine for themselves or fall into the trap of being relentlessly and mercilessly copied. Mosimann's Cuisine Naturelle can be said to be truly his own, offering versatility and daring eclecticism, as can, for example, Vergé's Cuisine du Soleil, Guérard's Minceur Cuisine and Minceur Exquise. All of the principal exponents, and a few others, established concept cuisines to differentiate themselves – and not merely present an agglomeration of exaggerated dishes strung into menu format. The menu provides narrative thrust; it is the ephemeral expression of the chef's inventiveness in the eye of the customer but has also to prove itself as a working and evolving tool.

The fashionable restaurant and fashionable menu genre kept haute cuisine buoyant in the latter part of the 20th century. Fashionable menus spawned by pioneer innovator chefs have secured the place of haute cuisine as a paradigm of contemporary culinary refinement. They have utilized the best of that which is time-honoured and have restyled it to remain relevant. But above all they have become much more customer profile-oriented, and conscious of themselves as arbiters of fashion and food. Cultivating exquisiteness and fashion, albeit fleetingly, while inspiring the mind and fostering a culture of improved (not impoverished)

Table 3.7 Origins of some classical menu terms

After restaurants

D'Antin	Paris restaurant which gives its name to a poached fish dish
Delmonico	Renowned New York restaurant which gives its name to a method of preparing potatoes and a salad
Maxim	This well-known Parisian restaurant has an egg dish named after it
Café Riche (Paris)	Method for preparation of fish, especially sole, and a sauce – 'Sauce Riche'; it also describes a method of garnishing small cuts of meat
Voisin (Paris)	Gives its name to a potato dish

After restaurateurs

Louis Bignon	Celebrated 19th century Paris restaurateur. An egg dish is named after him
Marguéry	Paris restaurateur, and creator of a sole dish carrying his name

After chefs

Antoine Beauvilliers	Opened one of the first restaurants in Paris in the 1780s and author of *L'Art du cuisinier*. A garnish for large joints of braised meats is named after him
Marie Antoine Carême	Celebrated chef and author of several books. Among dishes he created that bear his name are Perdreau Carême and Bécasse Carême
Pièrre Cubat	Chef to Emperor Alexander II of Russia. A method of preparing fish bears his name
Dugléré	Chef at the Café Anglais. Methods of preparing sole and turbot are named after him
Auguste Escoffier	Author and celebrated chef. Most of Escoffier's dishes were named for other people, for example Nellie Melba and Sarah Bernhardt. However, several sauces and a cold sole dish bear his name
Jean-Julien	The term Julienne describes a method of cutting vegetables into very fine strips. A consommé is also named Julienne, which contains the vegetables cut in this fashion
Laguipière	Chef to Prince Murat. A sauce and two fish dishes take the name. Carême also dedicated many dishes to Laguipière
Vatel	Worked for Louis XIV of France (reputed to have taken his own life because a fish course for a special banquet was not ready on time). A fish dish was created in his name

Table 3.7 continued

After gourmets/gastronomes

Baron Brisse	Writer and gastronome whose name describes a preparation for red mullet, sole fillets and a garnish for small cuts of meat
Joseph Berchoux	A consommé and a pheasant dish are named after this gourmet. He was also a poet and wrote a poem titled *Gastronomie*
Brillat-Savarin	Gastronome, magistrate, politician and author of *Physiologie du gout*. Jean-Julien created an enriched yeast cake which eventually had the 'Brillat' part of the name dropped and is today better known as 'Savarin'. Marie Antoine Carême also created a salmon dish, an omelette and a garnish in his name
Jean-Jacques Cambacères	High Chancellor of the Empire appointed by Bonaparte, he was later made Duke of Parma. Cambacères was a gourmet. A method of preparing salmon trout and a cream soup with pigeon and crayfish are named after him
Viscount François Châteaubriand	Gourmet and French Ambassador to England. Montmireil, his chef, created a method of preparing the head of fillet in his honour
Lucius Licinius Lucullus	Wealthy Roman General and gastronome renowned for his luxurious banquets. Several dishes carry the name Lucullus, most requiring elaborate preparation and costly ingredients
Charles Monselet	French gastronome and author of assorted gastronomic works, the best known of which was *Almanach des gourmands*. Many dishes are named after him: a distinctive feature is the presence of globe artichokes, truffles with potatoes fried in butter

dining, are the values to which these fashion leaders are dedicated. Whether it is perceived as a constraint or as a liberator, it is thanks to nouvelle cuisine that we are all now potential victims of culinary fashion. Luckily, in the hands of a select group of chefs, fashion may in fact be perceived to be a positive and challenging tool that moves cuisine and gastronomy forward.

3.3 Concept cuisines: impetus for market reinvigoration

In analysing the rise of concept cuisines and their systems of delivery and portrayal by certain of the culinary fashion exponents, it may be seen that the initial fashionability of the 1970s nouvelle cuisine wore thin as others mercilessly pirated menus and dishes. This has strengthened the development of concept cuisines, as the top practitioners fought to remain relevant. These new and clearly identifiable concept cuisines included a reinvigoration of the market, thus producing a following for fashionable restaurants.

The greatest attribute of a chef has been to create a successful and lasting fashion. This has been well demonstrated by the leaders of cuisine ancienne, including chefs such as Antonin

Carême (1784–1834), Alexis Soyer (1809–1859) (with whom the cult of the chef is perceived to have been seeded), Georges Auguste Escoffier (1846–1935), Édouard Nignon (1865–1935) and lastly Fernand Point (1897–1955). All of these were pioneers, visionaries and innovators (see Chapter 2). They also provide the antecedents for those who have followed. From the first decades of the 20th century, many pioneer innovators have been direct or indirect beneficiaries of Point's gastronomy. Early examples include Louis Outhier and Paul Bocuse, and one later example is Alain Senderens. Some of these chefs have undertaken pioneering work of their own. For example, Outhier and Senderens' early culinary work was with the use of unusual flavours and spicing. Fashion leaders Guérard and Mosimann visually and nutritionally simplified and clearly identified their cuisine with healthy eating, and Vergé made his name through the tireless promotion of Cuisine Provençale.

All the chefs mentioned here have been exponents of haute cuisine and nouvelle cuisine. They have all produced collections of dishes that have led to the compilation of fashionable menus, and they have all been plagiarized by other chefs. As inferior replications of their dishes flourished, these and other haute cuisiniers have responded by striving to further differentiate themselves through the formulation of new and almost entirely individualistic concept cuisines. In doing this these key chefs established niche markets, which are still developing. The new cuisines were given differing titles, some of which are listed in Table 3.8.

Table 3.8 Examples of concept cuisines

Name of cuisine	Simple meaning
Cuisine d'Auteur	My cuisine/the author's
Cuisine de Civilité	With courteous attention
Cuisine Courante	Current
Cuisine Etrangère	Foreign
Cuisine du Femme	Feminine
La Cuisine Gourmande	Gourmet
Cuisine Heureuse	Happy/joyous
Cuisine Improvisée	Improvised
Cuisine de Jus	Flavour-packed, using the juices
Cuisine Maigre	Lean
Cuisine du Marché	From the market
La Cuisine aux mille senteurs	With a thousand aromas/perfumes
Cuisine Minceur	Slim/slender
Minceur Exquise	Exquisite, slim
La Grande Cuisine Minceur	The highest expression of slim
La Cuisine Moderne	Modern
Cuisine Naturelle	Natural/healthy style
Nouvelle Cuisine	New style
Cuisine Parfumée	Highly aromatic
La Cuisine Réussie	Successful
Cuisine sans frontières	Across frontiers
Cuisine de Sensibilité	Sensitively balanced
Cuisine du Soleil	Of the sun
Cuisine Spontanée	Spontaneous
Cuisine du Terroir	Earthy

The originators of concept cuisines saw that these new ideas had to amass some significance and meaning. Through the use of basic techniques of market manipulation, they attempted to move their ideas on dish and menu production to the centre of people's attention, where, by careful placing, they could align with other phenomena in the public consciousness, including people's aspirations. Supported by this carefully targeted marketing and associated media endorsement, chefs sought to establish a distinctive following. They endeavoured to understand the particular needs of their clientele more fully. In turn, the clientele responded and gained more interest in the chefs who had cultivated, and to an extent, captivated their attention. What had not been thoroughly comprehended initially though was that the whole concept of fashion lies in its fluidity. It is engineered for change. Consequently even these singular cuisines would necessarily have to evolve through time to avoid dish and menu fatigue.

Concept cuisine development and realization requires financial input, the confident support of backers and the personal enthusiasm of internal participants (the kitchen brigade, food service staff, the management team and the upper echelons of the dining-out community). Much of the chefs' groundwork is involved in establishing their own credentials as individuals worth listening to. If the concept of chefs as stars is examined closely, it can be linked back to the perceived need of pioneering, visionary and innovator chefs to distinguish their cuisine as truly their own. Top practitioners remodelled or created anew not only their own dishes and menus but also their entire businesses. In this respect, for example, Mosimann and Blanc in Britain, Vergé, Bocuse, Guérard, Senderens and Robuchon in France, and Witzigmann, Müller and Winkler and others in Germany, can be likened to international products or brands that are so well known that they can exploit a seemingly endless consumer demand for new and fashionable ideas.

Once a reputation for quality, innovation and excellence has been established it can be built upon, and diversified with remarkably successful results. As brands, these cuisines also reflect idiosyncrasy at the heart of which is the perceived need of chefs to avoid culinary piracy and the denigration of their cuisine. Thus, these new concept cuisines have been ultimately and irrevocably associated with their individual founders, ensuring a virtual branding for the chefs and their businesses. These concept cuisines also reflect a need on the part of both chefs and customers for clearly recognizable products, which both meet and exceed their needs and expectations in terms of a desire for novelty.

3.4 The advance of fusion cuisine

The term fusion cuisine was first coined by Norman Van Aken, chef/proprietor of the renowned restaurant Norman's, located in the historic Coral Gables area of Miami. As with most evolutions in cuisine, the term has broadened in meaning as the movement has increased in momentum, and has also been confused and misrepresented en route.

Fusion cuisine came about in conceptual terms as a consequence of the amalgamation of gutsy provincial cuisine with the more academic or highbrow classic French cuisine codified as part of the Escoffier orthodoxy. This is what Van Aken was characterizing when he originally spoke about fusion. Van Aken was alluding to the harmonious blending of foods of various origins as a consequence of the convergence of contrasting cultures. He was in essence, like any good chef, studying market opportunities and reacting to where he lived. Fusion can of course take place anywhere, from Australia, New Zealand, Hong Kong, Canada and all over Europe. It has now become an umbrella term which chefs use when adopting aspects of disparate cuisines, fusing them together in harmonious dishes and in the process giving rise to a democratization of taste.

Like nouvelle cuisine (as discussed Chapter 2, page 62), fusion cuisine, *per se*, is neither new nor fashionable (of the moment or time), nor is it a voguish whim. Just as Guérard, and others, coined the latest representation of nouvelle, so Van Aken coined the term fusion, but fusion itself has been around for as long as nouvelle cooking: chefs have always created anew. Fusion in cuisine was conceived in the heady expressions of early power, influence, affluence and political battles for supremacy. It can be seen clearly in the Roman conquering and colonization of new lands and territories. They by necessity ingested what the locals consumed to supplement that which they brought with them. As a consequence methods and ingredients were woven into local culinary culture and incorporated in both directions.

Bringing the story forward in time, fusion can be just as easily detected by gastro-geographical and gastro-historical study of the cuisine of the Swiss, which had harmonized to the topography of the country and what could be grown or transported. Gastro-geographic research can identify various ethnic influences, including those of Germany, France and Italy. The cuisines influencing Switzerland also affected the evolution of other areas like the Mediterranean and the United States of America. Fusion then takes place not simply by national border incursions, but also over time. It can occur by stealth over hundreds of years, or at speed.

As the travelling public and chefs have become much more sophisticated through having sampled different foods en-route, and as global travel comes within both transport and fiscal reach, the travelling public and chefs have on the whole embraced ethnicity and new and evolving tastes with gusto. Through the attendant transport explosion, restaurants today have few constraints on the availability of raw materials. The rise of fusion cuisine is not then surprising, the more so since, as Ackerman (1995) has said, 'food has a powerful social component'.

Ingredients from around the world skilfully blended together from the cuisines of more than one country may at first appear odd, but the idea also makes good sense. A good deal of what are now acknowledged as essential elements of the various national cuisines of Europe are often imports. However, in developing new approaches there is a need for a culinary intelligence and an educated palate. This is to avoid dishes being created that lack the precision of an art or craft, or of culinary understanding, interpretation and stability. It is to avoid, for instance, dishes that reflect an agglomeration of random ingredients with disparate flavours, caused by culinary piracy without the stealth of logical intent.

Today's most highly skilled chefs do not create their dishes in a vacuum. They are sentient beings who watch, listen and interpret. Above all, they have an awareness of the culture and community in which they operate, as Van Aken has, and its gastro-geographical and gastro-historical roots. They also fully understand that the foundations in cuisine, as identified by Bourdin (see Chapter 1, page 8), are necessary before considering additional superstructural and strengthening elements in creative development. In many cultures and countries, great individual ingredients exist, but these are sometimes blended together in a coarse fashion more through habituation of taste than fault. Skilled chefs have taken individual elements and unloaded powerful spice blends in order to make them more subtle. They have been more sparing in the blending of herbs and they have also been more thoughtful in the choice of ingredients used. In the process they have created an appreciable impact.

Fusion cuisine is also arguably a concept cuisine to which it is difficult to apply the criteria that would normally prevail in assessing the cuisine of an individual region or country. A more cultivated individual analysis is required as the benchmarks from the culture(s) where the dish/dishes have come from do not apply, or at least do not apply in the same fashion.

As with any dishes, decisions need to be made on the visual appeal and the positiveness of the impact on the senses. Mouth feel is also important, but surprises may be in store in terms of how things might be expected to look and taste and how they actually physically appear. Of uppermost importance though is the balance of the dish.

Traditionalists (classicists) might never dream of putting smoked salmon or caviar on a pizza for instance, but this does not mean that it might not work. Classicists might also recoil in horror, for instance, at a dish available at the Hotel Arts in Barcelona (operated by Ritz Carlton). This is a wood-fired chicken curry pizza with soured cream and cucumber. This dish has been sampled on numerous occasions; it is packed with subtle nuances of flavour. The wood smoke penetrates the dough of the pizza base and the subtle chicken curry is light and refreshing, especially with the dressing and cucumber. The attendant atmosphere is of a five-star hotel, ocean front property, and open dining also plays its elemental part. Eckart Witzigmann's tiny baked potatoes filled with caviar and other exotic fillings are also a rare treat, as is the lobster taco served at The Mansion on Turtle Creek in Dallas. It is sometimes the getting away from what things should taste like, by enhancing or fusing them with further interest, which creates real impact.

As with nouvelle cuisine, there are bad attempts to construct dishes under the banner fusion, but fusion cookery is no fad or fashion. Food progression and experimentation in cuisine has not and does not cease. Gastronomy is concerned with all cuisine and not only with classic cuisine. Gastronomy is a broad church with many views expressed and firmly held. Importantly and somehow comfortingly, fusion cuisine is supported by some of the world's most classically inspired chefs. This may not only be in response to fusion's assimilation of new flavours, textures and mouth feel. It is also because the majority of techniques and prevailing standards are based on the classic (predominantly French) tradition, including with this the art of presenting ingredients of the highest possible quality, showing regard for texture (which can be of secondary importance in some ethnically inspired dishes), for presentation and also for a pronounced and recognizable bouquet.

Fusion chefs' predilection for the application of French traditions is evident in the choices they make in fusing cuisine for example:

Thai–French	Japanese–French
Chinese–French	German–French
Indian–French	Italian–French
Spanish–French	Belgian–French

This has come about partly as a result of the chef's own training, and partly as a response to the dominant perceptions of a well-travelled clientele, who equate French cuisine with the height of culinary expression, although there are many other cuisines equally deserving of the same respect and praise. Baudrillard (1993) has expressed the view that modern fusion cuisine can be seen as a contamination or virus, stripping a culture of its real identity. The most successful are clearly beyond this type of criticism, although there is a view that the approaches to modern fusion cuisine do need to be developed further.

3.5 A harmonious union – food and wine

In the same way as food, menu and restaurant operations have developed, so have wine and other beverage lists. The broadening of supply with the increasing availability of wines, from for example Australasia and the Americas, together with an increasing range of beverages, including for example designer lagers, and the modern flavoured alcoholic beverages (FABs, e.g. Bacardi Breezer), have all impacted on the modern beverage list construction. Additionally, diversification and rises in the range of demands from an increasingly knowledgeable and value-conscious clientele have forced the development of higher levels of professionalism in the sale of beverages.

Wine and drink lists are basically product guides assembled in a particular and recognizable format. They identify for the customer:

- the selection on offer

- the price of the item

- details such as measure in which the item is to be sold

- in many cases a description of the item if it is a wine, or unusual spirit or liqueur.

Wine and drinks lists now come in a variety of individual styles and size formats, which frequently indicate the type of establishment. The compilation of wine and drink lists derives from the consideration of a number of factors, such as the following.

- Careful consideration of the intended extensiveness of the list, as it can cost a vast amount of money to maintain.

- The layout and style of the list, including the overall design and packaging, which should be in harmony with the style of operation.

- The dimensions of the list, in order to make it easy to handle and use for both guests and staff, and the required durability.

- The time span for which the list will be in operation.

- Adaptability of design and construction so as to be able to modify the list as vintages change and for the incorporation of special promotions.

- The overall design and clarity of the list, which can contain illustrations, or insertion of a contents page if the list is sizeable.

- Provision of the information required to support customer needs as well as answering legal requirements.

- Consideration of the availability of supply, storage and capacity, and the capital investment required.

Wine and drink lists articulate the character of the operation. Style of presentation can mark one operation out as exceptional even though there may be comparable content to other operations in the vicinity. Equally, weak presentation can adversely affect customers' judgement of the business and the food and beverage product.

Wines and drinks incorporated into the modern list include:

1 non-alcoholic drinks including natural spring and mineral waters, aerated waters, squashes, juices and syrups;

2 cocktails, including non-alcoholic cocktails;

3 bitters as apéritifs and for mixed drinks and cocktails;

4 wines, including still wine, sparkling wines, alcohol-free, de-alcoholized and low-alcohol wines; fortified wines and aromatized wines need consideration, as do spirits and liqueurs;

5 beers, including draught and packaged beers and reduced alcohol beers, cider and perry.

The order of wines and drinks on lists tends, as in menus, to follow logically the order of consumption, or be grouped under types of wine or drink. This will include:

1 cocktails

2 apéritifs

3 cups

4 spirits

5 wines

6 liqueurs

7 brandies and port

8 beers, minerals and squashes.

Wines are frequently classified by area, with the white wines of one region first followed by the red wines of that region. A more contemporary style lists all the white wines available area-by-area followed by the red wines arranged in a similar way. Alternative approaches are to list wines by grapes or more specifically by light to heavier. This type of layout is frequently more useful to the customer. None the less, sparkling wines, and therefore the Champagnes, are commonly listed in advance of all other wines available.

Types of beverage lists

Bar and cocktail lists ● ● ●

These may range from a basic standard list offering the common everyday apéritifs, a selection of spirits with mixers, beers and soft drinks, together with a limited range of cocktails, to a very comprehensive list offering a wide choice in all areas.

Apéritif lists ● ● ●

These can be combined with the restaurant wine list – although they are more frequently today presented as a separate apéritif list along with digestif and liqueur lists. For apéritif lists it is common to include lighter, drier styles in wines and fortified drinks, although drinks with some acidity are useful to enhance appetite. The contents might include:

- Champagne – non-vintage, vintage, premier cuvées, Champagne Rosé
- Kir Royale
- Other sparkling wines, sparkling rosé
- Dry sherry – Fino, Manzanilla through to dry Oloroso

- Dry white wine – for example, Muscadet and New Zealand Sauvignon Blanc
- Lighter Mosel, Austrian and Swiss wine styles
- Pineau des Charentes
- Sercial Madeira, Rainwater, Verdellho
- Ratafia
- Vermouths
- Bitters
- White Port
- Dry Marsala
- Tawny port (served chilled).

Restaurant wine lists • • •

The content and presentation of the wine list says a lot about a restaurant. The prime duty of the list is to inform, although too much information is just as bad as having none. Examples of types of wine list include:

- a full and very comprehensive list of wines from all countries, but emphasis on the classic areas such as Bordeaux/Burgundy plus a fine wine/prestige selection;
- a middle of the road, traditional selection, e.g. some French, German, Italian together with some 'New World' wines;
- a small selection of well-known or branded wines;
- a prestige list predominantly with wines of one specific country.

Technical consideration in constructing a restaurant wine list include:

- the extent to which the list will allow suitable pairing with the menu(s) on offer;
- the range to be covered, such as the 'Old' and 'New Worlds', and including sparkling wines, Champagne, red and white wines, rosé and fortified wines;
- balance not only in terms of country of origin but also styles, prices, grapes, countries, tradition and fashion;
- the inclusion of a small selection of well-known or branded wines, where required;
- stating who the producer or merchant is and what the vintage is, if appropriate;
- the availability of some wines by the glass, half bottle, bottle and magnum;
- the inclusions of half bottles, which although in the main are likely to be taken up by individuals eating on their own, will also be of interest to individuals wishing differing wines with each course or to parties of guests with differing preferences, e.g. individuals who like a dry-red and others who prefer a sweet white or perhaps rosé wine;
- the opportunity for effective marketing of a reserve or special list of rare wines;

- ensuring that prices per item appear clear and unambiguous;
- the extent to which the list excites the customer and communicates commendable value.

After-meal drinks lists (digestifs) • • •

These are more frequently presented as a separate digestif or liqueur list. Digestif lists will usually comprise soothing, mellowing, heavier, sweeter, richer styles but also list settling beverages. The contents can include:

- really good sweet wines such as sweet German, Austrian, Loire and Jurançon wines which can refresh the palate;
- sweet fortified wines like port, sherry, Madeira, Marsala, Malaga, rich and liqueur Muscats;
- vintage and LBV port;
- a specialist range of Cognac, Armagnac and brandies and/or a specialist range of malt and older malt whiskies;
- a range of liqueurs;
- settling digestifs, including Chartreuse (the spirit held in the deepest regard by connoisseurs), richer bitters, Strega and good Cognac;
- a range of speciality liqueur/spirit coffees might also be included.

Banqueting wine lists • • •

For banqueting wine lists:

- the length of the list is generally according to size and style of operation;
- there is often a range of prices from house wines to some fine wines to suit all customer preferences;
- in some instances the banqueting wine will draw wines from the restaurant wine list – this reduces the need for double stocking;
- there is often a selection of popular wine names/styles on offer.

Essentially an operation is endeavouring to achieve ease of availability, strong gross profit margin and high recognition. There are certain technical considerations in drawing up banqueting wine lists.

- The list must allow suitable pairing with the menu(s) on offer, especially if there is a range of suggested standard menus.
- Because banqueting lists are often sent out months in advance of an event, care needs to be taken to ensure ongoing supplies.
- A disclaimer might be included which advises that an alternative may be necessary, or substitutions may be made if the client does not request that wines be set aside for their event.

- Sales mix data must be able to distinguish between banqueting lists sales and restaurant sales, as wines may appear to be performing more strongly simply through an order placed from a banquet.

Room service drinks list ● ● ●

These lists tend toward less formality. However:

- they usually offer a limited range of wines and other drinks, although it can be helpful if the customers can purchase from the main lists if required;

- there may be a mini-bar/refreshment centre or choice from a standard bar list;

- in some instances a fixed stock in sealed decanters is provided for VIP or CIP (commercially important guests) and other guests.

Other beverages lists ● ● ●

Cocktails, spirits, liqueurs, beers, cider and perry all make up the beverage directory on offer in many establishments. More recently the attention being given to other beverages has increased, with even the most simple operations offering a range of teas and coffees and other proprietary drinks as a matter of course. Additionally even the best destination hotels, restaurants and resorts are offering freshly prepared juices, some of which mimic the look and gravity of wines both red and white as an option.

Increased travel and growing numbers of European tourists have impacted on tea and coffee service in no small way. The impetus is towards ever-higher standards of fresh preparation and an accelerating demand for continental styles.

Offering a range of beverages other than wines and drinks often provides opportunities for increasing revenue, especially where these beverages are offered with additional revenue generators such as biscuits, sandwiches, scones, open or closed sandwiches, savouries etc.

Matching food and beverages

For the gourmet and gastronome matching food and wine (or other beverages) for consumption in the home is relatively simple. The wine is chosen because it is liked, neither too light nor too weighty, nor too young or too old, to accompany a meal. A common predicament for the professional in a restaurant or for the host however is when a party of three or four individuals or more choose different dishes from a menu. Europe has an extensive range of wine styles available, but it is still normally the food that is selected first, with two or more wines being singled out to complement different courses on the menu, or to consume throughout the meal.

It is common practice to sip an apéritif prior to dining. The term apéritif originates from the Latin *aperitivus* – to open out. In keeping with this, apéritifs are designed to open out and stimulate the taste buds and cleanse the palate in preparation for food. Another practical reason for taking an apéritif is that it can be an aid to relaxation, helping the diner unwind ready for the enjoyment to come. There are however some pitfalls which can spoil the chosen beverage. Peanuts, whether unsalted, salted or roasted, should be avoided as they can devastate wine flavours. Olives are generally too tart or pungent for the majority of wines, however they do accompany Martini and sherry well. More appropriate partners for apéritifs are for example, almonds, walnuts, pistachios, lightly salted crisps, gougères and mild cheese straws. It is also worth considering the avoidance of strong spirits as drinking too much can desensitize the palate.

The pairing of food and wine (or other beverages) can be complex as there are no absolute food and wine combinations. Pairing food and wine is a learned response; however, there are some helpful hints available. In essence it all rests upon personal taste and experience. The main intention is to achieve harmony between the food and the beverages. The achievement of this can be aided by consideration of:

- temperature
- the palate
- matching weights
- intensity of both food and wine
- flavour dominance
- texture
- cooking method
- garnishes, sauces and other accompaniments.

Temperature

Heat is discerned as both temperature and taste sensation. Cold can be discerned in the same way but can be a pleasing contrast to hot and warm foods, as in for example a cool refreshing glass of beer with a medium spicy dish or curry which acts as a compelling contrast.

Temperature is also important for wine storage and service. Serving a wine too warm or too cold is the surest way to spoil a bottle, which would otherwise be considered commendable. The serving temperature for wine can have a profound effect on the wine, transforming its smell and taste. Different styles of wine warrant serving at different temperatures to enhance their positive features. Examples of temperatures are given in Table 3.9.

The warmer the wine, the more extensive the evaporation of volatile flavour compounds from the surface of the wine in the glass. Figure 3.2 shows a wine temperature formula that readily explains the role of temperature and its effect on aroma, acidity and tannin. Basically this suggests that to heighten the impact of aroma (or bouquet), it is best to serve wines within their style at slightly higher temperatures. So red Bordeaux would have its aromatic features maximized at 18°C and this would accordingly minimize tannin and acidity. Above this temperature and most definitely at 20°C and above, wines will become unbalanced, as

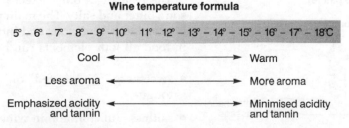

Figure 3.2 Wine temperature formula

Table 3.9 Serving temperatures for wine

Red wines

Red Bordeaux	18°C	Mature Pinot Noir	17°–18°C
Red Burgundy	16°C	Cabernet Sauvignon/Syrah	15°–18°C
Beaujolais	12°–16°C	Pale Rosé	5°–8°C
Light red	10°–13°C	Rosé	7°–10°C
Medium red	14°–17°C	Ruby/tawny port	15°–17°C
Full red	15°–18°C	Tawny port	9°–12°C
Tannic red	16°–18°C	Vintage port	16°–18°C
Quaffable Gamay/Pinot Noir	10°–13°C		

White wines

Full bodied white	12°–17°C	Mature vintage Champagne	10°–11°C
Complex dry white	12°–16°C	Fino and Manzanilla sherry	9°C
Medium dry white	10°–12°C	Amontillado/Oloroso	15°–18°C
Light white	8°–10°C	Sercial Madeira	9°–10°C
Full bodied sweet white	8°–12°C	Bual Madeira	13°–16°C
Light sweet white	5°–10°C	Malmsey	15°–18°C
Sparkling white	6°–10°C	White port	6°–8°C
Young lively Champagne	6°–8°C		

the alcohol content will begin to evaporate. Mature and rare wines should be served relatively warm.

The impression of cold in the mouth and throat is a component of the overall enjoyment, slaking thirst and being generally refreshed. Perception of cold and hot is due to thermal sensitivity, which is part of our tactile sense. The lips provide a thermal warning that can avert painful contact with the sensitive mucous lining of the mouth, the walls of the pharynx and oesophagus. At minimal serving temperatures of *circa* 8°C negligible volatile elements will evaporate and only predominantly aromatic wines will appear to have any aroma whatsoever. Faults in poor-quality wines can be partially concealed by serving the wine very cool. Generally speaking, a more assertive wine is required for hot food than cold food.

The palate • • •

Used for organoleptic evaluation, the palate is formed by the tongue, nose and retro-nasal passage.

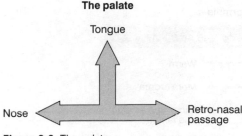

Figure 3.3 The palate

The palate can only detect four tastes: sweet, sour, bitter and salty. The main points to look for in wine are sweet, sour and bitter elements, but in food all four elements can be detected:

- sweetness is detected on the tip of the tongue;
- saltiness (uncommon in wine) is detected just behind the tip;

- acidity is detected on the sides of the tongue; and

- bitterness is detected at the back of the tongue.

(See also the notes on organoleptic skills in Chapter 1, pages 31–3.)

Matching weight • • •

The alcoholic strength and depth of flavour of a wine should parallel that of the dish; delicate food deserves subtle wines, hearty dishes require more substantial wines. Weight or body comes from the alcoholic strength, or the amount of fruit and acids. This is the backbone of a wine. Two wines can have the same alcohol content but have differing weight stemming from the fruit and acidity concentration. Pruning has its part to play in weight of a wine. The more individual bunches of grapes are pruned and smaller grapes removed, the more concentrated the flavours and thus the greater the weight. Pressing also has an effect – the more the grapes are pressed the higher the yield and the lower the weight or body of the resulting wine. A full and rich wine will almost certainly overpower a delicate food – fish or meat. Conversely a rich, well-seasoned dish will swamp a light and delicate wine. By way of example, a roast quail dish topped with Muscat grapes will be completely overpowered by a high alcohol, oaky Chardonnay as it would with a Barolo or red Hermitage. Figure 3.4 indicates the principles.

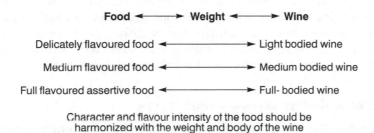

Figure 3.4 Food and wine weight

Intensity in both food and wine • • •

The simpler the food is, then the greater the likelihood that the wine will excel and dominate. Also the finer the food, the greater the likelihood that humbler wines will appear inferior.

Flavour dominance • • •

Flavour concentration may be linked to weight, but not inevitably so. For example, the finest German Riesling's can possess great flavour concentration and complexity, however are conventionally light bodied, low in alcohol and comprise a refreshing sorbet effect on the palate. Sauvignon Blanc can also pack fine flavour concentration but is rarely full bodied. Often a marked contrast in flavours can work well, in for example a spicy wine like a Late Harvest Gewürztraminer with subtly spicy food. In essence you have to look at the complete dish or menu and not the main food component in isolation. Consideration of the texture, cooking method, garnishing, saucing and other accompaniments will decide the wine. The principal dominant flavour component needs to be isolated and examined.

Texture • • •

After weight, intensity and specific flavours, there is the texture of some foods to consider. Some foods have a mouth-coating effect that affects the perception of any wines. Cheese, eggs and chocolate are particular offenders. Wine, as with food, comprises abundant flavours and textures and should be paired with the other elements of a meal based on those flavours and textures.

Cooking method • • •

Brillat-Savarin (as cited by Peynaud, 1996) identified the most desirable order of drinking wines, which is from the lightest styles of wine to the most full bodied and most perfumed. Cooking methods also range from simple lighter styles to heavier and richer more aromatic styles such as:

Light methods	Heavier methods
Poaching	Deep frying
Steaming	Stewing
Grilling	Braising

The cooking method employed is important in that there are many differing types to consider. Each of the cooking methods has a distinctive effect on foods, many of which will have subtle distinctions in the hands of different chefs. There are similarities with wine, in that the eventual taste of a wine can vary widely from one producer to another, and in different vintages and at different stages of maturity. Sweet dishes have instant impact but fade quickly. Methods that impart salty or acidic taste also instantly have an impact but this impact lasts longer. Very salty and acidic foods are difficult to match effectively with wine.

Garnishes sauces and other accompaniments • • •

Normally the central flavour in sauces dictates the wine, but other factors have to be considered. The regional cuisines of Europe have evolved strong partnerships with the wines of their region, in many cases not through the main ingredient but rather through regular garnishes and accompaniments and saucing. In this instance it is best to serve the wine of the region where available. Carbonnade de bœuf, cooked in beer, should be served with the beer that created the main flavour component. Hot spicy dishes can be accompanied by lager instead of wine. Chocolate, egg dishes and mayonnaise vinegar and oil dressings on salads and mint sauce are problematic.

The selection of food and beverages is invariably influenced by numerous factors. These include:

- preference
- gender
- occasion
- weather
- style of restaurant/other venue
- mood

- selling skills of contact personnel

- location

- previous experience

- ambience

- theme of the event

- cooking style

- time of day

- price sensitivity

- season

- marketing and other promotions.

Overall, it is the combinations that please the individuals concerned that are of greatest consequence. Many authors provide structure and definition, which identify a basic median with levels of compatibility or incompatibility. Tastes change with age and with every generation, and as individuals travel farther and experience new foods and new wines and other beverages. Regional foods with their region's wines are one thing, but ideas about classic combinations are changing as people are becoming more experimental and are fusing food from one culture onto another.

3.6 The changing nature of dining

There is emerging a new sophistication in restaurants that seek to stimulate all of the senses. This evolution in dining comprises holistic experience and entertainment. Architectural and interior design elements are to the fore and members of staff are enthusiastic, self-motivated, creative and less formal. These are the restaurants that subconsciously inform the guest, when walking thorough the door, that the right place has been arrived at through instant reassurance and individual cosseting. These are also the businesses that whisper evocatively 'expect an impressive and holistic experience'. It all starts with the person-to-person greeting (which is termed by the Mandarin Oriental Group the 'moment of truth'), and an unequivocally positive body language.

Great restaurants, along with good food and beverages, also have equally great guest contact personnel who are self-assured, have poise and credence. With the changing nature of dining servility now becomes a mythical concept, for it has no place at the table in these restaurants and hotels. Everything and everyone is supporting the other. The audible contentment of being in the right place should pervade the room (as described in the earlier example in Chapter 1, at Paul Bocuse, in Lyons, page 23).

London's Mandarin Oriental Hyde Park hotel opened after extensive renovations costing £43 million, half what Mandarin Oriental Group paid for the hotel in the late 1990s. Director and General Manager Liam Lambert, played an integral role in recruiting and training the property's employees. The group's customers comprise a blend of traditionalists, older conservative travellers, achievers, the young traveller or businessperson, the assertive and the ambitious. It clearly demonstrates the changing nature of the hotel and dining. It is a business focused on people, its own and its clientele, and it is centred upon setting world standards and meeting local needs. It has a more casual, but essentially elegant and international, approach to service and an environment where staff movement appears

The spa

A suite

Figure 3.5 Interior views of the newly refurbished Mandarin Oriental Hyde Park hotel, London

almost balletic in its professional smoothness. It is a business where design has been woven through every aspect from the spa to the rooms, to the restaurants and on to the cuisine, the cutlery, crockery and glassware. It is thus creating new sensations in the hotel, in the rooms, in the dining rooms, on the table and also on the plate.

This changing nature of dining is a feature not only of the chefs profiled in Chapter 4 but also of other equally prestigious and world renowned individuals, such as Alain Senderens at Lucas Carton, Paris; Joel Robuchon at restaurant Joel Robuchon, Paris; Michel Roux at the Waterside Inn at Bray, UK; Alain Ducasse at Le Louis XV – Hotel de Paris, in Monaco and at SAS Hotel Le Parc, Paris; Heinz Winkler at Residenz Heinz Winkler, in Aschau, Germany; Gualtiero Marchesi at the restaurant of the same name in Brescia, Italy, and many more. As the nature of dining changes, the service and setting must keep up with the food and beverage, and everything must form itself into one positive holistic impression.

Contemporary restaurants, design, staff and their clientele

Europe has a strong restaurant, hotel restaurant, brasserie and café tradition, particularly in cultured metro cities like London, Dublin, Paris, Munich, Madrid, Barcelona, Lisbon, Amsterdam, Rome and Copenhagen. Distinctive, imaginative and challenging new restaurant designs have been undertaken in recent years, but design can also have impact and become distinctive in terms of lighting and through the use of both subtle and richer colourways.

The chief aims of restaurant design appear now to be to:

- develop a facility layout to meet the operator's requirements (fitness for purpose);
- support the character of the food and service being offered;
- create atmosphere and ambience;
- create a consistently themed environment;
- entertain in safe and pleasant surroundings;
- set the stage for what is to come and provide experience;
- create an offering relevant to the wishes and desires of the targeted audience;
- market the aesthetics and engage the five senses;
- place a unique and memorable stamp on the dining environment;
- differentiate the goods and services offered from a sea of potential look-alike competitors;
- satisfy expectation and extend the business life cycle;
- reinforce and accentuate the most prized aspects of the businesses' qualities;
- assess future business needs and factor those in at the design stage;
- increase perceived value and therefore the price charged to users (you are what you charge for);
- serve the economic needs of the management to make the business successful.

There has to be a balance and a certain amount of drama, even if that drama is created from pared down Zen interiors or as in some eateries and trendy bars offering very good food in Amsterdam and Munich which utilize colour search lights to wash entire areas with light, adding dramatic effects and colour transitions to completely change the look of the dining and reception room(s). In design, attention to detail is also very important and a good deal of money is spent on artefacts, to set the theme.

Today there is a trend towards more open areas. The production of food in the kitchen fascinates people. A few years ago it was the norm to titillate customers by providing a glimpse into another world by having a window or glass wall near the entrance to the restaurant which gave an impression of this culinary engine-room and its buzz and bustle. Apart from the fact that chefs like to be on show and demonstrate their craft, in general the distance from the kitchen to the restaurant is today getting shorter. It is more streamlined and less complicated. In many cases the bar activities are also much closer to the restaurant than previously.

Nowadays hotel restaurants are also realizing what is happening in stand alone operations. They are moving in either of two directions to match these developments: by either franchising the business out, or keeping the facility and attempting to transform their restaurant operations. Michel Bourdin suggests that those who have chosen the franchising route 'have raised the white flag in defeat not knowing how to or even wishing to attempt to make a success of their restaurants'. Others, who have seen the opportunities, have recognized that in order to be successful, hotel restaurants should not be isolated, hidden entities that are badly or irregularly marketed or not marketed with sufficient vigour and appeal.

Those who have attempted to turn around failing hotel restaurants are also considering the opportunities to forge strong relationships with key customers and businesses that possess information critical to sustaining competitive advantage. Restaurants are for relaxing, for unwinding and having great food, recognition and great service. Excellent restaurant managers get to know their clients and are in tune with the psychology of their customers. They can, as Bourdin states, 'propose and the guest disposes'. The future of these businesses is seen as being connected with recognizing at least the top five customer groups whose opinions and ideas on the products and services are critical to business success.

Success in particular restaurants is also being generated through members of staff today being trained in the fine and professional art of detecting customer preference, through the ability to inconspicuously gather detailed information about what their customers like and dislike, share the knowledge and then proceed to introduce an increasingly personalized experience for them.

Just as cuisine has moved through different phases, restaurants have become more casual and this has become accepted by a percentage of restaurateurs and hoteliers. There are still exclusive restaurants but they are more and more expensive to create. Fine dining, as it has become known since the 1970s, has become more relaxed, warm and almost domesticated. The designed environment has promoted this. Design is also seen to be successful when it is matched to the building architecture, especially in some fine dining establishments where the architecture of the room has been allowed to dictate the interior design – including the fixtures and fittings, such as the mirrors, the chandeliers, the starched white linen etc. – all in keeping.

In addition to the requirements for service staff to have sound product knowledge, well-developed technical skills, interpersonal skills and teamwork capabilities, today's new food concepts require individuals who have been exposed to the new cuisine so that they know how it all fits together. There is a need to attract very talented and dedicated people. In mature organizations it is paying dividends to send managers, chefs and service personnel abroad, and to other establishments, to expose them to new foods, new styles and new trends (as Anton Mosimann does in London). During this period they mature and learn. Successful restaurant managers are also leading from the front. They have progressed through the profession in the same way as chefs. They have a passion and an ability to enthuse. They do more than merely recognize individuals who come to the restaurant frequently; they know that everyone needs to be treated with the same respect, care and attention.

Food and Beverage service is a living thing; it is changing all of the time. There is a framework to work within but there is also a requirement for being proactive as well as reactive. Hans Matthias Kann, Executive Assistant Manager, Food and Beverage, Oberoi Hotels, uses the following story to educate his service personnel:

> the lady on the trapeze in the absolutely gorgeous costume hanging there smiling radiantly, may not feel like smiling, she may be scared of falling, but you would never know it, her performance is carried out perfectly. That is the way we need to be.

Kann also says, 'the food service business is a radar business because you need to constantly be alert and scan'.

3.7 Gastronomic philosophy: meaning and symbolism in gastronomy

Philosophizing is principally a theoretical discipline, the essence of which is a search for understanding of the world and the nature of the individual and his/her place in the world. A review of this nature can disappoint those who expect philosophizing to yield final answers, intellectually satisfying to all individuals, for as the word suggests, it is about a love and search for wisdom as distinct from a love of knowledge. Philosophy is, in part, a critical analysis and assessment of conceptions and meanings. One of the principal tasks of the philosopher therefore is to examine and evaluate these, making their meaning explicit, to so determine the limits of their application, and to view the grounds on which they may be justified. As an enquiring attitude bred of curiosity, philosophy is virtually unrestricted in scope and subject matter.

Meaning and symbolism are allied to language use. They are also embedded in the cultural system. They are two of the weightiest acquisitions from society, since they provided the grounding for communications between persons, and therefore an essential requirement for a socially ordered environment. Meanings cover beliefs, values, symbols and signs. Some individuals might even argue that the rule-based use of meanings is a central feature of our social existence.

Food is central to our existence. It is essential and yet can also be a luxury; food symbolizes itself and more than itself. Mary Douglas (1966) has stated that food and culture are enormously important subjects, viewing food as a natural area of cultural symbolism, but adding the caveat that the meanings of symbols may vary within the social context from culture to culture. Food has many purposes besides its critical and nutritional base, and many of these superstructural elements built onto food are social and ceremonial in origin.

Wine and the vine also have significant ideological prestige and symbolism, from their blossoming in Bacchic ritual (Bacchus the classical Roman god of wine whom the Greeks called Bacchos, or more frequently Dionysus), to their significance in the Christian Eucharist. The vine with its discernible death in winter and its enthusiastic rebirth in the spring (in the northern hemisphere) becomes a markedly relevant symbol for the annual cycle of the death and rebirth of nature in its entirety. The emergence of viticulture and wine production itself was closely allied with the emergence of distinct religious experiences, in which symbols in the environment were used as routes for interpreting and spelling out the intricacies of human life. Distinctively, the vine emerged to be viewed as a potent symbol of death and rebirth, and its legacy, wine, as a way of coming into contact with the forces that were seen to govern human destiny.

In controlled quantities wine has been viewed as advantageous, leading to pleasurable experience. When taken to excess, however, it was considered hazardous both for the individual imbibers and also for society. The forces wine unleashed therefore called for codification of rules of behaviour, deemed by society to be judicious so that it would not lay waste to its very fabric. These rules, put together by the Greeks and Romans, were seen to be important in medieval Europe and are still impacting today (Unwin, 1991).

For sociologists there are no absolute meanings. A common link is the universal role that meaning plays in sustaining historical continuity and social order. A problem for the academic study of meaning is that meanings are constantly being created and changed. But changes in meanings provide the way of viewing the more general process of social change. If meanings are so important in our social life – and they definitely appear to be from the research with gastronomes – then we must consider how they might be grouped and utilized as a way of studying these people as a phenomenon. 'We must take the problems of objectively determining the social meanings of actions to the actors' (Douglas, 1966).

Gastro-symbolism and rich meaning

Use of symbols has often been regarded as a defining characteristic of human social behaviour. A symbol is a thing, be it an odour, a taste, sound, material object, colour, or the motion of an object, the value or meaning of which is conferred upon it by those who use it. The meaning of a symbol cannot be perceived by the senses alone. Symbols and meaning are essential ingredients in all beliefs, for they provide the most powerful images of life; with the myths that accompany them, they compensate for what is not comprehended. They also imply more than their immediate meaning, and the more that they imply the more potent they become.

The philosophy of Plato and Aristotle considered that humanity could and should arrive at the single, true, meaning of things, their *core*. However, today it is generally held that there are no *real or single* meanings, and meaning is really only ascribed to objects in terms of human use. To the casual observer symbolism can seem quite formal and potentially religious, but a symbol is a surrogate for a thing or event. It seizes something from the sensuous immediacy and fuses it in the mind, making it an object to be thought of at any time. This is one of the principal reasons why certain types of gastronomic events associated with specific individuals become fixed in the mind. Layer upon layer of meaning is attached onto the focus of the event – be it the chef and their cuisine, the environment, the companionship, or a distillation of all three. These events are also set apart through dressing up for them, the irregularity of them, and that they are generally expensive and have to be budgeted for.

Most individuals cultivate ideas that cannot be proved; they are the private convictions that give meaning to lives, and help establish the individual's place in the universe. It is the role of symbols to encapsulate these ideas, and for this reason they go back to the most ancient fantasies and needs of our species. This can be seen for example in the work of Lionel Poilâne, whose importance here rests solely in the fact that he is a prominent and internationally renowned user of symbolism and rich meaning in his writings and provides a classic starting point for anyone wishing to gain a grounding in its use within gastronomy.

Poilâne is a Paris bread-maker, philosopher and sculptor in bread dough. He is generally considered to be by far the most professional and virtuoso bread-maker in France and worked with the late artist Salvador Dali from 1968 on several projects – first making bread frames for Dali's paintings, and then sculpting furniture from dough. Poilâne has written several books on the subject of bread. His place here is to display some of the rich symbolism that has grown up around distinctive aliments; in this case, it is with bread. He considers fermentation to be a captivating field of enquiry and that it is openly responsible for the symbolism of bread.

The invention of leavened bread is ascribed to the Egyptians, who cooked flat cakes from millet and barley baked on heated stones. The symbolism in the fermentation used in wine and cheese production is full of association, which can be linked to sexuality and procreation. The three great culinary marriages of bread, cheese and wine, all requiring yeast spores, combine nature's offspring and man's resourcefulness, and all transpired by chance.

It has been posited by Poilâne that possibly Egyptian women took pieces of the old dough adding it to the new one, and so injecting life into the inactive mass making it rise by impregnating it so to speak with the seed. Down the centuries this has been identified with the rotation of existence, which has created a number of words and symbols in our language and creativity. By way of illustration, Poilâne (in Salinger, 1986) points out that 'in Spanish, yeast is called "madre" meaning mother. In Latin yeast is called "luvancm" which does not mean fertilising but solace, like in the language of midwives as she provides solace, comfort etc.'. Words like this can be found in all languages. In Germany small breads are called 'brot leb', meaning woman's body. In Italian they are termed 'angel's wee-wees', whereas in France they are called 'les miches' which means the buttocks, and in Britain they are called buns. In Britain and the United States of America, when a woman is pregnant she is said to have 'a bun in the oven'; 'in France they say when an unmarried woman is expecting a child that she has borrowed a bread from the baker' (Poilâne, in Salinger, 1986).

In terms of the baker's equipment, the cloths used to cover the bread during proving are called 'diapers', with precise synonymy of the word used for babies. The oven is also viewed as very symbolic because the 'four' (oven) derives from the Latin 'fornics': 'fornication a place where one goes back and forth, a warm place' where the breads are transformed from a dough containing the 'seed' (yeast) into a complete product in readiness for consumption (Poilâne, in Salinger, 1986).

From the examples above it can be seen that there are multiple symbols all with a similar thread of meaning, and this symbolism has been passed down throughout time, as have many of our aliments and cooking methods. They have, of course, been refined, with civilizing influences upon them to display this test of our progress, and acculturation, which has been seen in the transition from medieval cuisine to modern cuisines and the fashion today for serving food casually, bereft of adornment. Gastronomes in many ways are tuned into this symbolism and rich meaning to such an extent that they have evolved a meta-language (the prefix meta indicating usage at a higher level or on a different plane). Gastronomic meta-language also deciphers and explains menus, wine lists and conversational set pieces. This though is not the classic French language of cuisine, as that is a technical language existing to give direction on a specifically and largely unchallenged and unchanging path.

The symbolism of the beaux-arts goes largely unquestioned, and the symbolism associated with the arts culinaire does run, to a great extent, along a parallel path. Problems arise, however, when trying to express the symbolism and rich meaning associated with food and gastronomy to individuals who have not been duly sensitized – who are not aesthetes.

Aesthetics should above all be flexible, but this is not always the case when dealing with gastronomy, quite simply because food is viewed as belonging to everyone. What is seen is sometimes considered to be all there is to see and understand, and so the gastronome can tend to be less understood and can be criticized on many levels. There is more to artistic and aesthetic judgement than is first apparent; works of art are devised in conditions that advance meaning to the work, and many artists work layers of symbolism and rich meaning into their artistic endeavours. Each art form may have its technical and aesthetic codes and languages. Cuisine and gastronomy definitely do, and it is quite common to be able to appreciate several aesthetic codes within single art forms (Steel, 1985).

Gastronomic principles impose aesthetic codes of excellence, which govern interpretation and construct creative criteria but allow for some adaptability to deal with changes in fashion and through time. The chefs profiled in this book freely use analogies which bring them on to a parallel path with the artist; indeed both they, the media and (to a greater extent than in the past) the general public, refer to some chefs as artists. Mosimann has in the past used the analogy 'my plates are my palate' and he also states in one of his books, 'a really good cuisine demands a single-minded, almost holy, devotion. Success depends on perfection in the smallest details' (Mosimann, 1989). Bocuse, Vergé, Mosimann and Guérard, for example, use the analogy of food as an art form. Mosimann wrote in his book *The Art of Anton Mosimann* (1990), 'food and cooking are my art and my art is the means I have of communicating with people'. Other examples come from Guérard, who asserts, 'The best chefs are artists in their own right'.

Poilâne has often expressed surrealist symbolism in the production of his works in bread, a residue perchance from his time with the artist Salvador Dali. Bocuse uses musical similitude in expressing points. The chef's central island suite (stoves, ovens, fixed salamanders etc.) is in many cases contemporarily termed their 'piano', and 'piano suites' are now common in larger kitchen plant manufacturers' catalogues, and can be customized in much the same fashion as a musical instrument could for a principal or soloist players. These 'piano suites' can also now be colour co-ordinated and hand customized to suit the artistic chef and his/her temperament.

With the creation and articulation of a culinary philosophy that is undisputed, many outpourings from the individuals and groups function in the community of gastronomes to recount, elucidate, expand and titillate. In general, they can detonate subtle implications, encapsulate difficult arguments and quite simply be clever or funny. However, it is important in gastronomy and the study associated with it to develop the notion of an aesthetic attitude. The word aesthetic derives from the Greek, *aisthesis* – sense perception, i.e. things perceptible by the senses. The 18th century philosopher Kant (cited in Telfer, 1996) broadened the use of aesthetics to 'the philosophy of perception through the senses'. The view here then is that excellence, in this case in cuisine, is dependent on heightened sense awareness.

Symbol, sign and senses

There is more to gastronomic sensibility than good food and good beverages in good company. For many it has always been so, but the chefs, some restaurateurs and hoteliers and the guides have not always seen it in this light. The core product was food and beverage, or standard accommodation, but in many instances the attraction of diners, gourmets and gastronomes to distant establishments meant overnight accommodation. If the property was in another country, a short break or holiday could be built around the core component, making it more valuable and interesting (Gillespie and Morrison, 2000).

The pursuit of the finer things in life attracts more and more individuals today than at any time before. There is also a greater sophistication in the dining and travelling public. Hoteliers and restaurateurs are now catching on to this in a big way, but some hotels and restaurants have been quietly attracting the most discerning customers for many years and in a valuable and subtle fashion. To explore this it can be worth considering the application of semiotic theory (a rich and highly developed way of looking at patterned communication in all states of being). This would include, for instance, gestures, symbols, signs, non-verbal communication and much more. What this science does is illuminate the precise ways in which messages are put across to mass audiences. This has many potential applications for restaurants and hotels.

If media communication is to be believed, then it is easy to be seduced into thinking that the industry is all about the chains, and that the brand has top billing. Periodically, highly respected consultancy companies and industry bodies predict further consolidation and the death of the smaller, often independently owned, hotels and restaurants. Certainly, taking a wide screen view of the international hotel and restaurant industry, there appears to be much validity in these perspectives. However, further enquiry can detect a more discreet and intricate drama being acted out at the élite fringes of the industry where there has been recognition of the value of creating an aura of élitism, which has become implicitly and explicitly associated with these establishments.

This élitism has been created through a combination of product design and enduring elements, which can lead to the creation of a sense of place. These establishments send out semiotic carriers in the form of symbols and signs, and use sensory differentiation to attract a specific niche market. In the main, this niche is composed of wealthy, international, business and leisure, frequent travellers who are attracted by élite life style products that offer an enticing interweave of fantasy and reality. These élite hotels and restaurants are using design and fashion, and semiotic carriers, to connect at an emotional level with their guests.

Design and fashion ● ● ●

Élite establishments appear to have utilized the best of time-honoured hospitality tradition but re-styled to titillate and rejuvenate contemporary demand within a specific niche market. One commentator (Conway, 1998) has described this as 'putting a contemporary spin on "classic", sleek, understated five star hotels'. Undoubtedly, the design process is complex. As a consequence it has become more common for hoteliers and restaurateurs with élite aspirations to commission internationally renowned designers. The most successful restaurateurs and hoteliers and designers appear not to have compromised on their guests' desire for comfort, nor with the operational requirement for functional interiors. As Grace Léo Andrieu, owner of the Montalembert hotel in Paris, has stated, 'certain designers have a tendency to forget that a hotel, however glamorous to the outsiders, remains a working tool'. Thus for hoteliers and restaurateurs with élite aspirations, it is not quite as simple as buying into a certain design and/or fashion look. The right balance must be struck between minimalism and hedonism, and practicality and functionality.

Semiotic carriers ● ● ●

An illustrative sample of what is meant by the term 'semiotic carriers' is presented in Table 3.10. Consciously or unconsciously, design and fashion marry and result in a range of semiotic carriers being communicated internally to, and externally from, an élite establishment. For example, even the vocabulary of 'élite' or 'modern classic' has become recognized

Table 3.10 Semiotic carriers

- Self identity
- Value system
- Aspiration
- Escapism and fantasy
- Adventure
- Influence of trends, fashion and style
- Emotional connectivity
- Cultural influences/Service mannerisms
- Conscious dream symbols, food, bodily comfort, health, emotions and self-sympathy
- Conscious symbolism
- Symbolically resonating objects
- Collective unconscious
- Biological reaction to colour stimulus
- Biological reaction to designed environment

as a social badge, associated with a certain life style, providing guests with new worlds of experience bound up with personal status symbols. Thus the term 'semiotic carrier' refers to the way in which symbols, signs and senses are woven together to create a meaningful, common language between hotel, restaurant, the guests and society as a whole. In this respect, there is 'a heavy reliance on the design element – it is required to send specific messages about the product to customers' (West and Hughes, 1991). Who will understand this special language? Ideally, it will be individuals within the targeted market niches. They will receive the transmission and translate the messages according to their personalized points of reference, at specific points in time. In this way guests will emotionally connect, which has significant implications for purchasing behaviour.

Élite establishments ● ● ●

So it is that design, fashion and semiotic carriers are deliberately devised to combine towards the influencing of purchasing behaviour, and the satisfaction of both the psychological and physiological needs of the guests. In this way, élite hotels and restaurants can actively create a form of life style accessory, which can provide a stage on which consumers can enact their carefully designed identities. This is a formal strategy, distinguishing these establishments from the generally more formalistic focus on product and service of chain-owned brands.

In achieving this distinguishing strategy, élite establishments are applying one or more of the following (Gillespie and Morrison, 2000):

- **Traditional timeless elegance:** creating the fashion and style of the period for the property and considering the heritage in the design.

- **Exclusive fashionable minimalism:** being exclusive and individual with distinctive graphic imagery.

- **Exclusive dramatic and theatrical environment:** creating a unique environment that is both dramatic and theatrical.

- **Informal elegance and chic:** offering superior service that is informal, as opposed to generic, snobbish and remote, in an environment that promotes a cheerful atmosphere with suggestions of refinement and originality.

- **Unique luxury leisure:** offering privacy within an innovative interior and exterior design, creating fluid, romantic, vistas, which offer drama and flair; being competitive through not merely being centred on the product, but on criteria such as myths and values, sensory differentiation and stimuli.

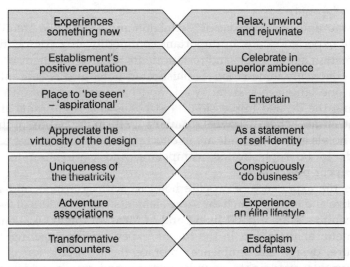

Experiences something new	Relax, unwind and rejuvinate
Establisment's positive reputation	Celebrate in superior ambience
Place to 'be seen' – 'aspirational'	Entertain
Appreciate the virtuosity of the design	As a statement of self-identity
Uniqueness of the theatricity	Conspicuously 'do business'
Adventure associations	Experience an élite lifestyle
Transformative encounters	Escapism and fantasy

Figure 3.6 'Élite establishments' sensory differentiators (after Gillespie and Morrison, 2000)

Establishments using a variety of these approaches, through virtuosity of design and fashion, are emitting semiotic carriers. These are then translated into powerful sensory differentiators (see Figure 3.6). Careful shifts in design and fashion emphasis, with an awareness of sociological changes taking place in society, allow sophisticated guests to contextualize these elements for themselves. This recognition of guests' emotional engagement is considered to be particularly significant, as consumer expectations are integral to the appraising of the overall experience of these establishments.

Élite establishments explicitly apply the concept of sensory differentiators to achieve significant competitive advantage within certain market niches. All hotels and restaurants have the potential to provide consumers, either deliberately or through serendipity, with a wealth and depth of semiotic carriers and sensory differentiators that can be used to benefit business performance. What is needed is a radical flip in marketing thinking from the traditional four 'P's approach to the three 'S's of symbol, signifier and senses.

3.8 The apex of the hospitality industry

At the apex of the hospitality industry a complex weave of related elements – physical location, the organizational culture, the human role and the delivery mechanism – are all prerequisites for success and achieving competitive edge. This is illustrated in Figure 3.7. These properties require a sense of place and endurance. With this in mind, a feeling has to be engendered that one has come to the right place and made the right choice, a feeling that should be confirmed throughout the stay, and overall design plays an increasingly important role and has to be integrated throughout the business.

Cultural criteria launch the business into a swirling orbit of subtly charged impressions, including semiotic carriers, which penetrate the human intellect, emotions and spirit on both conscious and subconscious levels. Furthermore, sensory differentiation influences purchasing behaviour, and during the hotel and dining experience guests add layers of their own micro-feelings to intensify emotional connectivity. Cultural cachet, in the sense used, implies that these hotels and restaurants offer cultivation, sophistication and opportunity for artistic and intellectual enrichment. Life style ambience and psychological needs all have to be met.

Hotels and restaurants offer persuasion, seduction and a symbolic identity. This is a time when memorable experiences are an important commodity in a competitive marketplace, and in the information age hoteliers and restaurateurs need to ask themselves whether they are really being effectively understood. Sophisticated hotel and restaurant guests comprehend more than one language system. Words and hotel and restaurant collateral are not enough in creating the desired impressions, and hotels and restaurants at the apex of the industry have introduced cues that, when combined, affirm the nature of the experience for the guest. These hotels and restaurants are in effect part of the experience economy and that experience needs to be sophisticated, compelling and captivating to ensure absolute enjoyment and repeat purchase.

So where does the experience of an élite hotel lie with gourmets and gastronomes? In essence, they utilize and engage much the same elements; connoisseurs of food and beverage also tend to be connoisseurs of good living and of form. In this book menu engineering is referred to for menu analysis, but in the future 'experience engineering' may be what to apply. Architecture, design and ambience embrace the manipulation of the five senses. Hotels and restaurants offer sights, sounds, textures and smells, which are registered in

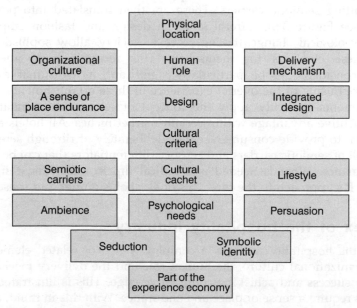

Figure 3.7 Key features of the apex of the hospitality industry

multiple forms from such things as the colour palate and the impact of the colour palate on other finishes, the effect of colour on space and of light on colour. This includes:

- Structural and interior materials, surfaces, finishes, tactile evaluation of materials and materials in their setting, textiles used, tactile elements like yarn, fibres and their construction and finishing, materials and their construction, graphic imagery.

- The aesthetics of decorative accessories, plants and artwork, signage and graphics.

- Acoustical sensing of recorded or live music, some areas providing different acoustics.

- Spatial differentiation of areas offering differing vistas, space, views of the exterior, and of the landscaping etc.

The more compellingly an experience preoccupies the senses, the more memorable it will be. Services transform into engaging experiences when combined with sensory phenomena. What today's top hoteliers and chefs have done is to design exactly the right sensations into 'cues' that transmit the unifying ideas from which sophisticated guests are attracted and return. Each positive cue is harmonized – visual, tactile, aural and olfactory impressions are integrated into an appealing theme, and so by the choice of restaurant or accommodation the individual is defined, and by their taste they are differentiated.

Successful hoteliers and restaurateurs fully comprehend conspicuous consumption and hospitality marketing. They go beyond hotel and restaurant functions and ergonomics to discover value in the hotel and restaurant experience on which they can capitalize in building brand and property image strategies. None the less, innovative and entrepreneurial hoteliers, like Liam Lambert of the Mandarin Oriental Hyde Park, London, utilizing detailed segmented data on clients, could see dominant but dormant brands lose their highest value clients to them, because they have developed strategies to fully understand their clientele and their reasons for purchase. Semiotic carriers, though lacking in tangible asset value, are assets as surely as capital, people and inventory for their power derives from symbols and rich meaning in the minds of clients. Clearly there is psychological symbolism associated with commercial hospitality provision, and the ways in which it is used to express certain meanings, emotions and social distinction and affiliation.

Pivotal leadership at the apex of the hospitality industry

Figure 3.8 shows a quality model of leaders in the luxury hospitality and resort market. It shows how delighting customers can lead to brand recognition and revenue from unique offerings, with profitability and growth-improved margins. It shows that brand recognition will lead to positive outcomes. Brand loyalty and retention and repurchase all lead to maximized market share and the enhancement of the product and business life cycle.

Before going on in Chapter 4 to consider profiles of some of the key contributors to modern cuisine and gastronomy, presented here is a profile of Atef Mankarios, Chairman and Chief Executive of Foresthills Hotels and Resorts, who has guided the development and management of some of the world's most prestigious hotels.

Atef Mankarios feels that

if you begin with the premise that if no two people are alike, why on earth would you want to treat everyone the same? Create so called standards that everyone would behave in the same way – and almost in some companies speak the same way and use the same

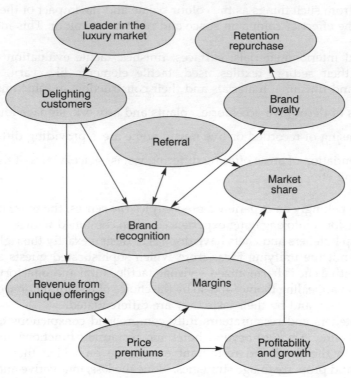

Figure 3.8 A quality model of leaders in the luxury market

phrases – and you are sending a clear message to the customer that you are exactly like the person behind you and the person that will come after you with no distinction. In this industry we are really selling experiences and relationships. We don't sell food and beds. We sell relationships and we sell building relationships. Whether the relationships are built between management and staff or between management and owners it is a relationship, it is the business of relationships.

Mankarios believes that you cannot call this an industry, 'there are no nuts and bolts and robots creating things'. He feels that if we revert to the behaviour of an industry, then we actually start believing that we should have manuals, and standards and everything should look, behave and act alike. And, therefore we can achieve the 'coveted' consistency in a hotel company or even in a hotel. 'I don't want to be served every morning the very same breakfast with the very same person, telling me the very same words. It's my pleasure! You are welcome sir! You take away the spontaneity and the creativity of staff when you put them in a strait-jacket called manuals.'

Mankarios feels that

you need to hire people based on their expertise, and their experience and their individuality (the entire package), and then you put them all in a mould and you start moulding them, most of the time in your own image and that's what I call corporate ego. Because at the corporate level there is all of a sudden ten to fifteen guys in the corporate office, all believing that they are the corporate gurus of the company and the gurus of the industry. They know everything there is to know, and therefore they try to clone themselves at the property level. It's an irresistible thing for one's ego. But as a consumer, do I really want to see that.

'Do you want to be served the same way by the same people seeing the same expressions and hearing the same words, and sleeping on the same beds and looking at the same television sets, sitting on the same chairs of the same shape and height. That so called consistency is almost against human nature to begin with. I think you get rewarded immensely when you let people apply their own judgement and their own creativity and their own style. Knowing that it is not a precise science. It is not a physics laboratory where you know a fraction of an inch would have disastrous consequences. If you allow people, especially young bright people to come through the ranks with a fresh outlook, you can either use that freshness, or you can get them to the same staid, stale concept that you created thirty years ago and you carry it through. Never allowing yourself to move with the times, to allow fresh air into your stale corporate offices or fresh blood into that main bloodstream that drives the company.

'I remember at a young age I always questioned, and maybe at the time I was more rebellious than visionary. You just resented being told what to do and how to do it eight hours every day. As you evolve through the years and through the business you start thinking well wait a minute – this may have worked for the last 50 years but I know of another way to do it. Why can't I apply it because if you even attempt it – then you are out of the manuals and out of the standards and in most cases you will even be punished, or banished, whatever.

'I think I have made a career out of going against the grain. I remember as I started growing into the management positions, and I received the sacred sets of manuals from corporate office, I used to take the contents out of them, throw them away and keep the covers on my bookshelves, so that every visitor from the corporate office would see the sacred manuals safely in place, but there was never anything inside of them. That was my own personal joke. It was my laugh on them. You guys think that you are going to shape my thinking after yours, and I am just going to be a little robot that you will control by remote control from your office. I started realizing that it was the people in each individual hotel that shape the style, that add their own personal style, their own personal creativity and their own personality to it, and, when I started travelling on my own I started searching and seeking places that have their own personality, that did not conform to some distant corporate office, and I think that these were the most important lessons I learned throughout my career and some of the most rewarding observations I had in our business is the things I learned from all over the world.

'The hotel business will only change when young graduates are permitted to use their own initiative, their own thoughts, their own ideas, even if they make mistakes and we all do. Heaven, I make mistakes every day and thirty years later I still make mistakes and that is how we learn. So if we try to make a mistake free environment, a sterile non-creative environment, that is what we end up with.

Atef Mankarios' core values are 'creating and preserving and respecting relationships':

At the luxury and individual end of the market you need to understand why these people that you have identified as your target customers would come to you and not the other one down the street or in the next city. When they come with you what do they expect, what is their expectation – it's a lot of homework, and that is something that we insist on with this team, it's doing our homework first. It requires a lot of time expended listening, asking questions but really listening. I guess the oldest adage in the business is to know your customer. Everybody says it but very few actually do it. You need to know what the customer wants so that you can craft the product around the customers' needs and expectations, so they can utilize it and pay you for it.

'What we do is create a pleasant environment, ensure that the people we employ are happy so that we make the people we serve very happy so they can get us paid. It is so simple, so basic it relies on instincts and common sense more than it really relies on skill and education; unless you are an engineer or have a particular and focused skill. But in most cases the business thrives on people with personality, with the willingness to serve which no one can teach – no one. You either have it or not, you need an innate sense of hospitality. I believe that hospitality is like playing the piano, unless your fingers are on the keys you cannot produce music; you will just be tickling the air.

For Mankarios 'the experience is the product and the creation of the product is the experience, and the quality of the experience is obviously the product.'

3.9 Summary

This chapter has considered the explosion in the range of diverse developments in operations, service and menu provision brought about by expansion in demand and serious reconsideration of the approaches to operations design. The modern influences on menus and their construction have been examined together with movements towards contemporary culinary refinement. The reasons for the development of concept cuisines have been examined along with the effects that these cuisines, including fusion cuisine, are having on the market. Influences on and changes within the development of beverage lists have been identified as well as information concerning the need for harmony between food and wine and other beverages on offer. The changing nature of dining has been examined and consideration has been given to the philosophical meaning and symbolism in gastronomy. Lastly, a portrait of the apex of the hospitality industry has been outlined and of management at that level as a precursor to considering the profiles of some of the key contributors to the development of cuisine and gastronomy in Chapter 4.

Contributors to the development of modern cuisine and gastronomy

This chapter builds on the historical perspectives detailed in Chapter 2 and the modern developments identified in Chapter 3, and profiles some of the most distinguished chefs in France, Germany and Britain.

This chapter is intended to help you to:

- identify the elements of the legacy of Escoffier

- view Fernand Point as the Father of Modern Gastronomy

- link the profiles of those who have laid the foundations of modern gastronomy to those who are laying the future ones

- examine profiles of some of the key contemporary contributors to the development of modern cuisine and gastronomy

- identify the distinguishing characteristics of contemporary modern contributors

- consider their contributions to the future.

4.1 Escoffier's legacy

We first mentioned Georges Auguste Escoffier (1846–1935) in Chapter 2 (page 60). As a platform for the consideration of what has happened since his time, we detail here the legacy he left behind. Escoffier was generally considered to be king of the cuisine ancienne and also the last exponent of that tradition. He handed over the doctrines of the classical cuisines to those who followed.

An axiom of Escoffier was:

La bonne cuisine est celle ou les choses ont le gout de cequelles sont.
(Good cooking is that in which things taste of what they are.)

This statement, which can be considered as being well before its time, neatly displays the transition from ancient to modern. It also remains today uppermost in the minds of all good chefs.

Escoffier, the son of a blacksmith, started work at the age of thirteen in his uncle's restaurant in Nice, which was quite near to his home, in the village of Villeneuve-Loubet. Escoffier trained with his uncle for six years and from there, at nineteen years of age, he went to Paris, where he worked for five years at the Petit Moulin Rouge restaurant as a commis rôtisseur.

After military service in the Franco-Prussian war he gained employment at the Hotel Luxembourg in Nice, before reappearing at the Petit Moulin Rouge, where he spent six years as head chef. In 1878 Escoffier attempted to go into business on his own, opening a small restaurant in Cannes. However, he decided this was not really for him as he missed the bustle of a large kitchen. In 1879 he became a director of an outside catering company, which he operated for five years; in the interim he assisted in the formation of the Société Culinaire Française, and, with Philéas Gilbert, in the founding and writing of the journal entitled *L'Art culinaire*.

Escoffier wrote in one of his diaries, 'Society had little regard for the culinary profession. This should not have been so, since cuisine is a science and an art and he who devotes his talent to its service deserves full respect and consideration.' His wish was to be granted, though sadly not in his own lifetime. Today's top chefs are indeed granted full respect and consideration, although some might comment that this has gone from the one extreme to another.

In 1883 Escoffier took over as head chef at the Grand Hotel in Monte Carlo, which was being managed by César Ritz. Ritz had lost his chef, Giroix, to the rival Hotel de Paris. At the close of the season both men transferred to the Grand National Hotel in Lucerne, where they spent the next six or so years. The Ritz–Escoffier twinning was to work like a magnet, with the dyadic coupling attracting to these early resorts a continuous stream of glittering nobility and aristocracy, including the likes of the Prince of Wales and the Emperor of Austria.

Ritz and Escoffier were greatly responsible for the universalized mass appeal and emancipation of gastronomy, through a transfer away from modest pockets of gastronomy in private houses, to the greater number of commercial enterprises now open to all, regardless of status or title. Ritz had a gift for making his guests most welcome. Escoffier added a further attraction in his magnificent cuisine, which was already associated with a break from the heavy sauces and garnishes of the 18th century.

Escoffier streamlined work practices and conditions to allow for the smooth running of his kitchens, just as he streamlined the food being served to clients. He banished drinking and smoking in his kitchens, did what was possible in his time to eliminate the extreme heat of the kitchen, barred the wearing of dirty chef's whites, and also the appearance in public of chef's dress. The shouting of kitchen orders was also eliminated. Escoffier's motto was *'faites simple'*, preferring simply cooked vegetables, lightly sprinkled with chopped parsley. He insisted that everything must be edible and gave up the tradition of ornamentation, which had prevailed with Carême. Out went *hatelets* (skewers) and architectural set pieces and in came simplicity. Analogies were drawn between Escoffier and Carême, stating that Escoffier was to Carême what the New Testament was to the Old.

Escoffier and Ritz played a massive role in the popularizing of the fashionable hotel, the classical *répertoire* and their large menus. In 1890 Escoffier opened the Savoy in London in association with Ritz and Echenard, where he remained until 1898. The *beau-monde* of Europe followed, for by now Escoffier was classed as a supreme talent in the kitchen. And Ritz was to become well established as the archetype model of the classic maître de table, maître d'hôtel and the professional hotelier throughout Europe, with major hotels still bearing his name today.

In 1898 Escoffier followed Ritz to take charge at the Carlton Hotel, at that time one of the most famous in Europe. Escoffier was said to have left for personal reasons. However, according to an archive uncovered by the British food columnist Paul Levy in 1985, both men had been dismissed by the Savoy for fraud. The Savoy Company records show the disappearance of over £3,400 of wine and spirits in the first period of 1897, and confessions of larceny had been signed by Escoffier and Ritz, and two former employees, in January of 1900.

It was, however, Escoffier more than any other who had handed over the doctrines of the classical cuisines of Europe into the twentieth century, with the publishing of *Le Guide culinaire*. This was published in 1903, when he was working in London. *Le Guide culinaire* became the definitive text until well into the 1970s, with the advent of nouvelle cuisine, and other serious reconsiderations of kitchen organization. His approaches to cooking, and to kitchen organization had travelled well beyond France and London and had become truly international.

The stratification and division of labour in the kitchen

The 'partie' system is a specific historical phenomenon credited to Escoffier. Since medieval times the kitchen staff had been divided into sections, each more or less separated. It had been highly stratified in the largest establishments with major, and basic divisions of kitchen labour. The system comprises highly skilled, semi-skilled and manual operators, including those who are involved in prolonged training, the latter spending this period progressing from corner to corner within the system until a desired standard is met. Unfortunately the system of indentureship had almost been lost, with few established organizations offering training agreements.

Whether operating the partie system or adapted systems (as for instance those used in country houses, small inns, private hotels, or generally smaller scale establishments) one thing remains paramount, and that is that under the 'partie' system, chefs are completely reliant on each other. Teamwork is essential and cuts across, above and below skill levels and the departments. The interdependence required has been a major feature of the 'partie' system, and it also has pre-eminence in unstructured operations. The full classical brigade is laid out and individually named Table 4.1.

The 'partie' system had always provided the means for sensitizing, stimulating, training and developing individuals to the stage where a thorough grounding and eventual specialism in the craft can be gained. The career path of a chef is influential in determining

Table 4.1 The complete grand partie system

The full brigade	
Maître Chef des Cuisines:	Executive Chef
Chef de Cuisine:	Head Chef
Executive Sous Chef:	Deputy Head Chef, with Executive Status
Sous Chefs:	Usually non-working chefs directing kitchen operations. Their status numerically imposed
Chefs de Partie:	Section Heads. Specialists. (See premier chefs)
1st Commis de Cuisine:	Directly responsible to the section head, takes over in his/her absence, and controls the commis working
Commis de Cuisine:	A cook in training, or assistant cook, not sufficiently skilled to be designated a chef. Their status is numerically imposed, i.e. 2nd 3rd 4th 5th etc.
Aprenti:	Apprentice

The premier chefs	
Chef Saucier:	Sauce Chef
Chef Garde Manger:	Larder Chef
Patissier:	Pastry Chef
Chef Rôtisseur:	Roast Chef
Chef Poissonier:	Fish Chef

The body of the brigade	
Chef Entremettier:	Vegetable Chef
Chef Potager:	Soup Chef or Cook
Chef Froitier:	Buffet Chef
Bouchier:	Butcher
Charcutier:	Sausage maker, pork butcher
Chef Rôtisseur:	Roast Chef
Chef Grillardin:	Grill Chef
Confiseur:	Confectionery maker
Glacier:	Ice-cream maker and ice sculptor
Chef Tournant:	Relief Chef
Hors d'oeuvrier:	Hors d'oeuvre maker
Chef de nuit:	Night Chef
Boulanger:	Baker
Volailleur	Poulterer
Poissonier:	Fishmonger
Saladier:	Salad maker
Trancheur:	Carver, always a skilled chef, normally from the larder
Chef de Garde:	Duty Chef
Chef de Banquets:	Banqueting Chef
Chef Communar:	Staff Cook
Patronnet:	Young apprentice pastry cook
Stagiare:	Chef or cook from another hotel or restaurant throughout the world gaining experience

The semi-skilled and manual sector of the partie system	
Aboyeur:	Kitchen barker, clerk
Annonceur:	As above (vide Escoffier)
L'econome:	Store keeper
Le secretaire de cuisine:	Kitchen clerk
Plongeur:	Pot washer
Cafetier:	Still room operator
Garçon de cuisine:	Kitchen porter
Vaisselier:	Crockery washer
Porteur:	Porter

the depth and rounded knowledge of cuisine, and this is usually gained by developing expertise founded on the production of classical dishes. Escoffier's own career path was analogous to the rise of large international hotels, and this came to be his medium. To some, however, his regime was also seen as a bureaucratically founded phenomenon, which had the potential to constrain innovation in cuisine.

The consequence of the establishment of the 'partie' system for chefs was that it contributed to the promotion of a culinary aristocracy, some of whom were able to achieve world-wide acclaim. Britain, Germany and other European countries benefited from injections of French talent at this time. The 'partie' system also provided a hierarchy, and therefore a training pattern that controlled the profession and provided developmental stages ('*parties*'), according to the level of skill. Specific skills had to be mastered and were a requirement for promotion. It was a means of managing the division of labour, but it also provided employers with a mechanism for breaking up the division of labour into more calculable units, thus allowing tighter cost controls. Inherent however to the rise of the modern chef was the partial rejection of the 'partie' system. This was because the system had the potential to stultify cuisine, limit the scope for creativity, and took responsibility away from the individual, giving it to the group.

Whatever view is taken of the 'partie' system, Escoffier's influence in the history of cuisine cannot be ignored. Many of his dishes are legendary. Some of these are:

- 'Tournedos Rossini', named after the famous Italian operatic composer Gioachino Antonio Rossini (1792–1868).

- 'Pêches Melba', created for Helen Porter Mitchell (1861–1931), the diva Nellie Melba, a stage name from her connection with Melbourne. The Australian soprano was a regular patron of the Savoy Hotel. The fresh raspberry coulis used in the preparation of this dish did not appear classically until several years after its creation and Pêches Melba were originally presented on the back of a swan carved from a single block of ice.

- A method of preparing poularde, created by Escoffier at the Carlton for Edward VII (1841–1910). There is also a 'Saumon Edward VII'.

- Dishes created for Alphonse XIII, King of Spain, including one in which Escoffier utilized fillets of sole, and a second utilizing poularde.

- Dishes named after Princess Alice, Countess of Athlone, and sister of King Edward VII. 'Alice' was another piece of famed Escoffier terminology used to indicate a method of preparing sole and also for a sweet dish.

In 1920 Escoffier was made a Chevalier of the Legion of Honour and Officer of the Legion in 1928, both given for having enhanced the influence and importance of French cooking throughout the world. Escoffier was regarded as the emperor of the kitchens of the world, a title conferred upon him by the Emperor William II, who spent a time on the steamer *Imperator* of the Hamburg–America Line, which Escoffier had joined to take charge of the imperial kitchens. In the course of a conversation with Auguste, the Emperor, in congratulating him, said, 'I am the Emperor of Germany, but you are the Emperor of chefs'.

Escoffier retired to Monte Carlo in 1921. He was now 73 years of age and had polished and pursued his art for 62 years. His writing, which carried great influence and authority, will best be remembered in works like *Le Guide culinaire* (1903), written in collaboration with Phileas Gilbert and Emile Fetu, and *Le Livre des menues*, published in 1912. In the latter, Escoffier sketched out the criteria that would emphasize a well-planned meal. These were:

- the season should be borne in mind;
- the meal should be appropriate to the guests and to the occasion;
- excessive dishes should be minimalized;
- the menu should be curtailed if time was short.

He also wrote *Le Fleurs en cire* (1910), *Le Carnet d'epicure* (1911), *Le Riz* (1927), *La Morue* (1929) and *Ma Cuisine*, published in 1934. He revised *Le Guide culinaire* four times and before he died he had also written the preface to *Larousse Gastronomique* (1938).

Escoffier died in February 1935, at nearly 89 years old. He is still viewed as one of the most important chefs who has ever lived. He was also deemed to be one of gastronomy's principal revolutionaries, and there are many of his most prized, and now classical dishes, still offered to this day. Most importantly it is with Escoffier that was associated the end of the excessive and luxuriant displays of medieval cookery. In his time and with his influence, gluttony had surrendered to gourmandise and quantity yielded to quality.

4.2 Fernand Point – the father of modern gastronomy

Escoffier had dominated the culmination of cuisine ancienne. Fernand Point (1897–1955) was to be recognized as the father of modern gastronomy. In Chapter 2 (page 65), Fernand Point is identified as having characterized the representation to the world of the high-class French restaurant, which endures to this day. He had a profound influence on the gastronomy of his time, as he has had on many aspiring chefs then and since.

Fernand Point was well known for statements such as:

A man is not a machine and a great chef gets tired – but the clientele must never know it.

In a way it was part of his professional signature.

The mark of Point's cuisine was not set by elaboration but rather by sybaritic and polished simplicity. Fernand Point was a marvellous and true master chef; for it is with him that the distinctive germ of nouvelle cuisine was implemented, without the employment of the public relations machinery, or promotions that would later attend it. It is thought that Point himself would not have lent his name to nouvelles cuisines, but the seed was sown in his pupils and it bore ample fruit. He was a man who thought it his duty to coach and train the young. It was indeed Point who started the breakdown of the secrecy among chefs, viewing such behaviour as generating sterility.

Point was single-minded with no interest other than cuisine. He was born in Louhans, where his parents kept the station buffet and where both his grandmother and his mother were in charge of the cooking. Quite how Point managed to lift haute cuisine to the levels he did is quite staggering, for he is reputed to have been on the brink of pathological insularity. He loathed travelling away from home and at no point did he ever seem to wish to travel abroad. He trained in Paris at Foyot's, where he became sauce chef, and also at the Bristol and Majestic hotels, then moving to Evian as fish chef at the Hotel Royal.

The family moved to Vienne, where his father Auguste opened a restaurant and two years after left it to Fernand, who renamed it La Pyramide in 1923, its name originating from the nearby pyramid from the time of the Romans in the region. The restaurant did not take long to become recognized by gourmets on their way to the South of France. Point focused his attention on the production of a cuisine that centred upon quality food enhanced by perfectionist provisioning, preparation and cooking. Point was indeed viewed as a genius, and the innovations that he undertook were seen as sound as they did not interfere with the foundations of the craft. As Point put it, 'Cuisine is not invariable like a Codex formula. But one must guard against tampering with essential bases.'

This modest man certainly returned cuisine to the indispensable bases, which had become blurred with excessive dogma. In 1933 the *Guide Michelin* awarded La Pyramide three stars – the first awards ever made by the Guide. Point's character had a lot to do with the restaurant's popularity; his warm welcome, humour, yarns, whimsicality, massive size and uncompromising nature all played a part. Many famous individuals travelled to Vienne to sample what Curnonsky termed 'the pinnacle of culinary art'. He was also important because he broke free of the conventional typecast brigade cooking that Escoffier championed. He changed his menus on a daily basis and worked as a soloist. He also cleared his larder each evening to make way for new produce.

Point was also renowned as being an excellent teacher. His pupils, many of whom became great chefs (namely Outhier, Bise, Georges Blanc, Roger Vergé, Raymond Thuilier, Alain Chapel, Paul Bocuse, and the Troisgros brothers), are all witness to his consummate mastery. Point's cuisine was sybaritic and of the classical model. One of his many catchphrases, for instance, was 'butter, butter, always more butter'. His biographer Felix Benoit entitled him 'the Pharaoh of the Pyramide at Vienne'. Point and his wife were also decorated after the war by the British and others, for the work they had done with the Resistance during the war.

After his death the kitchens at La Pyramide were supervised firstly by Paul Mercier and then Guy Thivard, but still under the ever-watchful eye of its administrator Madame Marie Louise Point, who must take a lot of the credit for turning the restaurant into a statement beyond food alone. The restaurant was run by the Point family up until 1986 and was taken over by the group La Foncière des Champs-Elysées in 1987, who chose Patrick Henriroux to carry on La Pyramide in Point's tradition. Henriroux has kept some of Point's dishes on the menu and also supplemented them with many of his own.

A tribute to Point comes from the chef Paul Bocuse, who outlines the respect the man was due among his peers and also from a much wider audience: 'There was no one like him. No one.'

4.3 Profiles of some of the key modern contributors

In the tradition of those who had gone before, a new age has dawned. In the same way as Escoffier and Point had laid the foundations of modern gastronomy, there are now those who, whilst continuing to build on those foundations, are also laying down the pattern for the future.

This section profiles some of the key contributors to modern gastronomy. These are some of the most distinguished chefs in France, Germany and Britain – those considered by some gastronomes to keep the gastronomic flame brightly burning.

These chefs are:

Nearly all of these individuals are or were chefs-patrons, being exclusive or part owners of their holdings. Their restaurants are considered to be temples of gastronomy, sometimes expressed in the famed rule of the five Cs (*Relais Gourmand*, 2001). These are:

1 Character

2 Courtesy

3 Calm

4 Charm

5 Cuisine.

It has been suggested that the very best chefs are born and not made. This thesis however stresses the heightened sense-awareness of these individuals, who have in many cases had upbringings where food was primarily respected, and a good deal of time or emphasis was placed upon food in the home or working environment. It is necessary to look no further than Roger Vergé and the influence of his Aunt Celestine, Anton Mosimann and his early love for the look and feel of ingredients (his family owning a farm and small family restaurant), and Michel Guérard, who played around pastry shops, enjoying the aromas of the foods.

Some of the top chefs profiled here are what could be termed 'chef tycoons', but not all of these chefs have settled in large cities. Some have based themselves in the countryside or smaller towns. None of the chefs who are described here has principal restaurants that might be considered modestly priced. However, they all offer dedicated attention to detail, excellent service and craft skills, individual and holistic gastronomic experiences, and complete harmonious enjoyment across food, beverage, service, decor, furnishings, atmosphere, lighting, etc.

Raymond Blanc

Raymond Blanc was born on 19 November 1949 at Besançon, the capital of the Franche Comte region. His secondary schooling took place from 1964–5 at Valdahon (CEP) secondary

school and from 1965–8 at the technical college at Besançon where he gained a diploma (BEPC). From there he worked as a nurse at Saint Anne's hospital in Besançon but decided it was not the life for him. He then worked for six months as a commis de rang, at the Nouvel Hotel in the rue Foch, Besançon.

From 1970–1 he carried out his military service and became a corporal. After this he returned to work as a commis de rang for one year at the Palais de la Bière. He had actually applied for a job in the kitchen, but was told that he was too old to train. He therefore quickly applied himself to the job of a waiter. He carried on the same job, gaining work experience for one year, in 1972–3, when he journeyed to England, ostensibly to learn the language. It was at his place of first employment, the Rose Revived in Newbridge, Oxfordshire, that he was to marry the owner's daughter, and worked for a time as a chef. During 1974 he spent six months in

West Germany at the hotel Wiesbaden as chef de rang, and finally, in 1975–6 he worked for an eight month period at La Sorbonne, Oxford in the same capacity.

In 1976–7 he became chef de cuisine, but also managed, Bleu, Blanc, Rouge, in the High Street, Oxford. In late 1977 he and his wife took over small premises in Oxford, naming it Les Quat' Saisons. It was here that Blanc really tutored himself by experimentation, determination and hard work, as he was now a chef proprietor and had to make it for himself. In 1978 Egon Ronay awarded the restaurant one star, as did the Automobile Association guide, and *The Good Food Guide* gave the establishment its Pestle and Mortar award. In 1978 Blanc also opened Maison Blanc, a highly successful pastry and bakers shop, of which he remained Director and Chairman until December 1988.

He was rewarded quite quickly for his efforts at Les Quat' Saisons, and by 1979 Michelin awarded it a first star, Egon Ronay gave the Restaurant of the Year award and two Ronay stars, the AA also presented two stars and *The Good Food Guide* made another Pestle and Mortar award. The second Michelin star arrived in 1983. In 1984 a new company was put together, Blanc Restaurants Ltd, and was to include, first, Le Petit Blanc, which was a one Michelin star restaurant and classed amongst the ten principal restaurants in Great Britain, but was to close in 1989.

Blanc has never cooked for a living in France, and like Olympe Versini in Paris (see page 145 below), he is an *autodidact* (someone with no formal training who is self trained). It is therefore all the more startling, and demonstrates the strength of character of the man, that today he is recognized as one of the finest chefs in the world.

If Blanc has been influenced by anyone else it has been Marc Meneau (see page 132 below), renowned chef proprietor of L'Espérance in Saint-Père-sous-Vezeley in Burgundy, which comprises an excellent hotel and restaurant, haunt of Europe's fine diners.

Raymond Blanc had a vision of opening an hotel and restaurant in perfect and holistic harmony and in 1984 he together with a group of partners purchased a 15th century manor house at Great Milton, calling it Le Manoir aux Quat' Saisons. Surprisingly to some, Blanc retained the two Michelin stars and in the process set a precedent.

Raymond Blanc describes his cuisine as authentic and honest. It owes little to his native region (Franche Comte), since his cuisine is light and distinctly flavoured, whilst the cooking of that region is peasant and country style food, which can be very rich, utilizing large amounts of butter and cream.

Blanc has appeared on television with his mother, who has been a great influence on him. She was an inventive home cook with a light cooking style, and has also influenced what is grown today in Le Manoir's vegetable garden. Blanc is obsessed by freshness and grows about 60 per cent of all the vegetables used (90 different varieties) and herbs (70 types) on 2 acres of land, many in poly-tunnels (plastic growing tunnels), which they are hopeful will receive the Soil Association's award for organic status. The extensive gardens at Le Manoir are overseen by Blanc's Head Gardener, Anne Marie Owens.

In 1990 the Le Manoir reopened after extensive expansion programmes had been carried out. This included a new kitchen, nine additional bedrooms and suites, and a conservatory. Le Manoir now has 32 bedrooms, which includes one superior suite, six suites, six junior suites, eleven superior rooms, five deluxe rooms and three standard rooms. In 1991 Raymond opened Le Petit Blanc Ecole de Cuisine, his own residential cookery school, which is headed by head chef Clive Fretwell. The School is unique in that it is the only cooking school in the world set beside the kitchens of a Michelin two-starred restaurant.

Blanc started writing: his book *Recipes from Le Manoir aux Quat' Saisons* was published in 1988. The book was an immediate success and remained on the *Sunday Times* bestseller list for two years, having sold 65,000 copies. It was also published in Australia, New Zealand,

à la Carte Menu

Hors d'oeuvres

Soupe de cabillaud fumé, huîtres au sabayone de citron
(Home-smoked haddock soup and native oysters in a lemon sabayon)

ou

Terrine de foie gras aux coings, gelée au vieux vinaigre balsamique
(Terrine of foie gras and quince; aged balsamic vinegar gelée)

ou

Coquille St Jacques, filets de rouget et St Pierre à l' escabèche de légumes au citron vert
(Warm fillets of red mullet, John Dory and scallop on marinated vegetables; herb and lime vinaigrette)

ou

Macaronis au beurre de Truffes noires du Périgord; grosses langoustines de petite pêche poëlées
(Macaroni in a truffle jus and pan-fried langoustines)

ou

Salade de cresson, foie gras de canard poëlé, boudin noir et pommes' cannelle et vinaigrette aux noisettes
(Watercress salad with pan-fried duck foie gras; apple, black pudding and roasted hazelnut dressing)

ou

Assiette printanière
(Lamb sweetbread and morels in a Gewürztraminer sauce: asparagus with a lemon sabayon)

ou

Raviole d'oeuf de poule aux truffes noires du Périgord; jus de volaille et beurre meunière
(Ravioli of herb purée and poached egg with Périgord truffles; meunière butter and roasting juices)

Poissons et crustacés

(All our main course dishes are served with vegetables)

Escalope de loup de mer à la vapeur; jus aux fuîtres et coquillages; caviar impérial
(Steamed fillet of sea bass on a herb purée; oyster jus and 'oscietra gold' caviar)

ou

Medaillon de lotte rôtie au jus de moutard et coquilles St Jacques poëlées à la crème de topinambours
(Pan-fried scallops and monkfish fillet, Jerusalem artichoke purée and mustard jus)

ou

Queue de homard rôtie, cannelloni aux herbes à soupe, jus de cuisson
(Roasted lobster tail in its own roasting juices; herb cannelloni)

ou

Turbotin rôti sur lit d'aromates; fumet de vin rouge et beurre blanc
(Roasted baby turbot on a bed of scented herbs; red wine jus and lemon butter)

Volailles, viandes et abats

(All our main course dishes are served with vegetables)

Pigeonneau d'Agen en croûte de sel
(Corn-fed squab baked in a salt crust, its own juices; pommes Maxime and pan-fried foie gras)

ou

Perdreau rôti, son, jus; boudin noir et légumes du jardin
(Roasted wild English partridge, its own juices, black pudding and seasonal vegetables)

Ballotine de queue de boeuf farcie braisée au fumet d'Hermitage et purée de panais
(Braised boned oxtail filled with shallots and wild mushrooms, in a Hermitage red wine sauce, purée of parsnips)

ou

Côte de veau de lait rôtie, son jus de cuisson
(Roasted wing rib of milk-fed veal, its own cooking juices and seasonal vegetables)

ou

Poêlée de rognons de veau aux escargotsde Bourgogne; fumet de vin rouge et chartreuse vert
(Pan-fried veal kidneys, Burgundy snails; red wine jus with green chartreuse; purée of shallots)

ou

Epaule de lapin braisée à l'essence de Pinot Noir et filet rôti dans sa panouffle; jus parfumé aux herbes et graines de moutarde
(Braised shoulder of rabbit in a Pinot Noir red wine sauce: roasted loin in a tarragon and mustard jus)

From the Rôtisserie

Carré ou selle de couchon de lait à la broche; jus de cuisson à la marjolaine
(Spit-roasted best end or saddle of suckling pig; marjoram juice)

A vegetarian à la Carte Menu is also available

A selection of dishes are available for children

Fromages

La ronde des fromages fermiers
(Farmhouse cheeses from France and Great Britain made in the traditional way)

Desserts

Charlotte aux poires William, glace à la vanille
(Caramelised William pear, baked in a thin brioche; cinnamon and vanilla ice cream)

ou

La pommes soufflée, croustillant et sorbet de pomme crue
(A Calvados soufflé baked in a Juna Gold apple; dried apple slices and raw apple sorbet)

ou

Assiette aux parfums de caramel
(A theme on one flavor – caramel)

ou

La palette de glaces et sorbets du moment
(Home-made ice creams and sorbets on a painter's palette)

ou

Millefeuille au chocolat Valrhona "Caraïbe" , pralines et pignons de pin, sauce au caramel citronné
(Leaves of Valrhona chocolate tuiles and ganache, pralines, pine kernels and almonds, lemon caramel sauce)

ou

Nature morte automnale
(A frozen autumn still life)

ou

Le Café Crème
(Concentrated espresso ice cream in a wafer-thin bitter chocolate cup topped with a Kirsch sabayon)

Figure 4.1 Raymond Blanc's à la carte menu 2001 at Le Manoir aux Quat' Saisons

Hong Kong and America. It was also later published in France in the spring of 1993 by Editions Laffont. Blanc's second book, *Cooking for Friends*, published by Headline, was also much lauded. It was published in 1991 and sold 71,000 copies in eight months. He has also contributed to many other publications.

Raymond Blanc is very much a food philosopher as well as being a businessman. He was approached by an assortment of major airlines but eventually elected to work, since October 1991, as the sole consultant chef for Virgin Atlantic Airways Upper Class. Virgin won *Executive Travel* magazine's award for best in-flight food, and Airline of the Year in 1991–92. They were also voted best in six other categories. Passengers are able to enjoy Blanc's vision of airline hospitality. He also selects the companion wines for his food, and passengers can take away recipes for home production. He also travels, sometimes working with other chefs on projects or giving guest appearances and demonstrations, and has been a consultant to the retail chain Marks and Spencer.

Raymond Blanc is a member of:

- Club des Cents
- Chambre Syndicale de la Haute Cuisine Française
- Commandeur de l'Association Internationale de Maître Conseils en Gastronomie Francaise
- The British Gastronomic Academy
- Restaurant Association of Great Britain
- Guild of Writers
- and he is Academicien Mentor de l'Academie Culinaire de France.

Le Manoir produces (three times a year) a publication coinciding with the seasonal theme titled *Le Petit Rapporteur*. The brochure, as opposed to a magazine format, is provided for guests and friends as the property's principal way of keeping everyone informed of what is happening. Le Manoir is considered to be one of Britain's greatest restaurants, and is most popular as a place for a steady trail of European gourmets and gastronomes to relax, dine and stay in a cosseting environment. The hotel is also very popular with chefs, other hoteliers and restaurateurs. In fact, one of Raymond Blanc's most prized awards has been from 'Restaurant Restaurateurs' (a professional association of restaurants and restaurateurs) which is one of the lesser known awards, however it is one of the most important as it is chosen by his peers (chefs). Blanc is a highly respected businessman and chef. Sixteen of his former chefs have gone on to gain Michelin stars and Le Manoir is seen internationally as providing an excellent training for chefs on a trajectory for greater success and innovation.

Paul Bocuse

Paul Bocuse has been variously termed 'the contemporary messiah', 'Lion of Lyons', 'King of chefs' and also the 'Ambassador of French cuisine'. He was born on 11 February 1926 in Collonges-au-Mont-d'Or, into a family of chefs, who had passed their restaurant from father to son since the 17th century. Bocuse's father Georges was also a chef and it was in 1942 that Paul was apprenticed to a friend of his father's, Claude Maret, at the restaurant de la Soirie in Lyons.

There was little doubt that Paul would follow his father into the profession. Bocuses had, for generations since 1765, been chefs in the fishing village located on the shores of the Saône at Collognes-au-Mont-d'Or, 5 kilometres from Lyons. With Claude Maret, Bocuse learned how to shop for produce and, because of the war in Europe, had also to learn how to get difficult-to-obtain items on the black market. They even sometimes had to slaughter and butcher animals themselves.

During the war Bocuse was a member of the Vichy youth and then fought with the Resistance. He was wounded by German machine gun fire while fighting with the Free French Army in Alsace and received treatment for his injuries at an American countryside hospital. He is now happy to recount that he has American blood coursing through his veins! The wounding ended Paul's active army career. Nevertheless, at the end of the Second World War he took part in the Victory March in Paris on 18 June 1945.

Following the war, Bocuse returned to his region to recommence his apprenticeship with La Mère Brazier, at the Col de la Luere restaurant, then in the 1950s at the three star Le Pyramide, where he learned to appreciate the significance of commodities with Fernand Point. Bocuse eventually finished his culinary schooling at Lucas Carton. In 1959 he took over from his father at Collonges, where in 1961 he gained a first star, and the accolade of Meilleur Ouvrier de France Cuisinier (best crafts-person in his trade). The second star came in 1962 one year after he had renovated his father's restaurant, Auberge. The third star came in 1965 by way of a just reward for his immense ability and achievements, having accomplished what is surely one of most chef's dreams, the award of the third Michelin star.

At this time Bocuse was alerted to the fact that he could no longer use the Bocuse family name for his restaurant, his grandfather having sold the rights as far back as 1921. He bought back the rights and the Auberge de Collonges was renamed 'Paul Bocuse'. In 1975 he was decorated with the Legion d'Honneur by Valéry Giscard d'Estaing, the French President. Bocuse stated that it was for this occasion he created his famed truffles soup, which appears on the menu to this day as 'Soupe aux truffes noires V.G.E.' (plat créé pour l'Elysée en 1975).

Bocuse has been quoted as being a hopeless romantic and believes cooking to be an art, like painting or music; he often uses musical similitudes to express his point. Bocuse feels that imagination and common sense must be employed in cooking, and a great respect for simplicity and tradition can be seen in his cuisine. One of his maxims is 'Great cooking through great produce'.

Bocuse is an author (selection of his works are included in the Bibliography), chef-tycoon, chef-patron

HIVER 2000 - 2001

ENTREES

Soupe aux truffes noires V.G.E. (*Plat créé pour l'Elysée en 1975*). 340.
Saumon frais mariné à l'aneth, pain de campagne grillé. 180.
Escargots à la bourguignonne en coquilles au beurre persillé. 180.
Foie gras de canard maison cuit en terrine, gelée au Porto. 195.
Dodine de canard à l'ancienne truffée et pistachée, salade de haricots verts. 180.
Soupe de moules de bouchot aux pistils de safran. 180.
Foie gras de canard chaud poêlé au verjus. 220.
Salade de homard à la macédoine de légumes, sauce cocktail au vinaigre de Xérès. 360.
Potage de légumes de saison. 70.

POISSONS

Rouget barbet en écailles de pommes de terre croustillantes. 230.
Loup en croûte feuilletée, sauce Choron (*à partir de 2 pers.*). 320. *par personne*
Gratin de homard à l'américaine. 310.
Filets de sole aux nouilles Fernand Point. 250.
Poêlée de coquilles Saint-Jacques au Noilly. 250.

VIANDES

Côte de veau bourgeoise en cocotte, petits légumes de saison. 250.
Filet de bœuf du Charolais poêlé au poivre. 230.
Carré d'agneau «Côtes Premières» rôti à la fleur de thym. 240.
Pigeon en feuilleté au chou nouveau et au foie gras. 240.
Volaille de Bresse à la crème aux morilles, riz pilaf. 240.
Pigeon entier rôti à la broche. 260.
Civet de chevreuil grand veneur, purée de marrons. 230.

Volailles servies entières pour 2 ou 4 personnes :

Volaille de Bresse truffée en vessie, sauce fleurette. 860.
Volaille de Bresse rôtie à la broche. 690.
Canette de la Dombes rôtie à la broche. 690.

Toutes nos viandes et volailles sont accompagnées de légumes de saison

FROMAGES

Sélection de fromages frais et affinés «Mère Richard». 120.
Fromage blanc en faisselle à la crème double. 60.

DELICES ET GOURMANDISES
Le choix de tous les desserts

Tarte aux fruits de saison
Ambassadeur aux fruits confits - Gâteau Président Maurice Bernachon
Crème au chocolat noir Bernachon - Œufs à la neige Grand-Mère Bocuse
Salade de fruits frais – Pruneaux à la cannelle et au Beaujolais
Baba au rhum «Tradition» - Crème brûlée à la cassonade Sirio
Glaces et sorbets maison - Petits fours, mignardises et chocolats

120.

LES PLATS QUE «OUS VOUS PROPOSONS SONT SOUMIS AUX VARIATIONS D'APPROVISIONNEMENT DU MARCHE
ET PEUVENT, PAR CONSEQUENT, NOUS FAIRE DEFAUT.
TVA COMPRISE (19,6%) ET SERVICE COMPRIS (15% SUR LE HORS TAXE

MENU

Soupe aux truffes noires V.G.E.
(*Plat créé pour l'Elysée en 1975*)
ou
Foie gras de canard chaud poêlé au verjus

Rouget barbet en écailles de pommes de terre croustillantes
ou
Filets de sole aux nouilles Fernand Point

Granité des Vignerons du Beaujolais

Carré d'agneau «Côtes Premières» rôti à la fleur de thym
ou
Volaille de Bresse à la crème aux morilles, riz pilaf

Sélection de fromages frais et affinés «Mère Richard»

Délices et gourmandises
Petits fours et chocolats

790.

MENU
(pour 2 personnes)

Foie gras de canard maison cuit en terrine, gelée au Porto
et dodine de canard à l'ancienne truffée et pistachée, salade de haricots verts
ou
Salade de homard à la macédoine de légumes
sauce cocktail au vinaigre de Xérès
ou
Loup en croûte feuilletée, sauce Choron
ou
Côte de veau bourgeoise en cocotte, petits légumes de saison

Sélection de fromages frais et affinés «Mère Richard»

Délices et gourmandises
Petits fours et chocolats

630. par personne

POUR NOS JEUNES CONVIVES
Moins de 12 ans

Suggestion d'une entrée et d'un poisson ou d'une viande
Desserts

110.

PAUL BOCUSE

PAUL BOCUSE ET SES MEILLEURS OUVRIERS DE FRANCE
ROGER JALOUZ 1976 - JEAN FLEURY 1979 - CHRISTIAN BOUVAREL 1993 - CHRISTOPHE MULLER 2000
FRANÇOIS °PALA, MAITRE D'HOTEL 1993

Figure 4.2 Menu at Paul Bocuse for winter 2000–2001

and entrepreneur. He has many business interests, including consultancies. He has been culinary consultant to Air France and to Royal Viking Line's *Royal Viking Queen* cruise liner. His books have been translated into many other languages, he has taught in Japan and has restaurants in Tokyo and elsewhere. He also lectures at the Culinary Institute of America (CIA). Bocuse has an expansive nature and in 1979 developed a line of first class delicacies in the form of own label wines, brandies, champagnes, digestifs, teas, preserves and foies gras, which he distributes through large stores housing Paul Bocuse boutiques, and throughout Japan by the company Daimaru.

Through numerous outlets he sells kitchenware emblazoned with the Bocuse logo, and also has his name on sleeves of recordings made on his collection of converted steam organs. He is involved in the manufacture and sale of preserves and chocolates, and in 1980 he acquired a Beaujolais vineyard at Letra. In 1982, at Disney World's Epcot Centre, he launched his American activities by opening Le Pavillon de France in conjunction with his friends Roger Vergé, who often accompanies him on foreign visits, and Gaston Lenotre, the world famous sugar and pastry work exponent. Bocuse has been described as a one-man multi-national organization. However, his place in the history books will be recorded as being the individual who is chiefly responsible for the social prestige and fiscal enhancement of the chef in contemporary times.

In 1987 he set up the first worldwide cuisine contest, which he christened the 'Bocuse d'Or', at which each winner collects significant prizes, ample kudos and a work of art by Cesar. In 1987 another honour was bestowed on Paul by Monsieur Jacques Chirac, the then Mayor of Paris; this was the Officier de la Legion d'Honneur. In the spring of the same year François Mitterrand luncheoned at Paul Bocuse, this being the first time that a President of the Republic in office had patronized the restaurant.

His principal gift to the progress of catering is as an innovator of cuisine nouvelle. It was he who helped moderate some of the excesses of French classical cuisine (see also pages 62–3). Though plentiful, his enterprises have not made him forget the origins of cooking. Bocuse has many spits used for roasting in his restaurants and uses them frequently to great effect. At L'Abbaye de Collonges, where Bocuse has a large banqueting room, guests pass a glass walled area where you can look into the kitchen. Guests then scent the wonderful aroma from a massive spit, and they tend to congregate, savouring the moment. (L'Abbaye also has a unique mechanical organ made in 1880 and equivalent to a 110-piece orchestra!) These are but some of the memories guests take away with them from Bocuse and L'Abbaye.

He has a solid base of great talent and dedication, which he shares with his sixty staff, under the guidance of Raymonde, his wife. His larger than life appeal brings rewards in that he is a natural with the media, and in early 1988, seventy television shows were taped in Germany entitled 'Bon Appetit'; a book was also released with the same title.

In 1989 Paul Bocuse was elected 'Chef of the Century' by Gault and Millau, and the restaurant promoted to 'The First Restaurant in the World' by the *Rich and Famous World's Best for 1989–1990*. He is famously quoted as saying that 'cuisine is like a fireworks display, nothing remains – it is *une fête rapide, ephemeral*. The man himself is a confusing mixture of seemingly disparate natures, a self-publicist who is also generous and free with his specialist knowledge to practitioners and other interested parties. On 2 December 1991 Paul Bocuse also became the first chef to be sculpted and exhibited at the Grevin Museum in Paris – the sculptor was Daniel Druet.

Bocuse is one of the many top chefs who takes stagières (work experience trainees) each year to work with him, and so learn about his craft and French haute cuisine at its most expressive. It could be implied that he has spawned a culinary aristocracy, which is simply one more facet of the art. Bocuse has, however, no time for slimming meals, preferring his own style, and stating that life is too fleeting to have time for the likes of his friend Guérard's slimming cuisine, stating 'dietetic meals are like an opera without an orchestra'. He was also quoted in the *Evening Standard* in 1985 as saying, 'the so called nouvelle cuisine usually means not enough on your plate and too much on your bill'. Bocuse definitely ensures that his guests leave ultimately satisfied in all respects.

Michel Guérard

Michel Guérard was born on 27 March 1933 at Vetheuil in the Val d'Oise, 42 miles northwest of Paris. His father died when Michel was two years old, and his mother remarried, to a butcher. Michel was brought up until the age of five with his grandmother. It was she who introduced him to cuisine bourgeoise.

At the start of the Second World War Guérard and his grandmother returned to Normandy. His stepfather then went to the war and Michel and his mother took over the running of the butchers shop. He took an interest in the job, helping with slaughtering the animals and learning to dissect the carcasses. In 1947, when his stepfather eventually returned, Michel went away for two years to a boarding school, the Lycée Corneille in Rouen, at the end of which he was forced to choose a career. The skills he now possesses were likely to have been developed from 1950 in the Normandy patisserie laboratoire, in Mantes-La-Jolie, of the exacting Kleber Alix, where he served his apprenticeship; patisserie was after all Guérard's first love.

After military service in the Navy, which lasted 27 months, he undertook a refresher course with Kleber Alix and worked in several famed Paris restaurants like Maxims, hotels including the Crillon and Meurice, in Paris, the Normandy in Deauville and Lucas Carton. It was whilst working at the Crillon hotel as pastry chef that he won the Meilleur Ouvrier de France Patisserie, in 1958. Guérard then worked at the Lido for the Clerico family where he stayed for six years, during which time he was highly acclaimed by Paris society. His next job came by way of opening a deluxe snack bar at Antonio's, a chic hairdressers, but by now he had the urge to enter business on his own.

It was in 1965 that Guérard opened Le Pot-au-Feu, a modest and previously bankrupted bistro/restaurant at Asnières in the suburbs of Paris, which he named himself. The business did not fare well and he had to assume much of the workload. The entire project seemed doomed until his mentor Jean Delaveyne stepped in and provided substantial guidance: 'he could not expect to survive selling that which everyone else was making a living from, and also he should produce the dishes which he himself wished to make'.

It was not long before Guérard redrafted his menu and the custom grew, mainly by word of mouth, to the extent that it became necessary to make a reservation at least one month in advance. His originality and virtuosity was rewarded through gaining his first Michelin star in 1967 and Henri Gault made Le Pot-au-Feu the fashionable place to be seen after his article in *Paris Presse*, concerning a review of Guérard's pâté of eel with a mousse of cress in 1968. Guérard was controversial and a bit of a rebel who circumvented the then constraints of classical French tradition but kept the well-proved attributes intact, and in doing so gained a second star in 1971.

Le Pot-au-Feu only seated thirty covers, with more than a little crowding. However the money being made was considered insufficient to cover his exacting and increasing standards. The restaurant did become one of the most fashionable in Paris but was closed and compulsorily purchased in order that a road could be widened, a deal in retrospect which actually made him some good money through hard bargaining with the authorities.

After several attempts to purchase property in Paris, Guérard went to work for the singer Regine, who wished to open a Russian cabaret. It was during this period in 1972 that he met his wife to be, Christine Barthelemy, during a cabaret dinner. Michel was 39 and Christine 28 and a graduate of the business school Hautes Etudes Commerciales. Her father owned several spa hotels and hydros. A change in location and culinary direction occurred in the same year as Michel and Christine married. She was running Eugénie-les-Bains, which she had received from her father Adrien, a self-made individual who had had the extreme good fortune to have invented the Biotherm range, and founded the first chain of spa resorts in France, which would grow to possess a 20 per cent share of the market. With Christine Guérard visited the spa which was her father's most prestigious hotel, Les Prés et les Sources d'Eugénie, and was struck by its clinical atmosphere and sparse cuisine.

In 1974 they restored the hotel, restaurant and spa complex. Some of the buildings and part of the hotel date from 1862, when the valley was discovered by the Empress Eugénie, wife of Napoleon III. The spa was a member of the Chaine Thermale du Soleil, which was the top 'village minceur' (village devoted to the awareness of lean cuisine). During this period the hotel gained the record of being the most visited spa by foreign visitors, which made up effectively 12 per cent of all clientele, and was awarded a Michelin star.

In 1975 Guérard's restaurant Les Prés d'Eugénie was awarded two Michelin stars, and in 1976 through the company Michel Guérard Conseil he became the international consultant to Nestlé, Switzerland (one of the world's best known food companies), to Findus, Chambourcy, Gervais, Sopad and other products. *La Grande Cuisine minceur* (Health Conscious Cuisine) was also published in this year and has since been translated into twelve languages.

Since their marriage Michel and Christine Guérard have spent the season, from March to November, in this part of southwestern France. In 1977 Guérard, whose cooking style at the time was most definitely cuisine gourmand, gained a third Michelin star for Les Prés d'Eugénie. He is classed as a most sensitive innovator by many chefs and gastronomes. The revolutionary method that he evolved for producing exquisite food for individuals who wished to remain slim and full of health was yet to develop. However, the link between high class cooking and health had been struck and from this evolved grand cuisine minceur (the health conscious cuisine) which transformed the outlook of many chefs on cooking, for it combined eye appeal, flavour and lightness. *La Cuisine gourmande* was published in 1978 (with the title in the UK being 'Michel Guérard's Cuisine Gourmand'). This book was also translated into twelve languages.

Michel Guérard

LA CARTE GOURMANDE D'AUTOMNE

La Soupe de Cèpes au Bouillon de Poule 170
et la Tartine au Haricot de Lomand
La Salade Baroque aux Crevettes Grillées 180
et les Croquignols d'Araignée de Mer à la Flute de Moutarde
L'Oeuf Coque Glacé à la Russe 220
Saumon Croisière, Jolie de Crustacés, Piccarpeso et Muscovite à l'Herbe Fines
Les Rillettes de Chevreuil au Vin de Margaux 180
Mousse de Cèpes et Piperacade Glacée
Les Ecrevisses en Gelée Blonde de Volaille 220
Vichyssoise à la Truffe et aux Feuilles de Salai
La Salade de Homard aux Aillets Verts 270
et la Rate et Asperges
Le Foie Gras Confit dans sa Graisse 190
et la Rate à la Marmelade de Figues

La Truffe à la Tartouffe 220
Chasse d'Épeautre au Beurre de Lauden et Légumes Verts Nouveaux

L'Oreiller Moelleux de Mousserons et de Morilles aux Asperges 190

La Daurade Royale au Plat 280
Tomate Brûlée, Sartralle et Jus Pris de Lomand
Les Filets de Lisette Grillés au Feu de Bois 270
et le Différencude de Choc Vert à la Truffe
Le Bar en Marinière de Légumes 290
La Friture Légère de Langoustines 290
Petit Syférons Grillés, Asperges et Merveilles Feuilletes
Les Coquilles Saint-Jacques Poêlées au Beurre Salé 280
en Neige de Thym Frais
Les Petits Rougets au Tamis de Bois 280
et la Marmelade de Tomates Soufflés Relevée à la Soubressade
Le Demi-Homard 240
Repère à la Chermule et Suplement Fana

La Grillade de Foie Gras des Landes 280
à la Moelle de Puor Muscade au Vin de Pêcheron
Les Cannelloni aux Herbes "Cueillies à la Rosée" 270
et la Monestrone de Ped de Lochon au Basile
Le Hachis Parmentier à la Truffe, à l'Oie et au Ris de Veau 420
Le Pigeonneau à la Diable Rôti Tout Simplement à l'Atre 280
La Poitrine de Poulette Grillée au Lard sur la Braise 280
Jus au Limon
Le Râble de Lièvre à la Broche 290
Relevé à la Crème de Lard Moutardée
La Tourte Rustique de Caneton 270
et de Pôtit Soulle au Foie Gras

Prix Service Compris (15% sur les Prix Hors Service)

L'ECOLE BUISSONNIERE
590

La Soupe de Cèpes au Bouillon de Poule
et la Tartine au Haricot de Lomand
ou
Les Rillettes de Chevreuil au Vin de Margaux
Mousse de Cèpes et Piperacade Glacée
Les Filets de Lisette Grillés au Feu de Bois
et le Différencude de Choc Vert à la Truffe
ou
Les Cannelloni aux Herbes "Cueillies à la Rosée"
et la Monestrone de Ped de Lochon au Basile
ou
La Tourte Rustique de Caneton
et de Petit Soulle au Foie Gras
Les Desserts et Douceurs Candies

JARDINS DE LA MER
660

Les Ecrevisses en Gelée Blonde de Volaille
Vichyssoise à la Truffe et aux Feuilles de Salai
ou
La Salade Baroque aux Crevettes Grillées
et les Croquignols d'Araignée de Mer à la Flute de Moutarde
Le Rouget au Tamis de Bois
et la Marmelade de Tomates Soufflés Relevée à la Soubressade
ou
La Friture Légère de Langoustine
aux Petit Syférons Grillés, Asperges et Merveilles Feuilletes
ou
Les Coquilles Saint-Jacques Poêlées au Beurre Salé
en Neige de Thym Frais
La Daurade Royale au Plat ou Le Bar en Marinière de Légumes
Les Desserts et Douceurs Candies

JOUR DE FÊTE AU PAYS
780

L'Oeuf Coque Glacé à la Russe
Saumon Croisière, Jolie de Crustacés, Piccarpeso et Muscovite à l'Herbe Fines
ou
L'Oreiller Moelleux de Mousserons et de Morilles aux Asperges
Le Rouget au Tamis de Bois
ou
Le Demi-Homard à la Cheminée
ou
La Grillade de Foie Gras des Landes
à la Moelle de Puor Muscade au Vin de Pêcheron
La Râble de Lièvre à la Broche
Relevé à la Crème de Lard Moutardée
ou
Le Pigeonneau à la Diable Rôti Tout Simplement à l'Atre
Relevé à la Vinaigrette de Simple
Les Desserts et Douceurs Cardies

Figure 4.3 Michel Guérard's Autumn Carte Gourmande 1999 at Les Prés d'Eugénie

In 1978 the first of the Comptoir Gourmand Michel Guérard opened in Paris. During the period 1980–4 Guérard became an exporter of French confectionery and chocolate products to the USA. In 1982 *Ma Recettes à la tele* was published after a series of television programmes. In 1983 through the company Michel Guérard Conseil, he became the technical adviser for hotel and catering to the Chaine Thermal du Soleil, he was also administrator of the Chaine Thermale du Soleil, and has been President of the Autonomous Spa Association, Syndicat Autonome du Thermalisme since 1981. He has been Vice-President of the supervisory council of the Compagne Française du Thermalisme, the premier private spa group in France, and a member of the Spa High Committee, Haute Comite du Thermalisme, and Administrator of La Chaine Internationale des Relais et Chateaux (the International Chain of Post Houses and Chateaux).

For Guérard cooking is as much an affair of the heart as a calling to a career. He is a culinary innovator, an expert on wine, and he is also recognized as one of the supreme talents of his age. In 1983 he purchased, with Christine, the historic Château of Bachen together with its ancient wine stores and vineyards in the wine region of Tursan. During 1985 they developed and replanted the vineyards, restoring, modernizing and extending the wine stores in co-operation with two young architects, Patrick Dillon and Jean de Gastines.

In 1988 the first harvest and production of his own Tursan dry white wine in two different vintages was ready under the labels Baron de Bachen and Château de Bachen. Michel Guérard feels that aesthetics and scents have a great and significant place in his heart, which he has carried over into his devout interest and love for wine. For seven months Guérard followed classes at the Institut d'Oenologie de Bordeaux (the Wine Academy of Bordeaux). These allowed him to explore further aspects of the richness of flavours. His in-depth research in this area is of primary importance to him, and he firmly believes that every chef should be trained in this, just as he believes every wine expert should cook. (The major strength in Guérard's wine list is in a collection of excellent Bordeaux wines.)

In 1987 Michel Guérard founded, together with a number of prominent French chefs, La Chambre Syndicale de la Haute Cuisine Française (the Employers' Federation for French Haute Cuisine), of which he remained president from 1988 to 1990. His book *Minceur exquise* (Exquisite Lean Cuisine) has been reported widely to tantalize every bit as much as his other works, and was written in collaboration with Alain Coumont, a Guérard protégé. The book has been critically acclaimed as being at the peak of crisp modernity in cuisine. It is easy to see that Guérard also comes under the classification of chef tycoon, while his honours are numerous and display the appreciation of his country. They are: Chevalier of the Legion of Honour, Chevalier of the Order of Arts and Letters, Chevalier of the National Order of Merit, and Chevalier of the National Order of Agricultural Merit.

Paul, Mark and Jean Pierre Haeberlin

The Haeberlins have had a restaurant on the east bank of the Ill at Illhaeusern for well over one hundred years. Originally called L'Arbre Vert, now it is called Auberge de l'Ill and is a Michelin three-starred restaurant where the Haeberlins serve what is arguably some of the most prized food in the world today.

Figure 4.4 The menu at Auberge de l'Ill, featuring a water-colour by Jean Pierre Haeberlin on the jacket

Auberge de l'Ill

Paul from an early age had a love of cooking, and his brother Jean-Pierre had an artistic nature and style. During the war Paul was conscripted into the German army and worked as a chef. He eventually left the German army and joined the Free French Army. Jean-Pierre was also conscripted and thus the terrible situation came about of two brothers fighting on opposing sides.

After the war Jean-Pierre went to study art and architecture at the École des Beaux-Arts at Strasbourg, while Paul went to Paris to work at La Rôtisserie Perigordine as an apprentice. He also trained under the great Édouard Weber, a former chef to the Tsar, the Rothschilds, the King of Spain and the King of Greece. The brothers are mentioned together because it is felt that neither would have achieved the heady heights of gastronomic excellence without assistance from the other. Paul insists, 'before you can teach youngsters in the art of cuisine they have to be fired with a passion for what they are about to undertake'. This is not hard to imagine from a gentle man who has had a single-minded love of cooking instilled in him by his Aunt Henriette since he was a youngster.

The produce at Auberge de l'Ill is regional, and Alsatian. Marc Haeberlin (Paul's son) has great flair, having worked with Paul for many years. He is already one of the most noteworthy chefs of France, and the Auberge is his inheritance. The restaurant at the Auberge is considered quite formal and highly sophisticated, and the members of the food service staff here are some of the finest and most professional in France.

The menu, which looks superb, has on its jacket a water-colour painting by Jean-Pierre, who is a gifted artist inspired by the Alsace landscape. (Jean-Pierre has in the past exhibited his work in Paris.) The menus at the Auberge have become smaller in size over the years. In the past they were collector's items – large and beautifully depicted, but also viewed as cumbersome. Customers had difficulty seeing each other over the top of them and glasses on the table could be knocked over accidentally.

There is also a great interest at the Auberge de l'Ill in beverages of all kinds, especially the great and under-played Alsace wines. The Haeberlins have a very good relationship with the Hügel family who produce excellent Alsace wines and their wines are a prominent feature on the wine list.

Marc Meneau

Marc Meneau was born on 16 March 1944, in the village of Saint-Père-sous-Vezelay, 3 kilometres southeast of Vezelay. His father died when Marc was seven. In order to survive, his mother Margerite converted the premises, which had been christened L'Espérance (the name means the Good Hope), into a café-deli. The premises had been handed down through the family, which is why Marc has kept the name alive.

By the age of nine, Marc had been charged with more responsibility, and during this period operated the cash desk. Progressively he took a larger part in the running of the business, in particular the administrative areas.

After schooling, Marc Meneau enrolled in the Strasbourg Hotel School, where he chose to major in hotel management. Having worked part-time for a small establishment, his next practical training was in a three-star hotel where he worked as a receptionist. After a period his school sent him on an entirely unsatisfactory job placement as a cook near Rheims. Three days later the Hotel du Nord in Chorleville-Mezieres gave him a job where he would have stayed if it had not been for his mother, who requested that he return home, as she was considerably overworked in his absence.

During his period of service in the French Army, where he was assigned to the running of the officers' mess in Joigny, he met his future wife, Françoise, who was clerk to a solicitor, and whose parents owned a restaurant approximately 40 kilometres away. When his military service was completed Marc married, and Margerite Meneau gave the couple the grocery store and café, which they immediately turned into a bar, with a brass counter and leather armchairs, and a luxurious dining room in what was reputed to be Roche Bobois style, with red velvet walls and copper covered illuminations. Marc feels that they had been somewhat irrational: 'It was classy, but we did not know how to cook. My mother-in-law was giving me cooking lessons over the phone! Their restaurant was always full and ours empty. This turned out to be a blessing for us as it gave us the impetus to do better than them.'

It was around this time that the couple began to exchange pleasantries with a friend of Françoise's family, Monsieur Vergeron, a regular customer of the restaurant and retired Michelin Guide inspector, who made a few gentle remarks and criticisms at the end of each month. When he thought that they were worthy of a distinction he mentioned the Meneaus to the management of the Michelin Guide. The first star was awarded in 1967. However, Marc's dwarfish kitchen was restraining him and something had to be done to secure new premises more befitting the ever-growing stature of his restaurant.

New premises were found in the form of a manor house with almost $2\frac{1}{2}$ acres of accompanying land. An added bonus was that it was not that far from Paris. Unfortunately though the sale had disadvantages, in that the property had to be acquired sight unseen. It was a considerable drawback but the couple went ahead and the banks kept their faith. It was soon self-evident why no one was allowed to visit the property prior to sale, as the entire interior structure was in need of reconstruction and re-fabrication. Françoise had gone to run a restaurant in Auxerre during this time. After the completion of what became mountainous repairs (accompanied by soaring interest rates), she returned to L'Espérance as the business was now substantial, and in 1975, due to their considerable efforts, L'Espérance gained its second star. After gaining a third star Marc became, as he puts it, 'riddled with doubts' about how he could stay ahead of the game now that he was on the top rung of the ladder.

Marc quotes three great masters who have influenced him and enabled him to progress the formation of his own cuisine:

Jacques Pic suggested we go and see the chef Alex Humbert, who had raised Maxims to three star level. He had just retired and it was only after the eighty-second phone call that we finally managed to track him down. He came down for three days to sample all of my dishes, without ever saying a word. Before leaving, he poured everything down the sink.

After three months of dedicated work by Marc, with one week spent reviewing the books and manuscripts stored in the Library of the Association of Master Chefs, Humbert returned to sample Meneau's cuisine again, and this time he committed himself to helping Marc.

Meneau's second master was Monsieur Bernard, who had at one time been chef to some of Europe's most respected houses; he was chef to Charles De Gaulle as well as the Shah of Iran.

The third master with whom he found inspiration is Andre Guillot in Paris, whose methods of learning about cuisine Meneau considered magical. Marc's impression of his own experience is that his seven years' practical learning was gained in an academic fashion, but that from Guillot he gained experience that would take him through the next ten years of his life.

Meneau is a chef who can view himself objectively, and he has considered himself in the past to be too laid back and lax. In order to correct this characteristic he pushes himself twice as hard as he does his team. To maintain a positive bloom and freshness in the job he took on a new challenge, and has been involved in devising menus for French astronauts and the restoration of foods in space, in collaboration with Patrick Boudry: 'I'm therefore under obligation to produce recipes for the Beleme enterprise', and so at the conception level, Marc has worked for both Beleme and L'Espérance on an equal basis.'

Meneau is known to have turned down many offers, despite his international reputation, to take contracts from manufacturers in return for the sponsoring of their goods. He does not lend his name to other restaurants around the world but does perform demonstrations, under the watchful eye of Françoise, during the period when L'Espérance is closed.

Many international gourmets and gastronomes consider L'Espérance to be a voyage of sensual discovery. On entering the heavy white gates, and then having passed the reception, a small boutique can be viewed selling various goods and products. On the right wing the chefs can be seen preparing the food. Windows overlook a river lined with trees, the branches of which contain thousands of tiny lights, brightening the night.

Meneau pays particular attention to his wines and L'Espérance has a list as well conceived as his menu. The china and table linen are also chosen from the very best available. As with some of the other top chefs, Meneau has become a wine grower, with his aim being to obtain the AOC (Appelation d'Origine Contrôllée) Vezelay Burgundy, and by doing so breathe life back into the Vezelay vineyard where Chardonnay and Pinot Noir grapes are growing once more.

He says, 'I am animated by innovation and feel that writing a recipe book is the best exercise for a chef'. He views it as important because of the value it brings to the individual and others, the discipline that accompanies its construction and also for posterity. Meneau also has a noted collection of antiquarian books, which he uses for reference. Meneau is almost entirely self-taught, and always puts into action that which he learns or excites him: 'I hate routine. If I wanted to live life like that I would lie in the sun with a fax machine and telephone by my side, giving instructions to my business manager on Monday mornings.'

Marc Meneau's publications include *La Cuisine en fêtes: les recettes originales de Marc Meneau* (edited by Robert Laffont, 1986); *Musée gourmand: le peintre et le cuisinier* (Marc Meneau and Anne Caen, 1992) and *La Cuisine des monastères* (Marc Meneau and Anne Caen, 1999).

Abats

ris de veau rôti à la broche crème d'oseille

vol au vent de cuisine bourgeoise (feuilleté, mousseline
de volaille, foie gras, ris d'agneau, crêtes de coq, truffes)

Volailles

salmigondis de pigeon à «la Contis»

fricassée de volaille citron aux merveilles

poularde de bresse à la serviette (2 personnes)

pigeon façon «Père Lathuile»

pintade «truffée» de persil, rôtie en cocotte
(2 personnes)

volaille marinée à l'huile d'olive,
sur oseille crue et céleri rémoulade

Viandes

bœuf à la ficelle, sauce vineuse

filet mignon de veau piqué de truffes, petits oignons confits
(2 personnes)

carré d'agneau rôti aux tartelettes d'abats

Fromages

fromages, galettes à l'écume de beurre, mendiants confits

Apéritif conseillé «le Soleil»

Hors-d'œuvre froids

huîtres à la gelée d'eau de mer

assiette de caviar, toast à la crème gratinée

lisettes marinées à la «française»

terrine de canard mère Denise, céleri en vinaigrette

nos foies gras, lobes et terrines, compote de figues

ambroisie de foie gras

les hors d'œuvre froids et chauds (8 petits plats)

crème glacée de tomate verte et son aspic

galette de crustacés au beurre de moutarde

Hors-d'œuvre chauds

soupe de homard au pain

consommé de petits pois à la royale

brochette de polenta truffée au foie gras

cromesquis de foie gras aux truffes

rissole de tomate «coquette»

tourte d'asperges au foie gras (2 personnes)

artichaut en soufflé de moelle, sauce au vin

Poissons

turbot rôti à l'arête, cuit oignons, champignons
et jus de viande (2 personnes)

turbotin poché au lait, sauce mousseline (2 personnes)

filets de rouget en pétale de pomme de terre

homard rissolé aux gousses d'ail, pommes sautées

bar au caviar, beurre de sardine

petit homard pané au riz, crème safran

grenouilles, écrevisses frites à l'échalote et persil

Figure 4.5 Marc Meneau's Spring/Summer menu 2000

Marc lost the third Michelin star in 2000. Nevertheless, he is lauded as proprietor of one of the best restaurants in France. Eating at L'Espérance is a once in a lifetime experience; every dish is memorable and founded on the hearty produce of Burgundy. He will surely regain a third star at some point, but no matter the rating, he is proprietor of a luxury Relais et Chateaux hotel with 12 rooms and two apartments. There is also a beautifully restored old stone mill with four rooms and four apartments. Marc Meneau is also the largest employer in the district and, in fiscal terms, one of the top restaurateurs in France, but still manages to retain an intimacy in the restaurant, which is a large part of this master's art.

Marc states that, 'work wise, we have always wanted to gain recognition for our skills and to do this we have to be at our guests' disposal twenty-four hours a day and ensure that they get perfect service'. Vegetables come from his own garden, similar to Raymond Blanc, and he cooks some of his dishes at very low temperature to maintain their inherent flavour. Quality has to be worked at, and he and many of his peers are constantly being judged. He feels it is the price of fame and it would be unfair to complain.

Anton Mosimann

Anton Mosimann is at the height of his career. He has the dual role of being both culinary ambassador for his native Switzerland and for his adoptive country, Britain. He says, 'I create, and for a time I am satisfied, then I am inspired to create anew, this is my art.' In the foreword to Mosimann's book *The Essential Mosimann* (1993) Sir Peter Ustinov wrote:

> Qualities of precision, of refinement and of fantasy lie behind the success of one of the country's most distinguished culinary ambassadors. He is not only an outstanding Chef de Cuisine, but also an arbiter of taste, a creator of ambience. The menu is proof of Anton Mosimann's great originality. His cuisine is neither traditional or nouvelle, nor is it enslaved by neo-Japanese minimalism, but is uniquely Mosimann.

From a child Mosimann wanted to be different, unusual, do exciting things and where possible be the first to do whatever he chose to do. He has a passion for perfection, innovation and creativity, and a firm determination and desire to be the best. These are qualities that are associated with most high achieving people, in whatever field of endeavour. However, in his youth there was also maturity with the realization of deferred gains being uppermost in his thinking. Mosimann was not looking for a quick-fix career that would bring monetary rewards but would be without substance. He adopted a laser targeted approach to career development, which resulted in a career path, taking him seemingly from cook as a child (he cooked for friends in his parents' restaurant on their day off), to chef within an impressive range of hotels and restaurants, and currently to businessman with the exclusive Mosimann's Club in London, and with a castle in Switzerland soon to open as a second Mosimann Club. He has also teamed up with Swisshotel Hotels and Resorts, to launch dining clubs, called Club M, at the Howard Hotel, London and the Swisshotel, Berlin.

Table 4.2 Anton Mosimann's career path

Dates	Title	Property	Country
1962–1964	Apprentice	Hotel Baeren, Twann	Switzerland
1964–1965	Commis Entremettier	Palace Hotel, Villars	Switzerland
1965	Commis Garde Manger	Cavalieri Hilton, Rome	Rome
1965–1966	Commis Saucier	Hotel Waldhaus, Sils Maria	Switzerland
1966–1969	Chef Tournant/Chef Saucier/Sous Chef	Queen Elizabeth Hotel, Montréal	Canada
1967	Chef de Froid/Sous Chef	Canadian Pavillion EXPO 67 Montréal	Canada
1969	Chef Tournant	Palace Hotel, Montreux	Switzerland
1969–1970	1st Chef Tournant	Palace Hotel, St Moritz	Switzerland
1970	Executive Chef	Swiss Pavillion EXPO 70, Osaka	Japan
1970–1971	Chef Entremettier	Palace Hotel, Lausanne	Switzerland
1971	Chef Garde Manger	Palace Hotel, Lucerne	Switzerland
1971–1972	Chef Restaurateur	Kulm Hotel, St Moritz	Switzerland
1972	Chef Rôtisseur	Palace Hotel, Lucerne	Switzerland
1972–1973	Sous Chef	Kulm Hotel, St Moritz	Switzerland
1973	Chef Saucier/Sous Chef	Palace Hotel Lucerne	Switzerland
1973–1974	Sous Chef	Kulm Hotel, St Moritz	Switzerland
1974	Chef Saucier/Sous Chef	Palace Hotel, Lucerne	Switzerland
1974–1975	Commis Patissier	Palace Hotel, Gstaad	Switzerland
1975–1988	Executive Sous Chef (June 1975) Maître Chef des Cuisines (December 1975) Director of Cuisines (January 1986)	The Dorchester Hotel, Park Lane	London
1988 to date	Proprietor	Mosimann's, Belgrave Square	London

When Mosimann travelled to Osaka, Japan to be Executive Chef at the Swiss Pavilion for Expo '70, it was here that he learned about plated art, which is something he has followed since that point, as can be readily seen in his books. It was coincidentally something that was also being learned and carried on around this period in France by men like Bocuse, the Troisgros, Vergé, and Guérard, and in Germany by Witzigmann and Müller and by others around Europe within nouvelle cuisine. This was a turning point for Mosimann. At the age of 23 he considers that he was too young to hold the position of Head Chef over 35 Japanese and ten European chefs. But he rose to the management and cuisine challenges. Furthermore, having been trained in the classical school, suddenly there was no cream, fresh butter, foie gras and truffles. This opened his eyes to the qualities of simply cooked fresh and natural produce.

After proving himself at the Dorchester Hotel for 13 years, where one of his restaurants, The Terrace, won him two Michelin stars (the second star awarded in January 1986) and Gault et Millau awarded 17 points, he decided to move on. He had by this time worked for five owners and ten managers and he felt it was time to 'do something different, go solo, but not just another restaurant, but something with wow!'. In April 1988 he established an exclusive dining club in premises originally built as an 1830s Scottish Presbyterian Church in London's Belgravia. Mosimann, the businessman, gained sponsorship for his private dining rooms from élite retailers with similar life style associations, for example, Fabergé, Gucci, Davidoff and Mont-Blanc (see Figure 4.6). He vividly describes the Davidoff room as, 'it is wonderful; the interior is just like being in a humidor'. Certainly it was a unique idea,

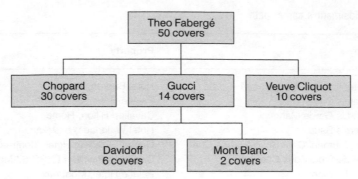

Figure 4.6 Mosimann's private dining rooms

inviting the retail sponsors to pay to decorate his restaurant. The Mosimann Club provides members with exclusive use and has become world-renowned as a sanctuary for the international gourmet in London. The wine cellar is situated where the organ once was, and is a major focus of attention as its wall of glass means that Mosimann's finest wines are permanently on view.

He said that the change of direction would provide more time to focus on his writing and broadcasting and this he has certainly fulfilled, with the assistance of a busy public relations machinery keeping him in the public eye and mind. His numerous books have been a tremendous success, as have been his television appearances.

His publications include: *Cuisine à la Carte* (1981); *A New Style of Cooking* (1983); *Cuisine Naturelle* (1985); *Das Grosse Buch der Meersfruchte* (1985); *Anton Mosimann's Fish Cuisine* (1988); *The Art of Anton Mosimann* (1989); *The Essential Mosimann* (1993).

Mosimann is a truly inspirational chef who will continue to surprise and enthuse us. He is currently at the height of his powers and is in constant public and media demand throughout the world. He has in the past catered on numerous important occasions, for instance for the British Royal family and prominent public figures worldwide. He has been winner of many international awards, including La Croix de Chevalier du Merite Agricole from the French Ministry of Agriculture 1988, personality of the year 1986, and honorary Doctorate of Culinary Arts from Johnston and Wales University, Charleston, USA. Mosimann has also been a highly skilled consultant for British Airways, and has been culinary consultant to The Old Course Hotel at Saint Andrews, Scotland.

Mosimann's party service was launched in 1989. The challenge was to create food with the same high standards as the club itself, but in different and unusual locations. For Mosimann, one highlight was a dinner in Prague, where he catered for guests including Prince Charles: Sir Georg Solti was conducting, Dame Kiri Te-Kanewa was singing and Mosimann was cooking! Mosimann caters for many banquets for state occasions at No. 10 Downing Street, and has cooked for the last three Prime Ministers.

It was a dream come true for Mosimann when in 1989 he opened his own Academy of Culinary Excellence, zealously committed to people nurturing and development. It was an innovative training provision through which he could share his experiences and expertise with the next generation of young professionals. He also created Creative Chefs, which acts as a recruitment agency and career consultancy bureau, which facilitates the placement of chefs globally. This is related to the philosophy underpinning the Academy, in that it is Mosimann's belief that for the human resources to become assets they must be allowed to 'live and breathe' outwith the company. He encourages his chefs to move out and on as,

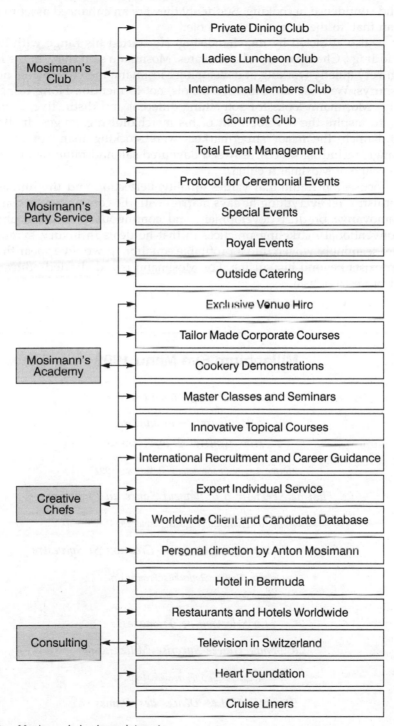

Figure 4.7 Anton Mosimann's business interests

'a few years later they will come back with more ideas, new innovations, certainly more experience and confidence in cooking. Suddenly they are an enhanced asset to the company and more than that, to the industry as a whole.'

Mosimann is also attracted by merchandising. He started his range with his vegetarian Christmas puddings, Champagne and chocolates. Mosimann said that, 'in the last few years we have been very quietly working at developing Mosimann merchandising, now it is being sold in Sainsburys, Waitrose and Harvey Nichols, not to mention Hong Kong and the Far East generally'. Mosimann looks for something different and distinctive, a unique design, taste or idea, to inspire the development of his merchandising ranges. In 1999, only two months after launch, the major supermarkets were stocking many of the items in the Mosimann range, including sauces, seaweed flavoured salt and rainbow peppercorns. Also available is a range of Mosimann china.

Mosimann focuses on traditional values, quality, perfection and the human side of the hospitality industry. Yet everything he says marries with the contemporary context of strong marketing, innovative product development and continuous innovation and vision. He challenges conventional marketing practices in that he deals in luxury, symbol, signs and senses that are seemingly woven into a profitable equation. It would appear that the real art of Mosimann exists beyond his cuisine. For Mosimann is a dedicated educationalist with integrity and professionalism.

Millennium Eve Menu 1999

Mosimann's Champagne Grand Cru Brut

Les Meilleures Gourmandises
Les Trois Gouttes D'or Rèveillon

Morton Estate Chardonnay Hawkes Bay 1997

Le Filet de St-Pierre à la Vapeur Sauce au Champagne

Corton Charlemagne Louis Latour 1995

Le Mignon de Boeuf Angus Sauté Crèation St-Sylvestre

Château Mouton Rothschild Premier Cru
Classe Pauliac 1982 Jeroboam

La Selection de Fromages

La Bombe Glacèe Surprise Millennium

Royal Tokaji 5 Puttonyos Aszu

Demi Tasse Les Délices des Dames

Mosimann's Rosé Champagne Cuvée Prestige

Figure 4.8 Anton Mosimann's Millennium Eve menu 1999

Grande Buffet de Gala 'Tour du Monde'

HORS D'OEUVRE

Scottish Smoked Salmon with Crab Meat, Herb Sauce

PACIFIC RIM

Selection of Sushi 'Expo 70'
Stir Fried King Prawns with ginger and coriander
Baby squid in Black Bean sauce
Scallops in Lime Juice
Boiled Yabbies
Dimsum Hong Kong 1983'
Roast Soy Chicken Singapore 1931'
Tandoori Spiced Chicken Bombay Brasserie
Lamb Gosi Kebab Goa 1995'
Thai Green Lamb Curry 'Oriental' 'Bangkok 1973'
Stir Fry Teriyaki Pork with Mushrooms 'Tokyo 1992'
Roasted Marinated Kangaroo Melbourne 1986'
Grand Rice
Shiitake Mushrooms and Chinese Vegetables
Bok Choy in Oyster Sauce Beijing 1990
Grilled Marinated Mixed Vegetables
Vegetables Patti Samosa
Dhrokla and Khandvi

EUROPEAN

Selection of Herring Stockholm 1925'
Summer Marini Villa Lorraine Brussels 1974'
Saucespiene Bündnerfleisch
Grand Assortiment de Charcuterie Rêve des Bouches
Crespelos'
Poltcakes with Parsley Sauce Belfrey 1988'
Aal in Grüner Sauce Hamburg 1985'
Griechenscholtes Kartoffelsch Lugano 1922'
Roast Ribs of Beef and Grazy Highlands 1989
Boiled Salverschle with Herb Dumplings
Tapas Marchildebise
Bauerenschieken im Gastflug St. Moritz 1971'
Wällser Rochette mit 'Gschwellti' Palace 1965'
Ravioli Casalonga 'Hilton, Rome 1985
Saucisses: Cumberland, Sage, Game, Duck, Lamb and
meat, Pork and Leek
Mele Melo con Wurst und Käse

AFRICA

Cape Pickled Fish
Güsh Babolie
Chicken Sish

CHICKEN SOCIETES

Chicken Socistes
Shish Kebab Turkish Style 1993'
Lamb Kofte
Kisir
Patti Kofte
Imam Bayildi
Boerewors
Crocodile Stew Sun City 1987'
Fricassé Springbok
Spicy Chickpeas
Hummous
Parsley Tabbouleh
Dawas
Feta Cheese with Olives
Semp
Hot Sos

AMERICAS

Manhattan Clam Stew New York 1965'
Sorvicho Ntexco 1968'
Main Lobster Cocktoil 'Albert Montreal 1957'
Bermuda Potatoes with Spring Onions Waterloo House
1594'
Seafood Jambalaya
Hawaii Smoked Yellow Fin Tuna 1971'
Alaska Crabmeat Legs
Shrimps and Okra Gumbo New Orleans 1988'
Cajun Spiced Barbecued Chicken
Roast Honey Glazed Chicken Napa Valley 1986'
Buffalo Chicken Wings with Blue Cheese Dressing
Peppered Pastrami with Dill Pickles
Chilli and Garlic Baked Spare Ribs
Moros Y Christianos
Feijoada a Rio 1980'
Chuchuacspan Beans, Texas

SALADES

Antoni Caesar with Carrolough Croûtons
Iceberg and Caraway Seeds 'Louisianne 1971'
Leaves with Blue Cheese Dressing
Celery, Apple and Walnut
Pickled Berry Beets
Corn and Smoked Bacon
Haricots de Soisons Parilles
Escroms with Shrimps
Kartoffel mit Koziedoressing
Pasta Venice 1985'
Aubergine Turkish Style

THE DESSERTS

Bread and Butter Pudding Sheffield 1984'
Zuger Kirschtorte 'Gstaad 1974'
Chocolate and Pecan Pie, Vanilla Ice Cream, Georgia
1987'
Pavlova with passion fruits 'Sydney 1986'
Peppered Pineapple with honey ice Cream
Crème Brûlée Cappuccino
Rumbof nach Grossmütter Art
Croquembouche Aveyolino France 1975'
Lemon tart with blackberries Coulis
Gugelhopf/Mere Olga
Baklava
Trio of Petit Fels
Passion Fruit Souffle Glace
Vacherin Glace Nesselrode
Apple and Blackberry Crumble
Zugerkirschtorle

THE BREADS

Mosimann Rolls
Grissini
Naan Bread
French Bread

THE BIRTHDAY CAKE

Carrot Cake, Raspberry Coulis

CHEESES

English and Continental

WINES

Champagne Mosimann Grand Cru
Degulny Arkahle, Tokay 1996
Mouton Rothschild en Jeroboam 1975
Champagne Domvielle Rosé Magnum

CAFÉ

Les Truiles aux Amandes
Mosimann's Champagne Truffles

Figure 4.9 Grand Buffet de Gala 'Tour du Monde' from Anton Mosimann's fiftieth birthday party held at the Natural History Museum in London for 630 guests on 22 February 1997

Dieter Müller

The Schweizer Stuben restaurant, situated in Wertheim, a quiet town in the north of Baden-Wurttemberg, has been in business since 1971. In Germany this restaurant had most definitely not to be missed. In 1988 it was recognized as one of the top two restaurants in the country. The Schmitt family owned it: Adalbert Schmitt, a confirmed gastronome and connoisseur, founded the restaurant and it was later to be directed by Andreas Schmitt, who had also developed his father's passion for gastronomy, and it was Andreas who arranged the phenomenal wine list at the Schweizer Stuben.

Dieter Müller is, however, the individual who attracted gourmets and gastronomes from all over the world to this sleepy town. As Maître Chef de Cuisine he fulfilled the role of an ambassador of German national cuisine during seventeen years at the Schweizer Stuben.

His love of cooking came from his parents' Black Forest restaurant. He has cooked elsewhere in Germany and trained at the Schweizerhofen at Berne, where he learned French methods. The backing of the Schmitt family meant that Dieter could provide his customers with the freshest of ingredients, many of which were available locally from the very fertile lands on the Main. Aberdeen Angus beef was shipped from Scotland, poultry and many cheeses came from France, and lobsters from the Atlantic coast. There was also an adjoining restaurant to the Schweizer Stuben, called the Schober, which utilized the same kitchen, but served less involved food.

Dieter Müller has stated that 'my cooking comes from the heart', and he has a definite individuality of style, which he feels is essential: 'my culinary style is however French nouvelle, which stems from my time at the Schweizerhofen, but applied to German tastes and aliments'. Dieter Müller's mentors are Escoffier, Fredy Girardet and Paul Bocuse. He travels annually communicating his philosophy, cooking for special events and giving demonstrations. Another pastime is in extending his skills to interested home cooks in Wertheim, where he cooks a meal and supervises others in its reproduction.

Dieter Müller had, however, for some time been considering a move and his new venture eventually came in the form of a Renaissance castle, originally termed the Wasserburg ('castle surrounded by water') rich in folklore and referred to as early as 1384. The castle belongs to the von Siemens family who have leased it to Althoff Hotels and Restaurants, owned by the Cologne hoteliers Thomas and Elke Althoff.

The castle, named Schloss Lerbach, is near Bergisch Gladbach and set in a 28-hectare park. The rooms and suites are individually designed and a new lease of life, and large injection of cash, have made it into a first class

Vorspeisen
Hors d'oeuvre

Vorspeise aus dem Menü **DM 48,–**
Hors d'oeuvre du jour

Gewürzlachsfilet mit Oliven-Tapenade, marinierten Artischockenscheiben
und Trauben-Senfsauce **DM 58,–**
*Filet de saumon épicé accompagné d'une tapenade d'olives, d'artichauts marinés,
et d'une sauce à la moutarde et aux raisins*

Gefüllter Schweinefuß und gebratene Gänseleber auf bunten Linsen mit Balsamicosauce **DM 58,–**
Pieds de cochon farci et foie gras d'oie poêlé sur un lit de lentilles, sauce balsamique

Trilogie von der Gänseleber – als Gugelhupf, im Baumkuchen und gebraten –
mit Feigen-Rosmarin-Brioche **DM 65,–**
*Trilogie de foie gras – se composant de foie d'oie, d'une terrine enveloppée d'un mameca de
Baumkuchen et de son foie d'oie poêlé accompagné d'une brioche au romarin et aux figures*

Marinierte Rinderfiletscheiben mit Périgord – Trüffel, Salatspitzen und Tête de Moine – Locken **DM 68,–**
*Tranches de fiets de boeuf marinées aux truffes du Périgord son bouquet de points de salade
et ses flocons de tête de Moine.*

Jakobsmuscheltatar mit Sevruga – Caviar von Petrossian auf Langoustinocarpaccio **DM 8,–**
Tartare de noix de St. Jacques au caviar Sevruga de chez Petrossian, sur un carpaccio de langoustines

Suppen/Zwischengerichte
Entrées/Soups

Entenconsommé à la chinoise **DM 38,–**
Consommé de canard à la chinoise

Cappuccino von Curry und Zitronengras
mit Meeresfrüchtespieß **DM 38,–**
Le Cappuccino de curry et de citronelle et sa brochette aux fruits de mer.

Kastaniencrèmesuppe mit Kalbsbries – Pilzravioli und weißem Alba Trüffel **DM 68,–**
Velouté de marron et de truffes blanches d'Alba avec sa ravioli de champignons et de ris de veau

Jakobsmuscheln mit Trüffelbutter überbacken
auf Chutney und Salace von Chicorée **DM 65,–**
Coquilles St. Jacques gratinées au beurre de truffe, sur, un chutney et sauce aux endives

Sylter Royal-Austern auf Kräuterzavarin und marinierten Rote-Betewürfeln
mit Safransauce überbacken **DM 58,–**
*Les huîtres Sylter Royales sur un savarin aux herbes accompagné de betterave rouges marinées,
et le tout, gratiné d'une sauce safranée*

Champagnerkuteln mit Kalbsbriespiccata auf Lauchkrautea **DM 48,–**
Tripes au Champagne, Piccata de ris de veau sur un lit de poireaux

Dieter Müller's Fischempfehlung **DM 48,–**
Spécialités de poissons Dieter Müller

Haupgänge
Plats principaux

Rotbarbenfilet mit Provencearomen und Thunfischsauce
auf sautierten Artischocken **DM 68,–**
*Filet de rouget-barbet aux arômes de Provence
accompagné d'une sauce au thon et d'artichauds poêlés*

Steinbutt mit Hummerhaube auf Schwarzwurzelgemüse und Basilikum-Orangennudeln **DM 78,–**
*Filet de turbot sous une croustade de homard, sur un lit de salsifis noir,
accompagné de nouilles Boulanghre au basilic et à l'orange.*

Kalbsfilet mit gebratener Gänseleber, Sauce Périgourdine
und gefülltem Kalbsschwanz auf Kartoffelravioli und Vanille-Karottenflan **DM 68,–**
*Filet de veau au foie d'oie poêlé, accompagnés d'une galette de queue de veau,
servi sur un ravioli de pomme de terre, d'un flan de carottes à la vanille
et d'une sauce périgourdine*

Galette und Geschmortes von der Ochsenbacke mit Balsamicojus,
Lauch-Kartoffelpüree und Ochsenmarkcrostini **DM 65,–**
*Galette et joue de boeuf braisée, accompagnée d'un jus au balsamique, d'une purée de pomme de terre et de poireaux
et d'un croustini à la moelle de boeuf*

Crépinette von der Etouffé-Taube
mit Blutwurstscheibe, grünem Spargel und Trüffelsauce **DM 75,–**
*Crépinette de pigeon au sang, tranches de boudin,
asperges vertes et sauce aux truffes*

Fasken vom Salzgraslamm und gefüllter Minikürbis mit Sauce von grünem Anis,
Provencegemüse und Schafskäse – Kartoffelroulade. **DM 68,–**
*ees prés salés a et sun mini patisson forci servi d'une sauce e l'anis vert, de légumes Provençaux et d'une
roulade de pomme de terre au fromages de brebis.*

Rehrückenfilet in der Brotkruste und geschmorte Schulter mit Holunder – Gewürzjus,
Rotkohl und Spätzle **DM 68,–**
*Selle de chevreuil en croûte de pain et l'épaule braisée accompagnée d'un jus au sureau épicé,
de chou rouge et de spätzle*

Fasan „Surprise", Eräte mit Moscato d'Asti – Kraut und Keulen mit Gänseleber
serviert in zwei Gängen **DM 176,–**
(2 Personen ca. 40 Minuten Zubereitung)
*Le Faisan Surprise en deux temps, sa poitrine à la choucroute au Moscato d'Asti e ses cuisses au foie gras .
(pour deux personnes, 40 minutes de préparation)*

Käse
Fromages

Käseauswahl vom Brett **DM 38,–**
Chariot de fromages

Vacherin au Mont d'or auf Kartoffelschnee mit Alba-Trüffel **DM 68,–**
Le vacherin de Mont D'or sur sme purée de pomme de terre accompagné de truffes d'Alba

Mit Rücksicht auf unsere anderen Gäste bitten wir Sie, auf das Rauchen von Zigarren, Zigarillos und Pfeifen
– bis 15.00 Uhr bzw. bis 23.00 Uhr – zu verzichten. Die Hotelbar steht Ihnen hierfür zur Verfügung.

Figure 4.10 Dieter Müller's à la carte menu 2000 at Schlosshotel Lerbach

Desserts

Mousse und Carpaccio von Zwetschgen mit
Süßholzparfait
*Parfait glacé à la réglisse sur un carpaccio de
quetsches accompagné de sa mousse*
DM 32,--

Charlotte und Eis von Holunderbeeren
auf geliertem
Moscato d'Asti – Holunderblütensüppchen
*Soupe gelifiée à la fleurs de sureau
et Moscato d'Asti, charlotte et glace aux haies
et fleur de sureau*
DM 32,--

Crème Brûlée mit Tonkabohneneis
auf Verveine - Weinbergpfirsichkompott
*Crème brûleé accömpagneé d'une glace à
la fève de Tonka sur une compote de pêches
de vigne parfumée à la verveine*
DM 30,--

Champagnercrèmesorbet "Moët et Chandon"
Sorbet au champagne crèmé "Moët eChandon"
DM 25,--

Dessertkomposition "Dieter Müller"
Assiette surprise "Dieter Müller"
DM 38,--

Milchschokoladen – Soufflé mit Himbeercreme und
Zitronen - Karameleis
(ca. 25 Minuten Zubereitungszeit)
ab zwei Personen
*Soufflé chocolat au lait accompagné d'une crème aux
framboises et de sa glace caramel-citron*
DM 36,--

Dessertempfehlung
Dessert en suggestion
DM 30,--

Figure 4.11 Dieter Müller's 'amuse bouche' and desserts menu 2000 at Schlosshotel Lerbach

venture. Dieter Müller had widespread involvement in the renovations of the restaurant area, and has brought his own preferences to the fore: 'I favour colours in harmony like blue, grey and salmon, which appear throughout in the carpets, drapes and wall coverings'. His interior design skills took in the purchase of Italian chairs and the use of Riedel and Zwiesel glasses. Gold medal winning cutlery was purchased from the Swiss company Berndorfer, and tablecloths and napkins were sought in a light champagne colour to give a harmonic effect.

Dieter Müller's cuisine is almost architecturally composed. He combines sophisticated technique with culinary design. He blends a Mediterranean ethos with French-Asian fusion cooking – which is masterly in its execution. It has been said of Müller that he is an articulate and consummate professional. His creativity is spurred on and interminably aroused by both domestic and foreign travel and an insatiable appetite for exploring all the recesses of gastronomic taste. His publication *Das Dieter Müller Kochbuch* (1988) gives an insight into his cuisine for those unable to experience it first hand.

Dominique Nahmias (Olympe Versini)

Dominique Nahmias (aka Olympe, and now remarried as Olympe Versini) is well known throughout France and the USA. Her renown is all the more special because, like Raymond Blanc, Dominique has no formal college or hotel background; she is an *autodidacte* (self-trained individual). Before turning to the kitchen, Dominique studied acting at the Toulon conservatory and also previously studied to be a lawyer. It is also unusual for a woman chef to achieve her peers' highest regard, more especially in France, where she has achieved so much in the professional kitchen in a country dominated by male chefs. Most startlingly, in the vigorously held male preserve of haute cuisine, Dominique became a prized pioneer.

Dominique, who was born in 1952, comes from a legal background, her father being a Corsican advocate. Dominique helped out in a family restaurant during her teens and gained considerable experience in doing so. In 1972 she opened her first restaurant in Montparnasse, the first Olympe, which was operated by both Dominique and her first husband, Albert, who was an academic sociologist. Dominique's mother and grandmother hail from Italian (Corsican) stock, and she has featured many pasta dishes over the years, although both mother and grandmother had given Dominique instruction in the art of French cookery. Chez Olympe's cooking style was light and creative, and her cuisine radiated freshness; she was constantly changing her dishes and remodelling older ones. Her mastery of the art was levelled at a 'cuisine parfumée', which pulls

Vins Blancs

Mas de la Bégude Vin de Pays des Coteaux de Ardèche	140 F
Cassis Blanc de Blancs Domaine Caillol 1999	170 F
Bourgogne Blanc Domaine Jarnal 1998	190 F
Châteauneuf du Pape Château Mont-Redon 1999	250 F
Fillette Edelwicker (46cl)	70 F
Cassis rosé Domaine Caillol 1998	150 F

Vins Rouges

Côtes du Vivarais Mas de la Bégude	Magnum	1997	220 F
Côte de Brouilly Domaine de Chavannes		1999	140 F
Chinon Domaine Du Colombier		1996	140 F
		1996	280 F
Bourgogne Cuvée Gravel Claude Marechal	Magnum	1999	170 F
Château les Jésuites Premières Côtes de Bordeaux		1998	160 F
Château Brillette Moulis en Médoc		1993	300 F
		1993	540 F
Châteauneuf du Pape Château Mont-Redon	Magnum	1996	280 F
Saint Joseph Bernard Gripa		1998	190 F
Séduction Rouge (50cl) Vin de pays des Coteaux de Ardèche		1999	70 F

Vins effervescents

Champagne Gosset	340 F
Cidre Père Jules	70 F
Champagne Gosset Grande Réserve	390 F

Apéritifs

Kir Alsace 12cl	30 F
Coupe Champagne Blanc de Blancs Barbier 12cl	50 F
Banyuls Léon Parcé 6cl	50 F
Gin - Vodka - Ricard 5cl	45 F
Tonic - Jus de Fruits 20cl	25 F
Pietra (bière Corse)	30 F
Crèmes Carton : Cassis, Framboises	
Whisky Jack Daniel's	60 F
Whisky Michel Couvreur 5cl	

Digestifs 5cl

4 ans	50 F
12 ans	60 F
Vendanges Tardives de Gewurztraminer	55 F
Calvados - Cognac - Armagnac - Poire - Vieux Kirsch - Mirabelle	70 F
Café - Thés - Infusions	20 F
Eau de Saint-Georges	30 F
Grande Source de Volcan	30 F
½ Saint-Georges	20 F
½ Volcan	20 F

Menu Carte 210 Francs

A l'Apéritif, l'assiette de Saucisson de l'Ardèche (45F)

Foie Gras de Canard à la Vanille (+6F)

Croustillants de Boudin Maison

Galette de Farine de Châtaignes, Oeuf Poché, Beurre Fondu

Cocotte de Légumes au Lard

Crème de Potiron au Foie Gras

Farci de Pied de Veau, Vinaigrette au Poivron

Sardines à la Vénitienne

❧❧❧❧❧❧❧❧❧❧❧❧❧

Calamar Sauce Bourride

Bar de ligne, Chou Fondant (+4F)

Épaule d'agneau de Sisteron au four (2/3 pers.)

Thon au lard et aux oignons

Mignon de Porc Sauce Acide et Douce aux Épices, Choucroute

Raviolis de Canard au Jus

Pintade Fermière, Lasagne Champignons Sauvages, Parmesan

❧❧❧❧❧❧❧❧❧❧❧❧❧

Fromage Corse

Fromage Blanc à la Crème ou aux Herbes

Fondant au Chocolat

Paris Brest

Croustillant de Pomme ou de Poire, Caramel Beurre Salé

Crème Brûlée aux zestes d'orange

Crèmes Glacées ou Sorbets Maison

Figure 4.12 Casa Olympe menu 2001

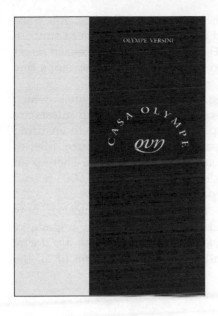

together flavours, aromatic elements, temperatures and textures in an exciting and sensual fashion.

She used light Middle Eastern and oriental aromatics to full advantage, sometimes imprisoning their delicate aromas and odours in filo pastry or en papillote, to be then released at the table. Her 1920s style restaurant featured fixtures from the great liner *Normandie*. Chez Olympe more than favoured the colour plum; it appeared everywhere, on the lacquered walls and matt ceiling, fabrics and china, which was plum and white, even the exterior was painted in gloss plum with plum awning. The wine list, finance and administration were her husband's responsibility. A successful flirtation in Geneva with another restaurant ended because it took her away from Paris and her family for extended periods of time.

The Nahmias also ran a nightclub restaurant called Les Bains-Douches. Most of the dishes served here had been at some point successful at Olympe. Dominique took part in twice-weekly radio programmes in Paris and authored *Les Parfums d'Olympe* and *La Cuisine d'Olympe*.

Dominique has in the past held one Michelin star, but this was taken away because she was no longer in sole charge of the restaurant; her husband Albert playing a leading role and turning Olympe into a chic bistro. This led to a subsequent depreciation in the restaurant's sophistication, although the à la carte menu still generally pleased and contained some original signature dishes.

Gault Millau have said of Dominique Nahmias (Olympe Versini) that she is the foremost practitioner of 'cuisine du femme' in the world. Like many of the other chefs in this book, she has juggled many different projects at one time, and one of her projects was for the Virgin Megastore on the Champs-Élysées, which although viewed as a diversion, was applauded heartily and seen as a resounding triumph.

She is now known as Olympe Versini, and the contemporary Casa Olympe, her no-frills restaurant, is the setting for her clearly defined menu, which features masterly French dishes like steak tartare. It is well worth a visit.

Jean and Pierre Troisgros

As with many other great chefs, the influences of the Frères Troisgros have come from their own. Their father, Jean Baptiste, was a café owner as also was Jean Baptiste's father before him. The original café was in Chalon, but in 1930 their father moved to purchase a small commercial premises, a hotel in Roanne in central France. Jean Baptiste was a great innovator. He was one of the very first restaurateurs to serve his food plated. He was also one of the first to serve young red wines cool, a custom, which today is common, and one that improves the beverage immensely.

The young Troisgros were sent to train at Lucas Carton and then to La Pyramide to work with the great Fernand Point. Roundabout 1954 the brothers returned to Roanne to put into practice what they had learned from the great chefs, and by 1957 they had gained their first star in the Michelin Guide. It took another ten years before they gained their second star and another three to gain the third.

The brothers have their own label wines and lend their name to sell wine, foie-gras, truffles and preserves. They are also TV personalities, and have travelled to other countries to perform special dinners. The untimely death in 1983 of Jean Troisgros caused great distress in the culinary world, but he had already helped to develop the restaurant's fine reputation, which has continued.

The restaurant is contemporary and distinctive, having a palette of earthy hues, which match the cuisine of the Roanne region. Dishes are very carefully executed and guests are warmly welcomed by a talented group of food service personnel committed to ensuring distinctive service. Signature dishes include escalope of salmon with sorrel sauce, fillet of beef, pot-au-feu, with creamy horseradish, and a thick cream soup of frog legs. There is an excellent cellar at Troisgros, stocked with some 80,000 bottles of which about 25,000 are sold each year. There are eighteen luxurious bedrooms at the premises.

Pierre, President de La Chambre Syndicale de La Haute Cuisine Française, now collaborates in the kitchen with his sons Michel and Claude, and a kitchen brigade of approximately twenty. In their collaborative work *The Nouvelle Cuisine of Jean and Pierre Troisgros*, the brothers wrote 'Cooking should be a carefully balanced reflection of all the good things of the earth.'

Roger Vergé

Roger Vergé was born in Commentry, France. He originally thought of becoming an aeroplane mechanic but pursued a culinary career instead and has been the accomplished and exemplary talented patron of the Moulin de Mougins since 1969 (Mougins is just inland from Cannes). His third Michelin star was gained in 1974. The pull of the culinary industry stems from his passion for perfection in taste and texture. He was always one of the most visible members of the 1970s culinary brat pack, which transformed eating habits in France and around the world. He has a second restaurant in Mougins village, called L'Amandier, which is also used as a cooking school. Vergé is most definitely a chef tycoon. His business interests are truly international, and have taken him all over France, and beyond to Japan and to the USA, aided by the fact that Moulin de Mougins is internationally renowned. He had worked in St Moritz, Casablanca, Jamaica, Monte Carlo and South Africa, before taking on Moulin de Mougins.

His empire takes in other restaurant ventures in Luxembourg and Denmark, although these are no longer in his control, and he has also had joint ventures with Gaston Lenotre and Paul Bocuse to service Disney world's Epcot complex in Florida. He has a partnership with the manufacturers of glass and china under the name of Denise (his second wife) and Roger Vergé. The Vergés have also had a café in the Galerie du Sporting d'Hiver at Monte Carlo. Many of his outlets sell branded gifts, including a range of oils, eaux de vie, herbs, teas, tapenades, preserves, wines, liqueurs, glasses manufactured by Riedel, vinegars, mustards and much more. At La Cave du Moulin, an old olive oil warehouse in the village of Mougins, which dates from the 13th century, he has a treasure storehouse of 5,000 bottles of fine wine and other objects relating to wine and alcohol in general.

One thing he continuously reiterates is that one of the most important things for a chef to know and understand is how to choose the best products. He also states that aliments should be true to their region of origin. He is a firm believer in his country's traditional flavours and aromas and of regional produce, especially that from Provence which features highly in his Cuisine Soleil. Vergé has a very large brigade in the summer, running to the mid seventies. He has been reported as referring to the kitchen brigade as 'catering's chorus line'. He states, 'the main ingredient in the making of a good cook is good taste, and natural appreciation, both oral and visual of the art of good eating and drinking'. Art is a passion for Vergé, and he has art works by Arman, Cane, César, Folon, Pagès and Tobiasse on display.

Vergé is a Meilleur Ouvrier de France; Chevalier de la Legion d'Honneur; Chevalier des Arts et des Lettres; Chevalier du Mérite Agricole; Maître Cuisinier de France; Honorary Doctor of Culinary Arts, honoris causa, from Johnson and Wales University and, a gold medal recipient and member of the Academie Culinaire de France. Vergé has written several books, which have all created a great deal of press attention throughout Europe and the man himself has given many interviews. He is also a gastronomic philosopher, which adds considerable depth to his public speaking. He states, 'a cook is creative, marrying ingredients in the way a poet marries words' and also, 'cuisine heureuse, which consists of marrying natural products with one another, is the antithesis of cooking to impress'.

Roger Vergé's publications include: *Cuisine of the Sun* (1979); *Entertaining in the French Style* (1986); *Roger Vergé's Vegetables in the French Style* (1994); and *Les Fruits de Mon Moulin* (1997).

Eckart Witzigmann

Eckart Witzigmann, born 4 July 1941 at Bad Gastein, Austria, is Germany's answer to a Mosimann figure. He has been one of Germany's tycoon chefs, and a culinary ambassador in Germany. After trade school and his initial cook's apprenticeship at the Straubinger hotel, he continued his training and travels, which took in Bad Reichehall, Pontresina, Königswinter, Davos and Bad Ragaz. He then travelled further afield and spent time with the Haeberlins in Alsace at the Auberge de l'Ill, in Illhäusern. It was they who were the springboard for his training and further development. They introduced him to Paul Bocuse and the Troisgros brothers, and then to Roger Vergé, where he was to gain further experience and inspiration. He had now developed a distinctive interest in nouvelle cuisine and continued gaining experience and gathering necessary stimulus by working in Stockholm, Ettlingen, London, Brussels and Washington, DC.

While in Washington he was approached by Fritz Eichbauer who wanted Munich to have a fine dining restaurant in time for the 1972 Olympics. He left Washington in 1971 and took over as head chef at Munich's famous Tantris restaurant, and it was he who was to introduce the principles of nouvelle cuisine throughout Germany. He did, however, become sceptical about much of what has been written about this crusade, and the fashion in which it has been generally misused and capitalized on.

His meteoric rise and the culinary creations that evolved at Tantris made Witzigmann responsible for opening much wider horizons in German cooking. He was seven years at Tantris and gained two Michelin stars in that time.

After leaving in 1978 he opened his own restaurant, Aubergine, in the Maximiliansplatz, in October of that year. It was classified as one of the best restaurants in Europe, and after only one year of operation gained the legendary three Michelin stars, the first restaurant in Germany to do so. And the three stars were to be annually renewed by Michelin. Similarities with Mosimann extend to Witzigmann having worked alongside Germany's premier medical nutritionists in devising menus for the West German Olympic team at the

Seoul Olympics; Mosimann had done similar work with top nutritionists at the Open University in Britain.

Aubergine's original trademark in decor was minimalist, which inspired concentration on the food. However that image was later lost, with wonderful floral displays and chandeliers giving the room warmth. Witzigmann's restaurant was to a large extent for expense account dining, with prices high and service well executed. Witzigmann's only diversionary projects have been his writing, though his books are not translated into English, possibly because of pricing – one of his books in Germany costs the equivalent of £78.00. His works though are a worthwhile 'investment' for the gastronomically minded. Currently Witzigmann has published fifteen books. His innovative recipe serial can be regularly seen in specialist journals like *Feinschmecker* (Gourmet) and the *SZ Magazin* (supplement to one of Germany's biggest newspapers the *Süddeutsche Zeitung*).

Because of his magnificent skill and his affinity for French cuisine, and its reinterpretation for a German market, Witzigmann was decorated with the medal Chevalier des Arts et Lettres by the French Secretary of State for culture. Additional awards are the medal München leuchtet – Den Freunden Münchens (Munich shines – to the friends of Munich) in 1991, he was also awarded the Prix Culinaire des Regions Européens in 1992 and in 1993 the Prix à l'Art de la Cuisine by the Académie Internationale de la Gastronomie. In 1994 Gault Millau crowned this with the award of 'Cook of the Century'. Witzigmann is now free to act in an advisory, consultancy capacity since he now has no fixed base. He is in great international demand and is able to respond to that which excites him. Since 1997, Eckart Witzigmann has advised three hotels and restaurants on the Spanish island of Mallorca, coming originally as adviser to German investors. He is also advising the Munich delicatessen and restaurant company, Käfer.

One of his latest ventures has shaken the cobwebs and stuffiness out fine dining in a dramatic fashion. It has been a startling evolution for one of Europe's most renowned chefs, and its success was assured from its initial conception. It premiered in August 2000 and is called 'Palazzo dell'Arte & Gusto' on the Waterloo Place in Hanover. In essence it is a dinner show in a high quality mirror-tent with what Witzigmann describes as first-class partners in gastronomy and selected artistes. The performers include jugglers, balancing acts, comedy waiters, magicians, contortionists, entertainers, hoola-hoop dancers, comedians, singers and musicians. These individuals enrich the programme, giving it unmistakable colour and vibrancy. The objective is to provide an unforgettable experience that maximizes the appeal to all of the senses. The philosophy behind Pallazo is incredibly simple:

- First class gastronomy
- First class programme
- First class location
- First class ambience.

The magic word today is 'event' gastronomy, which really does not fully explain Pallazo dell' Arte & Gusto. Palazzo is a holistic work of art appealing to all of the senses. The name refers not only to the commedia dell'arte and therefore to the artistic, but it is also a homage to the art of service and cooking. Here unique and magical events are created, which will be consigned to long-term memory.

Considering this profile of Witzigmann and the progression he has made one can only be left to ponder what will be next from him, and many of the others profiled here. Their creativity appears to be boundless, and they are continually setting new standards in the production and presentation of food.

4.4 The distinguishing characteristics of the key contributors

What distinguishes chefs from other individuals is their ability to physically participate and function with highly appreciable skill levels in their given area of expertise as well as possessing vastly significant theoretical knowledge. The symbiosis of skilled practitioners' knowledge and wisdom combined with theoretical, and in some cases academic backup, is what creates the top chefs.

What distinguishes these chefs from other chefs?

What distinguishes those profiled in this chapter from other chefs is that which defines these principal chefs. Many chefs are not particularly interested in what they are doing; it is viewed as a job like any other, where time must be put in to receive remuneration for the hours of service to an employer. The job may be being carried out with skill and attention to detail, but they may not also possess the 'love' and willingness to take their knowledge out of the kitchen and immerse themselves in a gastronomic career for the rest of their lifetime.

All of the chefs profiled in this chapter have by their very nature as human beings, a distinct personality, but they possess some of the characteristics that are elemental to the makeup of a leading chef. These top chefs truly 'love' what they do. They have genuinely enquiring and curious minds when dealing with their subject matter and its related fields. They tend to live the job, are enthused by it and will generally spread this enthusiasm amongst those with whom they come into contact. They are prepared to spend long hours associated with their work and also tend to be seekers of knowledge and wisdom on their subject area.

Some are self-publicists, others are great writers and TV personalities, and all of them have mentors from earlier times whom they will freely refer to and to a greater or lesser extent revere. These premier chefs also keep in frequent contact with each other. They are technician craftsmen and women and innovators with perfectionist tendencies. They are also sufficiently au-fait with their given subject area that they can philosophize freely and in so doing enrich their world with meaning and symbolism. This has often been seen as problematic for academic research, however it is such a rich and fertile area in itself that it cannot be overlooked indefinitely. These principal chefs are stimulated by the need to express themselves in generosity, which needs encouragement, recognition and praise, and they all possess a certain shrewdness.

The working principal also needs immense endurance, strength and determination. The great specialists are funds of knowledge, but they also have a tendency to be piratical: for some creation is entirely cerebral, but for others it is technically inspired. Some of the chefs have been seen to be truly international figures, with immense cognisance of cuisine sans frontières, but who are also repositories of domestic cuisine and culture. Some can truly be called chef tycoons. In general these individuals are daring, and do things that other chefs may merely dream of; in general they also tend to be more open concerning how they go about what they do.

The archetypal features of the key contributors

From the profiles presented in this chapter, it is clear that these chefs share a number of characteristics in terms of life, experience and interest. These are that the chef may:

1 be internationally known;

2 be a media personality;

3 be an author;

4 be patron of his/her own restaurant;

5 regard food and cookery as symbolic philosophy;

6 believe in the need for heightened sense awareness;

7 travel to promote self/business and to enlighten others/give dinners demonstrations etc;

8 merchandise their own products/endorse ranges other than their own;

9 have oenological pursuits/interests;

10 view dining as a holistic experience, much more than the provision of good food;

11 be stimulated by gastro-history/gastro-geography;

12 be classified as a chef tycoon;

13 have experienced childhood trauma;

14 have been stimulated from childhood by a significant adult in culinary pursuits;

15 be viewed generally as principal chef or culinary ambassador of their chosen country;

16 have or had parents or relatives owning restaurants or other hospitality venture;

17 own three star Michelin rated properties;

18 lecture at home or abroad;

19 have his/her own distinctive cuisine;

20 have no formal craft/hospitality training, and

21 have been influenced by past or present masters/mentors.

To explore this further, Table 4.3 lists these 21 characteristics against the name of the chef, as follows:

(A) Anton Mosimann
(B) Raymond Blanc
(C) Dieter Müller
(D) Eckart Witzigmann
(E) Paul Bocuse
(F) Michel Guérard
(G) Marc Meneau
(H) Dominique Nahmias (Olympe Versini)
(I) Roger Vergé
(J) Paul Haeberlin
(K) Jean Troisgros[1]
(L) Pierre Troisgros

---

[1] Jean Troisgros died in 1983. However, enough is known and written about the man for inclusion, and his place amongst the modern masters is unquestionable.

Table 4.3 The archetypal chef – analysis chart (see text for key)

	A	B	C	D	E	F	G	H	I	J	K	L
1	*	*	*	*	*	*	*	*	*	*	*	*
2	*	*	*	*	*	*	*	*	*	*	*	*
3	*	*	*	*	*	*	*	*	*	*	*	*
4	*	*	<*>	*	*	*	*	*	*	*	*	*
5	*	*	*	*	*	*	*	*	*	*	*	*
6	*	*	*	*	*	*	*	*	*	*	*	*
7	*	*	*	*	*	*	*	*	*	*	*	*
8	*	*	*	*	*	*	*	*	*	*	*	*
9	*		*		*	*	*	*	*			
10	*	*	*	*	*	*	*	*	*	*	*	*
11	*				*	*	*					
12	*	*			*	*	*		*			
13					*	*	*			*		
14	*	*	*	*	*	*			*	*	*	*
15	*			*	*							
16	*		*		*					*	*	*
17	< >	< >	*	*	*	*	< >	< >	*	*	*	*
18	*				*				*			
19	*			*	*	*	*	*	*			
20	*						*					
21	*	*	*	*	*	*	*	*	*	*	*	*

<*> Dieter Müller has only been a chef patron since early 1992.

< > indicates the lack of three-star status. Anton Mosimann took himself out of the grading system when he became owner of a private club; prior to that he had two Michelin stars. Raymond Blanc has two stars. Dominique Nahmias (Olympe Versini) has had one star.

Notes on Table 4.3 • • •

It can be taken as read that the chefs in cells numbered 1 to 3 are indeed internationally known, are media personalities and are authors. This is borne out by the fact that they were chosen from amongst professionals and amateurs in all three countries for inclusion in this book. Multi-media documentation exists for them all, and the ready availability of their own publications is sufficient testament.

With cells 4, 7 and 8 it can be noted that of the chefs in the study, all are patrons. This would seem to be the norm. However, it was not possible to dismiss a trend, which witnessed some chefs (though none included in this book) making the transition from chef patrons back into hotels. If chefs are asked, in general what would be their principal desire, it is usually recorded as, 'being their own boss', and 'becoming a chef patron'.

Cells 7 and 8 reflect the view of chefs as promoting their hotel/restaurant (the chef in many cases seen as part of the product to be marketed). Many chefs travel both to learn new skills and techniques and to promote their business, which is usually caught up indissolubly with themselves at this level (e.g. Le Prés d'Eugénie and the Auberge de l'Ill would not have the same focal attraction without Guérard and the Haeberlins respectively).

Cell 18, regarding those chefs that lecture at home or abroad, should be seen as just one other way of promoting self and business together, extending that which chefs consider gastronomic and, in many cases as referred to in cell 19, extending their own distinctive cuisine. The chefs are astute enough to observe this, and the fact that their industry has a dynamic. They cannot be seen to stand still and expect lifelong loyalty from their clientele, if that clientele is not stimulated by the dining experience. The merchandising of own label product ranges is one simple and very effective way of doing this. (More and more chefs nowadays lucratively endorse other merchandise, equipment, plant and companies.) In many cases the range is sold in-house (as is the case with Blanc, Guérard, Mosimann, Vergé, and others) and can be taken away, thereby extending the chefs link with the client. If sold externally in boutiques and shops (as is the case with Bocuse, Guérard and Mosimann) it can introduce new custom to the quality standards the chefs set for themselves and their business, as well as the obvious extension of income. There is however an obvious requirement for careful and sensitive packaging and marketing of the range. This hints at the extent to which the formation and image building of the chef as 'star', takes place. In general this has been accredited to them by a contemporary food media hungry for copy, however it is also self-cultivated.

Cell 15 links into the passages above in that again it is the multi-media, i.e. food press, general press, food writers and critics, radio, and television, that assist in promoting the chef, who has quickly learned the nature of the beast and can milk the media, often ably assisted by the chef's own marketing department, machinery or personal assistants, to such an extent that we now have 'stellar' chefs who are seen to represent their country, as virtual culinary ambassadors, e.g. Mosimann in Britain, Witzigmann in Germany and Bocuse in France.

Cell 13 'has experienced childhood trauma' can be seen from Table 4.3 to have directly affected one-third of the sample, and therefore cannot be ignored. In general one can posit several views:

(a) Can this really be seen as a defining element in the formation of some chefs? Many of the chefs had indeed difficult young lives which could not however be interpreted as having been traumatic.

(b) It should be ignored and seen as an irrelevance.

(c) It has been character-forming, and strengthened the resolve of the individual to strive for success, and make it against the odds.

(d) It was a function of the times in which they lived – 'the war years'.

What is being suggested here is that an amalgam of (a), (c) and (d) may have affected the outcome, but these specific chefs were all also stimulated from an early age by a significant adult or adults in the culinary arts, and this brought about a desire to please others and succeed in their chosen careers.

However, perhaps the most important elements that bind chefs together is their system of beliefs and attitudes, particularly as they relate to:

(a) the creation and articulation of 'culinary philosophy' and

(b) conviction that excellence in cuisine is dependent on heightened sense awareness.

Contributions to the future

The chefs profiled in this chapter have all contributed immensely to the future of gastronomy. They also get the best possible from their colleagues by effective communication, enthusiasm, motivation, teamwork and leadership. Many people do not want to be managed – they want to be led. Leadership however requires a suite of skills. Examples of this leadership are in Raymond Blanc having sixteen of his chefs go on to become Michelin-starred chefs in their own right. It can also be seen in Mosimann setting up his own 'Creative Chefs' business for international recruitment and career guidance.

The chefs here also have influence over the dining public and over chefs worldwide. Today's premier chefs need more than culinary genius to survive as the business becomes more complex and customers more demanding. All of the chefs mentioned are leaders who have sought successfully to elevate the image and prestige of gastronomy and have the following in common:

- They have something of value to sell.

- They target and are targeted by those who value it.

- They communicate benefits clearly.

- They understand how people purchase.

- They differentiate themselves on value, not cost.

- They listen hard and sell soft.

- They sell to individuals and not a mass market.

- They view quality not as accident, but rather as always the result of intelligent effort. Great cooking only comes by securing great produce.

- Their people learn by design rather than by chance.

- They energize and inspire their profession – now.

- Their protégées will be the ones re-energizing the profession – in the future.

- Strategic imperatives enable them to lead by example.

- They connect with their employees and customers in a meaningful and substantive way.

- They elevate the needs of their employees as well as the needs of their customers.

- They exceed at generating customer satisfaction and identify and retain profitable customers.

- They are highly identifiable figures at the apex of their industry.

There are many others who are also contributing to the development of cuisine and gastronomy in the same way as those profiled in this chapter. Limitations in time, space and the availability of information have also restricted the potential coverage of others. This is not to say that their contribution is less profound.

4.5 Summary

This chapter has considered the legacy of Escoffier, as the king of cuisine ancienne, and the person who represented the turning point for the advent of the modern cuisine. Fernand Point was to become the father of modern gastronomy and also create the model for the internationally renowned French haute cuisine restaurant. He was also to affect the development of cuisine through those who came into contact with him as direct beneficiaries, and those who they themselves have influenced. Profiles have been presented in this chapter of some of the key contemporary contributors to the development of modern cuisine and gastronomy, and the chapter has identified the distinguishing characteristics of these modern masters.

Into the 21st century

The chapter provides an epilogue to the text, consolidates and reflects on the material and also looks to the future.

This chapter is intended to help you to:

- consider the potential key influences on the development of cuisine at the beginning of the 21st century
- explore the status of the chef in modern society
- identify the importance of design, vision and leadership to the development of food and beverage operations
- consider entrepreneurial skills as a prerequisite for the development of food and beverage businesses, beyond the ordinary
- recognize the need for the application of firm foundations and the development of knowledge and discipline to the exploration of gastronomy
- review the characteristics of those who have contributed most to the development of cuisine and European gastronomic culture
- define and validate the title gastrosopher
- encourage emphasis on, and recognition for the exploration of gastronomy as a rich source of material for legitimate study.

5.1 Influences on cuisine

The history of cuisine and the hospitality industry in Europe is closely affiliated with travel, either through migration or tourism. Travel for whatever reason expands the horizons. People always take with them their fundamental need for survival, but in the lives of many people food and drink play a significant role beyond this. Just how individuals satisfy this fascination varies from individual to individual, but it is a safe bet that with the gastronome care will be taken in the choice of food and drink and the accompanying experience.

This expanding interest comes from simply having sampled different foods and beverages on travels and also observing how these different foods are arranged and cooked. The demand of experienced travellers and the effects of migration have also influenced the types of cuisine on offer in contemporary restaurants.

The resurgence of travel came with the Enlightenment, when the wealthy and noble classes became able to move with greater freedom and with new modes of transport. They also tended to transport their own attitude to foods and cookery with them, but also somehow assimilate some of the foods and methods that they found in new lands, into their own cuisine. This was evidenced in the progression of fusion cuisine, as discussed in Chapter 3.

In the 18th century there were numerous French chefs absorbing influences in Russia that were then taken into the classical *répertoire*. Testimony as to the way in which cuisines tended to travel from one part of the world to another can be seen with, for instance, the Greeks and Romans as discussed in Chapter 2. Also the intermarriages of royal families in Europe, for political alliance and state reasons, blended not simply custom, but also social etiquette and cuisines. For example, Catherine de Medici, wife of Henri II of France, and Marie de Medici, Queen of France to Henry IV (Le Vert Galant) were chiefly responsible for bringing Florentine influences and wider Italian practices into France. Again the number of Florentine dishes in the classical *répertoire* attests to this.

Just as improvements in the accessibility and availability of travel has made it less demanding for individuals to reach new destinations, and therefore new aliments and alimentary experiences, it is now swifter, easier and cheaper for the foods from the world's markets to reach the chef and the larger stores in their own countries. Improved technology and methods of transportation have assisted growth in this area as much as improved techniques in the storage of food, to prolong the quality, nutritional value and shelf life of products. Studies in gastro-geography can show transport being made easier from one geographical area to another and across countries, so that foods once considered seasonal in one geographical location can be obtained anywhere. Improvements in nutrition through more balanced diets, resultant from this opportunity and inspired by chefs, have seen old cooking methods dropped and new ones established. This development in the direction of the internationalization of food and beverage, of cuisines and eating habits, has and is becoming more commonplace now at the turn of the century than at any time before, and is being further promoted through the growth in industrial large-scale food and beverage trading.

The food industries employ more people across Europe than any other and consume a quarter of all wage packets. Gradually, over a period of some thirty years, and peaking sharply in the last decade, the whole idea of health conscious eating has gained ground again, as it has with peaks and troughs since medieval times. In tandem with this, individuals on higher disposable incomes were ripe for the public relations and marketing machinations of the contemporary food chains, food companies, hotels and restaurants. People could be seen exploring objects of conspicuous consumption with which they could display their new-found wealth: enter designer foods and beverages like Häagen-Dazs, isotonic drinks, gourmet logo foodstuffs, functional foods, designer water and bottling, with attendant clubs. On to the scene came nouvelle, naturelle and other restaurants, themed rooms in hotels and much more, catering and appealing in many cases to both markets in tandem – consumer desire and the wish to remain slim and healthy.

Chefs and other food and beverage specialists have also contributed to the transferring of styles, practices, experience and foodstuffs around the globe and in doing so have contributed to the general diffusion and deconstructivist approach of modern European cuisine. The transfer of aliments, sometimes caused by the migration and colonization that

Table 5.1 Summary of some potential developments that may affect cuisine and gastronomy in the 21st century

Sociocultural	• Further establishment of the link between the living habits of the population and the trend towards smaller family groups, leading to increasing demand for food and beverages away from the home, either to be consumed away from the home, or to be used as sources of convenience foods
	• Food and beverages, and meal occasions, remaining central to the cultural development of society and the focus for celebration and integration
	• Increased linkages between health and diet, and health promotion booming of greater importance to both the developed and the developing worlds
	• Greater emphasis on the balance of the availability of food resources across lands and peoples
	• Further development of cuisines and gastronomy being driven by advances in travel, tourism and in social development
Economic	• The balance of availability and accessibility of foodstuffs increasingly being used as a measure of the economic prosperity of individual nations
	• The hospitality industry becoming central to the economy of more countries
	• Growth in niche marketing based on the application of sensory differentials for product promotion (signs, senses and signals) and competitive advantage being achieved primarily through differentiation
Political	• Emphasis on the safety of the food chain and the protection of food and beverage supplies, becoming central to political policies
	• Greater recognition and support for the activities of the hospitality industry, simply because of the significance of the contribution it makes to the economies of various countries
Legal	• Greater legislative controls on foodstuffs, especially in newly developed food technologies, alongside controls designed to ensure food safety
	• Greater legislative controls supporting ecological issues
Ecological	• Protection of the natural environment being much higher up the political agenda, and with this the protection of varieties of foodstuffs and endangered species
	• Energy conservation being rewarded and energy waste penalized
	• Food waste caused by political and economic pressure groups ultimately seen as potentially criminal
Technological	• New technologies developing to enhance the availability of food across the globe
	• Heightening of tension between the arguments of food manufacturers for increasing yields and profit, and the ensuring of the safe use of technologies to protect mankind

has taken place throughout European history, has meant the gradual development of what is now recognized as the reality of cuisine sans frontières.

However, there is of course the danger in all generations that people do not look forward enough. There are many changes in cuisine going on all the time but there is always the pressure of conservation, which also brings with it the danger of fossilization. The encouragement and development of fresh ideas can also be stultified and quashed by tradition and by those who urge caution rather than experimentation and learning. Equally all food and beverage professionals must be aware that the ferment of culinary aims should not become so disastrously rich that eclecticism and innovation goes on simply because it is expected by the media.

The development of cuisine, and the approaches to it, is not likely to be squashed by tradition. The dynamics of both the culture and nature of it and its changing forms will prevent this happening in the 21st century, as it has done over the times before. The enterprise, experiment and go-ahead spirit of worldwide food and beverage specialists has created masterpieces and masterworks. Individual characters driven equally with respect for tradition and fresh thinking have been the foundation of a glorious art, which is set to further light up the decades to come.

To reflect where cuisine is today is to consider where it has developed from and where it is going. That is what this book is about. By way of a summary and a consideration of what is happening now and maybe to come, Table 5.1 attempts a summary of some key potential developments that may affect cuisine and gastronomy into the 21st century.

As a result of improved education, increased travel and the increasing ease of international food transit, individuals have in general become much more positive about food and beverages. It certainly looks that there has been, and will continue to be, an air of discovery.

5.2 The status of the chef in society

There has been an increase in the number of chef proprietors developing new means of communicating their art through simplicity and subtlety. There has also been a tendency toward individualization, which is a distinguishing feature of contemporary societies. It is clearly displayed by the chefs who have established their own culinary niche within contemporary culinary culture. They have identified in their diffusion of haute cuisine, and the spawning of a worldwide miscellany of concept cuisines, through their own unique coinages. Examples can be seen in, for instance, Mosimann's Cuisine Naturelle, Nahmias' (Versini's) Cuisine Parfumée, Guérard's Cuisine Minceur, and Vérge's Cuisine du Soleil.

What is also apparent is the fact that Europeans have always had a romantic notion of culinary culture and food's place in their lives, having had a love of food for centuries. However they have not always been sensitively in love with it and fully understood its transmission through time and culture. The Revolutionary period in France can be documented in historic menu strategy. The French were always affected by their own writings and ideas on food. Individuals were once ranked, amongst other things, by their ability to read and write. The written word provided a gateway to differing styles of living and opportunities to learn and advance in all things, including cuisine. What is clear is that the French in cuisine are concept led, and have been from well before the Revolution. Cuisine nouvelle was concept led and was in fact a cuisine improvisée, stemming from cuisine bourgeoisie, and haute cuisine. It was a singular idiom given a new look by the first real designer chefs to utilize diverse materials to create plated art works ranging from the sophisticated to the wildly eccentric.

The modern head chef and the management team must now be able to field many enquiries successfully. Food and beverage operations cannot be run by single individuals alone. Managers must be sought and head chefs and service and other professionals found who are highly skilled and motivated. They must also be able to deal with the pressures of having a busy or absentee proprietor. Additionally they must be self confident enough to handle, for some operations, the fact that the proprietor or principal chef will take all or much of the publicity.

As chefs in general have taken the ownership of a restaurant or a hotel dining room away from its original focus, the passing of the restaurant manager has in many instances been mourned. The restaurant manager was the focal point in the restaurants of old, but the food was not always of equal merit. Today there is a lack of recognition and promotion for the service management as there has been in the past, quite possibly because the chefs, or other business managers, who have to admit that he or she cannot focus entirely on all areas of specialism, have supplanted them. However, it is also true that any of the famous restaurants mentioned in this book, and others in the industry, are offering not simply food and drink, but holistic experiences. The essential contribution to the creation of those experiences by the other food and beverage professionals should not be underestimated. Today service managers and assistants should surely have comparable attention focused on them as the chefs. This century might see this happening.

Today there are chefs using public relations teams, publishers, or private secretaries to promote their books and their businesses, and the media are just as likely to seek the opinion of a top chef as that of a gastronome. Chefs use lexivisual imagery. This lexical imagery stems from the menu, from their writings, press and publications, from the rich meaning and symbolism they employ, which they link to visual imagery and stimuli to add weight and substance. Some of the chefs' books reviewed for this book could be considered works of art in themselves. Witzigmann, Mosimann, Bocuse and Müller, are principal examples that may be cited.

The chef of modern times has to a large extent shaped gastronomy and gastronomes, although it is doubted if they would wholly agree with this statement. In doing so they have followed in the tradition of those that have gone before them and are also contributing to the developments that are to come.

Developing chefs for the future

Achievement begins with attracting the appropriate quality of educators. It commences with the individuals who initially enthuse, motivate and inspire us – the people who give instruction and who instil a desire to enter into a career with tremendous opportunity for the right candidates to progress toward a goal that may lead to independence and the ownership of a business, or who can lead a team of individuals toward ultimate success.

It all starts with career guidance which neither overstates the positive or negative elements but operates from a position of genuine knowledge applied with honesty and professionalism. What is required is information about occupations and the local and national market; advice about education and training; assessment and guidance to help plan the individual's future development on the basis of their existing capabilities and potential; counselling and advice about how to obtain qualifications or credit towards them on the basis of skills and knowledge that they already have through accreditation of prior learning (APL). Careers advice will also support potential candidates not just with CV compilation but also through helping them to know themselves through the exploration of:

- short and medium term goals;
- preferences for working as part of a team or on their own;
- ability to work atypical hours;
- enjoyment in assisting other people;
- seeking a working environment where training takes place;
- preferences for working for a small or large business/organization;
- desire to work in a variety of different areas or focus on one;
- seeking of early responsibility;
- ability to pay attention to detail;
- extent of being goal driven.

This means that careers guidance staff by necessity must make contact with colleges and universities and with the wider industry. It also means that industry must involve itself at this level and ensure that time is spent sending out the correct messages to those who initially sensitize career opportunities to youngsters.

There are a great number of eminent and authoritative chefs, food service and beverage management teachers and writers on cuisine and the hospitality industry. The quality of individuals holding positions of prominence in the field today is greater than ever before. However, for many tutors it is not their inherent ability that is in question but rather the importance of the amount of money and other resources set aside to provide sound, industry-relevant education. Attendant to this there needs to be both a determination and significant vision from governments and individual institutions to enable individuals to operate at their maximum potential. A lack of financing together with a lack of leadership potentially stultifies enthusiasm and maximum engagement with the task of educating. Luckily there are a small band of champions for the hospitality industry around Europe who are determined to make a lasting impression on the individuals they train and help to develop.

Funding for craft-based courses should be the same or similar to funding for other scientific courses. After all, what is the value of management training when the very individuals management will be responsible for are not receiving proper opportunities for success? It is astounding also that an industry which seeks to employ individuals from courses around Europe does not more frequently involve itself with education, except when it requires new blood. There are, of course, positive exceptions to this general rule, which have shown startling results, for companies that ensure that they maintain regular contact with education. Benefits include enthusiastic and motivated employees who have become sensitized not only to the company and its brand, its operating style and systems, but also to the company culture, key players and personnel, and expectations. The individuals are thus more relaxed and attentive, able to land on their feet running, knowing what they are getting involved in. From the companies' point of view, they have the benefit of having followed the candidates throughout their training and of having had an input into and an influence upon the training.

Every European country has its trend setting, inspirational and supremely ambitious and dedicated chefs and other food and beverage specialists, who inspire through not solely their own personality, but from having excellent training programmes for young chefs and other staff.

Anton Mosimann's advice for newly appointed head chefs is to make money first by filling the restaurant, and to aim for the fulfilment of more independent ambitions such as accolades and stars afterwards. 'You also need a creative business mind and the support of your brigade. This comes from being totally committed and remembering that there is an instructional or teaching element in being a head chef which cannot be achieved if the individual is not ready and cannot inspire, lead and develop a team.'

Michel Bourdin was appointed head chef at the Connaught in London at the age of 32, having become a head chef at the age of 30 in Paris. As an individual who is keeping alive traditional custom and practice he laments the disappearance of the rigorous apprenticeship schemes which provided young chefs with comprehensive underpinning in all sections of the kitchen prior to ever contemplating promotion.

If the restaurants and other businesses in this industry are to survive, a continuous supply of individuals who are enthusiastic and highly motivated is required. Michel Bourdin, when asked what the key elements were for him when employing a commis chef for the Connaught Hotel stated:

> The commis' training background is important. For me this is the college they come from, the parental supervision and their love of food. I still think we need to have school leavers interviewed with their parents first and the apprentice next, because if the parents are good parents they will like food, they think food is important and the youngster will also like their food. This is 80 per cent of the potential success. I will also take a person on the recommendation of a colleague.

When asked if there were key differences in his approach to hiring a chef de partie or sous chef Bourdin stated:

> I would generally promote for example a chef de partie from inside the business and according to the number of areas the individual had been working in. If it was someone from outside, I would be interested in which type of place they had come from. These are the most important elements. It is true that I would prefer chefs who had been working with people I know are good mentors and places I know are good training places. I am not interested in people who have done a stage [work placement] that lasted a short period merely to collect their star or distinction or whatever. For me this is not part of the main issue. The main issue is the time they have spent in their last job, what type of department they worked in and who they were working with.

Anton Mosimann was also asked what he thought of the career opportunities for young chefs. He was given the four options: college trained; self-taught (*autodidact*); to work with a rising star, or to work with a Michelin chef. His response was that he always believed in a good basic training:

> If it is college, if it is a restaurant in an hotel, if it is one day a week at college, it depends on the individual – I still believe hands on training has helped me a lot. I did an apprenticeship and one day a week at college for an afternoon and that is how I did the rest of it. . . . I would say half and half, or an apprenticeship with a good chef, whether he is a Michelin chef or not, he needs a good attitude and a good way of training people. That for me is very important. For anybody who is young and wants to go into the

industry, it is vital they go with someone who is determined to make a good pupil out of that student and eventually make a good chef. Good attitude is also important. For the basics of cooking, the chemistry of cooking, college or university is vital, even though hands on experience is equally important.

Mosimann feels that there are excellent opportunities for young chefs today. He feels that young people should be congratulated for entering the profession, they should be given opportunities, and guidelines, and he firmly believes that if they work hard in themselves, there is tremendous possibility to travel the world and to give pleasure to other people.

A hierarchical stratification of chefs

Today's premier chefs are a new breed – respected and admired for their skill, craftsmanship and artistry. The elevation in the standing of the chef has been useful to attract accomplished and imaginative people to the industry, providing a steady supply of new professionals for this expanding industry. Figure 5.1 is an attempt to indicate the various types of chefs that there are, through the identification of a hierarchical stratification.

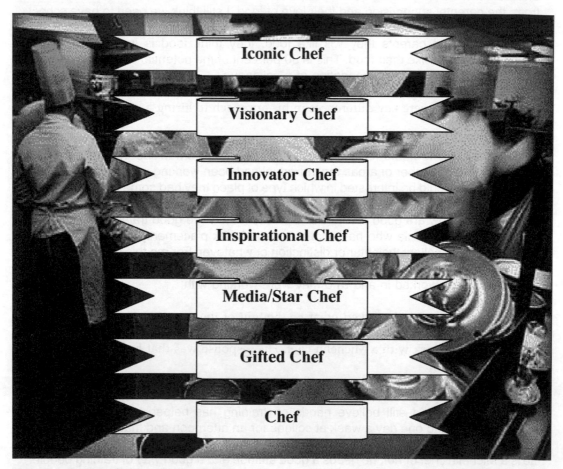

Figure 5.1 A hierarchical stratification of chefs

There are countless good **chefs**, and these form the majority in the trade. There are of course also some poor ones – some of whom, perhaps, will never have been given guidance or opportunity to improve. There will be others who are simply interested in a wage packet.

Next come **gifted chefs**, who are talented and often on a trajectory to greater things. It is worthwhile noting however that not everyone who is gifted will become eminent, as they must be first of all identified and trained to capitalize on their gift.

Media and star chefs are at their best supremely talented and give pleasure by having an agenda to educate and at times delight. They are exuberant, enjoyable to watch and are an excellent form of entertainment and learning. The alternative view is that, at their worst, they are pointless and cheapen the art by becoming meaningless pyrotechnicians, offering nothing but animation and padding between better programming, much of which is the fault of the production companies and not necessarily the TV chef.

Inspirational chefs motivate, inspire and stimulate other chefs and their public; they can energize and galvanize a brigade of chefs and a loyal band of customers behind them.

Innovator chefs are likely to bring in new ideas, make changes and possibly restyle and update existing practices. All the chefs outlined in this book can certainly be classed as innovators and some have gone still further establishing themselves as true visionaries.

Visionary chefs have a strategic style, which is expressed through strategic activity. Visionary chefs are leaders, who have created, designed, introduced or established something new or atypical and are either in the process of evolving or have already evolved it. Evolution refers to the premeditated nature and progress of evolution of a vision. Their vision may have come about through inner reflection or interaction, as is the case with many new dishes and menus.

Finally there is the **iconic chef**, a grand title, but this is a rare breed indeed. For example, Anton Mosimann is an ambassador for cuisine in the UK and in his native Switzerland, Eckart Witzigmann is an ambassador for cuisine in Germany and Paul Bocuse is an ambassador for cuisine in France. Additionally, all of the chefs mentioned in this book may be considered, along with others, as icons of the age. They represent the pinnacle of expression in the art and science of cooking and are at the apex of their industry. Here creativity implies visualizing and conceptualizing; they have all brought into being something that did not previously exist. Their continuous curiosity and observation has inspired interest in gastronomy beyond the boundaries of their own countries. They are niche players with an international profile for themselves and their operations. They are recognized by both practitioners and customers, they are gifted, provide inspiration, innovate and are truly visionary.

These iconic chefs have amassed impressive artistic capital and leave a priceless legacy for the world to enjoy. There are many others who are also contributing to the development of cuisine and gastronomy in the same way as those identified in this book. It is only limitations in time, space and the availability of information that has limited the potential coverage of others. All truly great chefs produce original imaginative and innovative work, often sustained for years, and their contribution is such that they enjoy a prolonged appreciation and reputation, which stretches beyond their own life span.

5.3 Design, vision and leadership

Design

In architecture and interior design, 'design' as a term describes the alchemy of all of the decisions determining how a particular object space or building will appear. Design can distinguish one restaurant from another and also allow determinations of preference, one against another. Virtually every feature of the food and beverages we ingest is affected in some form or other by design. When Raymond Blanc employed interior designer Emily Todhunter in 1998 to design for Le Manoir, he stated 'my problem was that most designers have egos even bigger than chefs. Emily Todhunter was willing to put her ego into a suitcase and work with my ideas. I gave her my dreams and she took them and lifted them.' Blanc had requested rooms that would reflect the subtlety of his food.

At the turn of the century the culture and design of food itself has become more sophisticated and has fascinated not only an eager dining clientele, but also spawned greater interest in the hospitality industry as a sound career choice. The central nature of food and beverages to daily life, tradition, culture and civilization makes it a particularly influential and meaningful vehicle of other kinds of significance. Food and beverages today are required to do so much more than merely fill stomachs – it also, as has been suggested, feeds the senses. What people eat, where and how they eat, describes who and what they are and how we may like to be viewed.

Telfer (1996) determines that the pleasures of food and beverages are not typically found in isolation, and that in some cases the significance of food and eating depends on the eaters' intentions. Eating can bind families together, a practice potentially in decline as fewer meals are taken around the family table, it can strengthen friendships and cement business deals. It can also be treated as overt expression of affluence, hedonism or self-indulgence. It can be viewed as an expression of civilization, style, elegance or luxury. Eating is an integral aspect of social activity, in this way it is also significantly about life skills and citizenship, an aspect, which has never been more important than it is in this century. Food and beverages, and approaches to them, are reflective of the times. It represents humanity and it identifies human-kind. Design then plays an obvious role, as it had done through the ages, in not only creating the stage for these important occasions but also in the management of the experience.

Menu, beverages and meal preparation also involves the alchemy of intricate design decisions – from concept to eventual execution of a dish and its final skilful service and communication to the customers. The creation of distinctive shapes, odours, tastes, textures, colours, mouth-feel and presentation in different combinations are required to create a pleasing whole. This practice is analogous to the working process of a designer. Design is also engaged to create the interior environment that enhances our enjoyment of food and beverage. So enjoyment of food away from home has as much to do with where it is eaten as with how the offerings on the menu and beverage lists are laid out and communicated. The careful proprietor, manager or chef who has unlocked menu architecture and beverage list and design has also become more adept at providing a holistic environment where every possible aspect of the dining experience is considered.

Vision

Business directors and gurus apply the concept of vision to underscore what Mintzberg *et al.* (1998) term 'a desired future state' for their businesses. The starting point, however, is a required investment in a visioning culture within the business, with the final or ultimate achievement being the vision. But vision alone is insufficient for a business to succeed. Visionaries are always alert, scanning and sensing the environment to elicit events and a broad range of phenomena around them. Anything encroaching on their short- or long-term effectiveness is likely to be vigorously scrutinized. Visionaries, however, should not be seen as solitary, remote figures working independently to determine the future of the business. Observation of the most successful businesses and organizations shows that it is dynamic visioning *cultures* that appear to prevail.

The most significant and persuasive vision is a vision shared. Vision comprises so much more than a mere management approach for strengthening the leadership and the efficiency of a high performance restaurant or hotel business. The visionaries observed in this book are all a priori (unconventional) in their approach. What they have established are distinctive individual destination restaurants and hotels with individual personalities. They have also ensured (for some a difficult and lengthy passage) both business and operational success. For them, vision has been an inspirational concept (state of mind), giving them insight into how their business should be formed, how they might evolve in the future, in other words being switched on to identifying and capitalizing on opportunities. Vision is used to perceive both trends and opportunities, and as visionaries they also tend to possess creative imaginations, and are able to see specific results ahead. What distinguishes these individuals still further is the acknowledgement of a nucleus of key management players who work together and are involved in the long-range process of visioning. They also have the strength of character to let their people shine, as viewed in Raymond Blanc's comment 'it is through the dedication and commitment of the whole team at Le Manoir that we strive to meet the guest's demand in every way. We aim to touch excellence in all we do here, whoever we are and whatever we do.'

It is clear that the vision requires assimilating into the core strategy of the business. Consequently visionaries need to assemble around them a formidable team of professionals. This team acquires further skills as they feed off each other (the principle of synergy). It is however essential that they share the same vision and the same guiding philosophy. Communicated and shared core values and beliefs should be sufficient to drive the organization forward. Once the key members of the business share the vision, a dynamic and clearly focused way forward is achievable as key players imbed the norms and culture, values and behaviour of the business with clarity of purpose and intent.

Many of the businesses outlined in this book are motivated by success, not just fiscal success, but the success in having created a great restaurant(s) and or a great hotel. It is about having customer focus, emotional value and emotional connection to your customers, customers delighted to the point of returning and becoming loyal patrons. It is also about having peer recognition, and peers taking notice of what is being done. It is making staff happy to be with them, having low staff turnover, fulfilling their career goals with them. That is what these individuals call success.

Vision is the essence of what the business is about and what it is there to achieve. A vision is more than a simple slogan or mission statement and has to be based on actions as well as words. Many attempts at creating a verbal statement of a company's vision have proven to be empty rhetoric, not recognizing that a live vision is a complex mixture of aspirations, values and how the company does business.

A live vision is more about actions, which take place on an ongoing basis and an amalgam of a number of small events including everyday communication of the key business aims and objectives, daily enthusiasm, and the creation of empathy at all levels. Vision needs to be shared. When a handful of people thinking in the same way come together then the vision will be created which will form the basis for everyday actions within the business. The visionaries are developing the vision, communicating the vision and driving the vision.

Leadership

In the first year of the 21st century over 2000 books were published on aspects of leadership. Leadership necessarily indicates a group phenomenon – the interaction of multiple individuals. The term leadership has only been in common English usage for around 200 years. The term leader from which it originates has however existed since about 1300 AD. The field of leadership theory is highly charged, and many theorists have over time become somewhat disillusioned. Prentice (1961), looked at a range of pitfalls and misconceptions in studying leadership, which were apparent earlier still. He calculated that many individuals were not in point applying themselves to leadership at all, but were investigating the likes of popularity, power, showmanship or wisdom in long range planning. Prentice saw that certain leaders displayed these features, but they were not part of the essence of leadership.

Some of the many definitions of leadership are outlined in Table 5.2. From this table it can be seen that there is no one most desirable method of behaving and no one most desirable

Table 5.2 Some definitions of leadership

Author	Definition of leadership
Clark KE and Clark MB (1994)	Activity/activities, visible to others occurring in a group, organization or institution entailing a leader and followers who by choice subscribe to common purposes and work together to accomplish them
Katz D and Khan RL (1952)	Leadership is the influential increment over and above mechanical compliance with the routine directives of the organization
McGregor Burns J (1978)	The mutual process of mobilizing, by persons with particular motives and values, diverse economic, political and other resources, in a background of competition and conflict, to realize goals separately or mutually held by both leaders and followers
Prentice WGH (1961)	Leadership is the achievement of a goal through the direction of colleagues. Individuals favourably guiding colleagues to achieve specific ends are leaders. Great leaders are individuals who can achieve this long term in a comprehensive range of circumstances
Drucker P (1992)	Leadership concerns work and performance, beginning with thinking through the organization's mission and articulating it, setting goals and standards. One who views leadership as a responsibility as opposed to a rank or privilege. Leaders also need to earn people's trust
Yukl GA (1981)	Leadership entails influencing task objectives and strategies, influencing commitment and compliance in task behaviour to achieve these objectives, influencing group maintenance and identification and influencing the culture of an organization
Wright PL (1996)	Leadership presupposes the existence of followers. The activity of leadership can't be carried out without followers to lead. What leaders do is to direct the behaviour, beliefs and feelings of other group members in an intended direction
Zaleznik A (1966)	Leadership necessarily requires the use of power to influence the thoughts and actions of other people

combination of personality traits to produce leadership effectiveness and success. However, possessing the competency to lead is often viewed as essential to managerial success. There are also many leadership styles, authoritative to participatory, no one of which is likely to be effective in all circumstances. The effectiveness of leadership style should vary according to the situation and benefits from a good degree of flexibility on the part of the leader. There is a definite need, however, to avoid seeming to be inconsistent in style, and so changes in regular style need to be relayed effectively to followers. (General terms applied here are subordinates or followers; for the benefit of this book, the term followers is applied.) The way in which leadership is exercised (leadership style) can have a strong influence on the performance, motivation and morale of followers.

Leaders are more known to initiate rather than merely respond. They are by nature highly competitive types, charged with the need to succeed. There is also a toughness to leaders, a function perhaps of their concentration on the job and the constant demands on their time. Leaders must point the way ahead, lead from the front, an action viewed as superior to pushing from the rear. Leadership also displays two active, crucial and interrelated traits: expertise and empathy. True leaders develop organizations that foster the exercise and cultivation of leadership. The work of leadership is therefore both personal and organizational and includes for example the degree of shared decision making, importance placed on task performance and the taking into account of followers' needs. Communication is another important aspect of leadership, and, for example, for the chefs mentioned in this book approximately 70–80 per cent of their time is directed toward various forms of communication.

Effective leaders understand the purpose of their business, its goals and objectives and are in a position to satisfy them, understanding in the process the implications of their actions. By necessity effective leaders appear to be consistent and clear in their decisions. If followers don't understand the leader it will make no difference how able the individual may really be. It will be difficult to follow the lead of someone like this. If, on the other hand, followers have been fooled and the leader merely appears to have these qualities, individuals are still likely follow the leader until they discover their error. In other words, it is the impression the leader makes at any one time that will determine their influence on followers.

Mintzberg *et al.* (1998) recognized a number of skills which he viewed as fundamentally important to business leaders:

- Communication skills: as Maude (1978) also identified, the importance of continuous communication, with colleagues, followers, media and others.

- Information skills: the ability to acquire, adapt, annotate, present and broadcast information.

- Management skills: the ability to direct followers and get the best possible standard of work from them.

- Disturbance handling skills: the ability to manage interruptions, resolve conflicts, manage crises etc.

- Decision making skills: the ability to arrive at quality outcomes from alternatives and information obtainable. The ability to find the best approach for reaching decisions, e.g. by committee, individual decision, consultation etc.

- Resource allocation skills: the ability to earmark time and other assets to rival demands in a business-like way.

- Entrepreneurial skills: the ability to react quickly, to identify opportunities, innovate and take risks.

- Reflection skills: the ability to conceive and plan their own and the organization's future.

Many breakdowns in leadership can be tracked back to oversimplified misperceptions on the part of the worker or to the leader omitting to recognize the context within which his/her actions will be understood by the follower. Prentice (1961) gave an example from the work of Asch (*Forming Impressions of Personality*, 1946):

> If I describe a man as warm, intelligent, ambitious and thoughtful you get one kind of picture of him. But if I describe another person as cold, ambitious, thoughtful and intelligent you probably get a picture of a very different sort of man. Yet Asch had only changed one word and the order of a couple of others. The kind of preparation that one adjective gives those that follow is tremendously effective in determining what meaning will be given to them. The term 'thoughtful' may mean thoughtful of others or perhaps rational when it is applied to a warm person toward whom we have already accepted a positive orientation. But as applied to a cold man the same term may mean brooding, calculating, plotting. We must learn to be aware of the degree to which one set of observations about an individual may lead us to erroneous conclusions about his other behaviour.

Visionary leadership

Management is the formal process of decision and command. Leadership is one important aspect of management's job, but it is not all of it. Leadership is also about the ability to influence the attitudes and behaviour of others to work toward the vision.

Visionary leadership takes ability and versatility, but the real challenge, and the real reward, is to take who you are and what you are capable of doing, and create the means to achieve your dreams. Self-reliance, to acquire the stamina to persevere, and to develop the vital qualities necessary for success and self-awareness – a powerful human resource – is beneficial. Self-awareness means having a valid opinion of yourself and being aware of all your positive qualities, without arrogance or conceit. A good self-image (the perceived self or the self one supposes oneself to be) contributes to the successful attainment of your goals and determines the way you live your life. Successful people still encounter disappointments and frustrations, but it is the way they respond to problems that makes them different from those who are overwhelmed by difficult situations.

A key aspect of leadership is the provision of guidance and inspiration to others in the business. The visionaries mentioned in this book have had the ambition (or passion) to achieve, to lead an acknowledged team in a determined, productive, profitable and positive enterprise. The inspirational qualities of the visionary leader often require them to use subtle persuasion to motivate and inspire others. This is usually always carried on by the use of simple language infused with rich meaning and metaphor to capture imagination. Communication is all-important for visionary leaders; they often fuse awareness and insight with symbols to evoke emotional responses, which form a richer connection between the visionary and the followers as well as between the idea and action. Anton Mosimann, like many of the others, is a master of this form of cleverly couched communication in such statements as (Gillespie, 2000):

'You never get a second chance to make a first impression' – First impressions are essential at the apex of the hospitality industry. Failures to immediately connect, impress and show the quality of your organization have cost, time and energy implications, which are avoidable. In essence, getting it right the first time is the core priority.

'A great pleasure in life is doing what people say you cannot do' – 'This gives me such a lot of satisfaction, to come back and say "yes we did it, yes here it is". I learned the discipline of adapting businesses to the needs of your customers. If you can't come to us, we will come to you.'

'Good food is not enough, good service is not enough, perfection is the answer' – A realization here that hospitality needs to be approached holistically. If everyone in the organization is working to peak performance and quality, perfection will follow. As Mosimann says: 'Excellent companies are brilliant at the basics.'

'Everything simple is beautiful, everything beautiful is simple' – 'My philosophy has always been simple – use the very best, the very freshest ingredients, but above all keep it simple. A nice quote, but when you unpack it, it can be about a plate of food, accompanying wine, a design, a logo, but with simplicity its essence.'

Once the visionary has the right product team assembled, future vision is usually crafted together with key personnel. This group needs to be 'in sync' to progress, for unless they all understand what they are trying to create, nothing can be created that is of any use. Real understanding comes from working with the operations team. These individuals like the visionary leader are astute lateral (not convergent) thinkers, gathering and processing information about the external environment and the business opportunities, which may allow them to create market advantage.

To summarize then, visionary leaders:

- Are advocators of change
- Have strategic focus
- Are lateral thinkers
- Search for better ways to do things
- Generate new ideas
- Take risks
- Continually learn
- Are customer focused
- Are commercially aware
- Are good at progressing projects (action oriented)
- Understand customer needs/desires in changing environments
- Have awareness of strengths, weaknesses, opportunities and threats
- Are hard working and risk taking.

The visionary's prime competitive advantage is their passion for the business – the hospitality business. Atef Mankarios, Chairman and Chief Executive of Foresthills Hotels and Resorts,[1] when asked what hospitality meant to him replied:

> it is the art of service and the art of creating a pleasant and welcoming environment for those who are out of that environment. When you come to my home and I give you a nice welcome and a good drink. I happen to know what your favourite beer is so as soon as you come in I reach into my fridge and I pull it out for you, I make you feel welcome because this is not your home it is mine. Then you will sit and relax and that would be a good hospitality experience. If I put you on edge, ask you pointed questions, make you feel uncomfortable, you will sit on the edge of your seat and you will wonder when you can leave and how fast you can get out of here. In this case I will have failed you as a host. So, I think that is the art of making people feel comfortable in a different environment.

Handy (1992) identifies the ability to develop a vision with competent leadership behaviour. He established five conditions, which, in his mind, need to be met for competent visionary leadership:

1 The vision has to be different (a view not shared by all theorists). A vision has to reframe the known scene, to reconceptualize the obvious, connect the previously unconnected, dream a dream.

2 It is imperative that others understand the vision. It may be challenging, but ultimately be able to be realized.

3 As well as having ease of comprehension, the vision needs to be memorable.

4 Leaders will both champion and exemplify their vision by their own behaviour and obvious commitment.

5 The leader must bear in mind that if the vision is to be fulfilled it must be one that is shared.

A consequential feature of the visionary leaders cited in this book is the prospect real or imagined that they are a consequence of the historical moment, a product of their times, of their followers, of their opportunities.

5.4 Entrepreneurialism

For gourmets and gastronomes the innumerable features of our well being (welfare, health, happiness, comfort etc.) in hotels, restaurants and other hospitality situations are sustained and elevated by artistic, social and aesthetic entrepreneurs. In this context the entrepreneur is not only the entrepreneurial proprietor but also the food and beverage professional who possesses entrepreneurial skills.

[1] During over 30 years in the hospitality industry Atef Mankarios has guided the development and management of some of the world's most prestigious hotels, which include the Lanesborough in London, the Hotel Bel Air in Los Angeles, The Mansion on Turtle Creek in Dallas and Las Ventanas al Pariso in Los Cabos, Mexico. Some of his views on hospitality management are also given in Chapter 3 (pages 109–12).

The origin of the word entrepreneur significantly hints at the activity. The early French economist Richard Cantillan (1725) is believed to have first used the word, coupling it to those who carried the risk in the economy. It can thus be posited that it was the individual who took the risk between the supplier and the customer. The *Oxford English Dictionary* defines the term entrepreneur as: '. . . a person who attempts to profit by risk and initiative'.

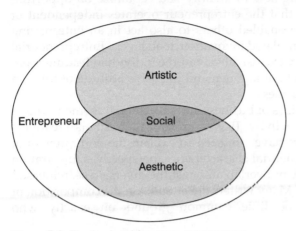

Figure 5.2 The food and beverage entrepreneur

In food and beverage operations, at any level, the business has been developed by visionaries with sufficient leadership ability to turn the vision into reality. They have seen the opportunity and have commercialized it, though this was just part of their strategy as all of them are far from what would be termed conventional entrepreneurs. In which case the question is begged – what kind of entrepreneurs are they? Figure 5.2 attempts to identify the specific makeup of food and beverage entrepreneurs. These individuals require energy, dedication and the right psychological disposition, and so it is not for everyone. However, a greater number of individuals could be more enterprising than they are. Entrepreneurial companies need not by force of circumstance be occupied by genuine entrepreneurs but can be entrepreneurially charged in such a way that rudimentary inducements are targeted to the pursuit of opportunities.

In commercializing opportunities, businesses of whatever size in the hospitality industry require great persistence and diligence in operational, management and strategic detail. Significantly for chefs in particular, capital originates as a consequence of the dissemination of their intuitive artistic and visionary talent. Lucrative hotels and restaurants operated by artistic, social and aesthetic entrepreneurs of the 20th and early 21st century have flourished. However, the entrepreneurs behind businesses identified in this book, and others in the food and beverage field, are most unlikely to be remembered for their money or astute business sense, but for their productive, original and artistic contributions to the hospitality industry. For their value, qualities and skills are affiliated with people's perceptions and gastronomic discernment.

For the food and beverage entrepreneur, as proprietor or as specialist applying his/her entrepreneurial skills to someone else's business, their legacy lies in their unlimited inspiration to successive generations, their establishments, their protégés and those they have trained. For some it will also lie in their publications, the wealth of material written about them, their generosity of spirit and their overriding dedication to quality detail precision and consistency. Anton Mosimann when asked how he wanted to be remembered stated:

A hard question to answer! – an innovative creative person, someone who helped to improve certain standards of food. I have been lucky I have had lots of 'children', my term for those who have worked with me, who are now head chefs in their own rights. It is a good feeling to be 'father' to so many children who have taken the Mosimann concept, the Mosimann system, the Mosimann style of cooking – whatever, to go further, and for me that is a pleasant feeling to be able to state. Also to be one of the youngest chefs ever in a large hotel. Those things are really landmarks.

The vast majority of these imaginatively talented individuals rarely view what they do as arduous or demanding. This can be seen in statements like Anton Mosimann's 'when I wake up in the morning I can't wait to get to work, I love it – every day brings something new'. These professionals do what they do as a result of the pleasure and satisfaction they derive from the job.

True entrepreneurial skill emerges in being able to identify and capitalize on opportunities. It would be wrong however to think that the entrepreneur operates independent of others. The most successful appear to have enabled others to also act in an enterprising manner, which has enhanced loyalty, and stimulated innovation at all levels. Entrepreneurial businesses are not just about size nor are they exclusively about the individual leading them or managing within them. Rather, they are about an open and inclusive attitude of mind, a philosophical process that permeates the business.

Entrepreneurship arises in all forms and sizes of business and its essential theme is one of innovation, giving rise to fresh economic activity. It is a process that entails creativity, teamwork and change. Innumerable authors have ventured to explain the entrepreneurial psyche by attempting to determine entrepreneurial characteristics, perspectives, inspiration and behaviours. Although there is a measure of overlap amongst the diverse research based contributions, conflicting views also remain. Many writers are at odds on the composition of entrepreneurship and there appears to be little common ground on exactly who entrepreneurs are.

Morrison *et al.* (1999) found that it was unrealistic to pursue homogeneity as entrepreneurs come in many contrasting forms. In addition to the differences of opinion on the existence and configuration of personal qualities in entrepreneurs, there is also disagreement as to the degree to which such attributes are present genetically, are societally influenced, or evolve through learned behaviour. One common feature is the fact that these individuals belong to a minority group, with some estimates put at from 1 to10 per cent of the population being genuine entrepreneurs. Bolton and Thomson (2000), who have looked at artistic, social and aesthetic entrepreneurs from other industries and callings, are of the opinion that entrepreneurial talent has to be located before it can be developed and allowed to flourish. They go on to state, 'unfortunately our culture and our education system inhibit the flowering of entrepreneurial talent, it also positively discourages it'.

Entrepreneurs show tremendous proficiency for expanding their own ability and in developing enterprising behaviour in their own people. They pinpoint the most appropriate opportunities accessible to them and use their talent to good advantage. Food and beverage professionals are also artistic, social and aesthetic entrepreneurs who provide abundant encouragement to others. Aesthetic appeal is part of their task, but these professionals are likely to engage other aesthetic agencies, like website designers, graphic designers for letterhead and menu productions and other business stationery, and other aesthetic and image creation consultants, such as interior designers, advertising and public relations specialists, as aesthetic and artistic capital brightens people's lives and lifts their spirits. These businesses play a social and artistic role in bringing like-minded individuals together to celebrate, amongst other elements, good food and good beverages in good company. They play an aesthetic role in making customers feel comfortable in well-designed and sensitive environments as customers are stimulated by art and design. When the atmosphere is right customers relax and if the atmosphere meets their impression of self and the world they live in, they are likely to return. The comparative weight and significance attributed to each aspect of atmosphere creation is, however, a matter of individual perspective and judgement.

Two Swiss hoteliers, Ruch and Tuor, contributing to *Professional Knowledge* (Backman, 1951), wrote the following: 'Anyone who follows this profession of selling food and drink without being a real host to guests, is on the wrong tack.' They continue: 'pleasant relations between head and staff infuse hotel and restaurant with a friendly spirit and the staff perform their task with a feeling of inner satisfaction; this creating a friendly pleasant atmosphere in which the guest feels at home.'

5.5 Gastrosophy – the new science?

In Chapter 1 we identified (see pages 14–15) that the two key determinants of modern gastronomy are:

1 Gastro-geography

2 Gastro-history.

It was suggested there that either or both of these, and/or the elements within them (see pages 17–18) could provide starting points for gastronomic explorations. Within this book we have identified and explored a range of issues related to these two key determinants and the complexity of the interplay between them. Additionally, at the beginning of this chapter we have returned to these key determinants in order to explore the potential developments in cuisine into the 21st century (see pages 159–60).

Also at the beginning of this book we identified four subdivisions of the subject of gastronomy (see page 17). These are:

1 practical gastronomy

2 theoretical gastronomy

3 technical gastronomy

4 food gastronomy.

These subdivisions or perspectives can be adopted for the exploration of the developments within gastronomy and we have, within the book, considered the topic from a number of these perspectives and a combination of them.

In this chapter we have also considered the role of chefs in society and the importance of design, vision and leadership in contributing to the development of food and beverage businesses and, for the food and beverage professional, the necessity for entrepreneurial skills, which make the difference between the ordinary and the inspired.

The foundations laid by Chapter 1 of this book also identified the diverse nature of the subject, with Table 1.1 (page 3) giving thirty-eight examples of subjects, callings, professions and trades which are associated with it. The question has to be posed as to the extent to which this is satisfactory for a subject, which is so central to life and the development of society. There is evidence in this book of those who have made more than substantial contributions to the development of cuisines and gastronomic thinking in their age and beyond. These people combined more than a good knowledge of food and beverages. They have contributed beyond the ordinary. To call some of these people, such as Brillat-Savarin, simply a gastronome, or Escoffier simply a chef, is to minimize their contribution and lasting achievement. These people were more than this. They have been the individuals who have observed, have thought and have had something to say about food and beverages, and through this they have contributed the most to the development of European gastronomic culture. They are also philosophers of their age and again more than that. Fortunately the literature already combines these characteristics and qualities and provides for us the title of **gastrosophers**. This title recognizes the fusion of all the qualities, the skills and the knowledge these people have applied, and through that, in turn, the people this title identifies are those who define the term. The use of such a term also provides the opportunity for a re-evaluation of exploring gastronomy as a legitimate focus for disciplined study, and of giving recognition to those professionals in the food and beverage industry who have and are contributing to this science.

In extraction, gastrosophy is the process of enjoying and reflecting on food, drink and service: the practical and academic interwoven, and complementary. The gastrosopher is an individual who combines theory and practice in the hospitality field, or as Baron Vaerst, a German aristocrat and writer put it (1851): 'This is indeed, along with the practical working knowledge and wisdom in a given area, the most particular duty of the gastrosopher.' Vaerst also proposed that the gastrosopher can be an individual with a great and private love of food and drink, or be the prophet, writing about and sharing their meditations and philosophies on food and beverage, appertaining to their jobs, or areas of specific interest within the spectrum of hospitality. This can be achieved on two levels; first the cognitive (private) level, and secondly, for what is perceived as the greater good of others, the public level.

The word gastrosophy comes from the Greek root 'sophos' meaning wise: if one combines wisdom with the practical skills associated with the affairs of eating and hospitality then one is dealing with gastrosophic concerns. The modern gastrosopher is he or she who works practically in some field appertaining to food and beverage, and who would therefore also be classified as an industry professional of some note. Examples could be in the areas of service, professional cooking, food and beverage management, restaurant or hotel management, science or technical fields, farming, supply, oenology (for example a master of wine), sommelier, negoçiant, brewer, supplier, wine writer or journalist, export director and specialist importer and distributor.

The two fields of gastronomy and gastrosophy are inextricably linked. They both deal with gastronomy, the difference between them being that in the case of the gastrosopher, a considerable knowledge base exists in some area of the hospitality industry. Gastronomy without professional input, and vice-versa, breeds sterility. One side cannot survive without the other. On both sides there are those who view their knowledge base as superior as opposed to complementary, continually seeking supremacy rather than accord. Discordant notes sounded by some gastronomes have become one of the main reasons for applying the label gastrosopher. However, there are distinctive differences and concerns in the two subject fields, just as there are distinctive similarities.

One of the main barriers to membership of gastronomic bodies is that the professional is not welcomed and membership is not therefore given. Other barriers to entry can be to those involved in the academic field and industry education. This applies not simply to professional chefs and waiters but also to the majority of hospitality professionals. There are very few organizations with a mix of professional and amateur joined under a gastronomic banner. Noted and prominent exceptions are La Confrerie de la Chaîne des Rôtisseurs, Ordre Mondiale des Gourmet Dégustateurs, and the Academie de Gastronomie Brillat-Savarin.

A central difficulty facing gastrosophers is the fact that the word cuisine itself is open to a medley of differing interpretations, as has been evident throughout this book. In general it alludes to the manner or style in which food is prepared and produced. As a piece of hospitality terminology its affiliation is usually with a particular nationality, such as French, Germanic, Italian, Spanish, Danish, Belgian or English. However, it also relates to the cooking styles of regional localities, such as French Provençal or Lyonnais, North German,

Bavarian, Scottish and Welsh. It also pertains to general cooking styles like haute cuisine, cuisine nouvelle, cuisine gourmande and cuisine parfumée, and to cultural clusters such as, Alsacienne, Basque, Bordelais, Lorraine and Picardian.

Cuisine holds a lot more for the individual than feeding alone portrays, and has symbolic significance. It is easy to contemplate commensality (eating at the same table, togetherness) and hospitality to be at the heart of sociality. Gastrosophers in many ways have not invested enough time in this area. In many cases people no longer go out simply to eat a meal; as demonstrated in this book, many other things come into play. Eating is a social activity and includes culturally valued characteristics such as fraternity, companionship, the rite of inclusion, rites of passage (significant birthdays, confirmations, bar mitzvahs etc.), pleasure, wealth, appeal to the senses, savoir-faire, kudos, the confirmation of a bond, reciprocity, celebration, business, to cement agreements, networking, to be seen in the right venue, family gatherings, ceremonial, special events and so on. It is also an addendum to the promotion of tourism, but can sometimes be used by the solo-eater, the lonely seeking company and companionship, or by those seeking reconciliation.

Gastrosophy is hindered by its lack of common usage. In many cases it would seem to suffer from having a similar coinage as gastronomy, in that it is a word only commonly understood by those who work with it. Gastrosophers have to a greater or lesser extent laboured to avoid habituation of the senses. What they failed to predict was the sheer volume of inexperienced practitioners who would piratically obtain their methods. It was not the fact that copies were being made; it was the fact that in many cases they were not always true to the original work. Cuisine nouvelle is a case in point; the movement gained momentum so quickly that interpretations were made which bore no resemblance to the original ethos. For example, the structure of a menu should have the occurrence of varying sensations in-built. In nouvelle cuisine some practitioners fed their diners on, for example, purées of vegetables, which were, of course, brilliant in their execution and correct in their inclusion at the source, but in the wrong hands many individual gastronomes and clients were sickened by habituation, and by the unadorned brutality of the cuisine.

Binding and contrasting features of gastronomy and gastrosophy

The common threads binding gastrosophy and gastronomy are that they are both linked to hospitality. They both deal with food and beverages; they both require skill to perfect; they both deal with a subject matter that is continually changing in the short term, and they both require commitment and a love of the subject to obtain optimum benefit from what will be a lifelong process of education. Rich meaning is hypothesized here to be a central linking feature of the commercial and domestic existence of gastronomy and gastrosophy.

Gastrosophers and gastronomes have for centuries banded together forming *confreries* (brotherhoods), both professional and amateur, which split up through time. In contemporary society those that still exist and those which have been newly formed, have much looser links founded on amity and healthy competition.

There are historical differences between gastronomy and gastrosophy. A major consequence of this is that gastronomy, in the sense of haute cuisine specifically, has a poor image. Gastronomy and gastrosophy also differ in that gastronomy is generally carried on by amateurs, no matter how enthusiastic, or by those with independent means. Gastrosophers, however, are professionals, and chefs and other food and beverage professional gastrosophers in particular earn their living from hospitality. Gastrosophy is a specialism for professional expertise in gastronomy and hospitality and both gastrosophers and gastronomes have enriched their specialism with alimentary philosophy.

Gastrosophers like gastronomes are fired by a passion for good food and beverages. The driving force varies from individual to individual, but the gastrosophers and gastronomes identified in this book are, and have been inspired to be, the best they possibly can be. Gastrosophers and gastronomes share a skill and wisdom in matters of eating. Gastrosophers like the gastronome are concerned with the assessment and improvement of the quality of food and beverages in the context of the occasion.

Gastrosophers are every bit as propagandist as gastronomes, and their literary output is much more sizeable than that of gastronomes. However, in journalistic terms, the gastrosophers today have more similar opportunities. In the past there was a total reversal where chefs did little or no promotion of themselves or their businesses, and their publications (apart from a small number of notable exceptions) were few. Today the chef gastrosophers use public relations teams, publishers, or private secretaries to promote their books and their businesses, and the media are just as likely to seek the opinion of a top chef as that of a gastronome.

The gastrosopher can clearly be an individual with a great and private love of food and drink, but in general the gastrosopher's is a profession more in line with that of the prophet, writing about and sharing their meditations and philosophies on food and beverages, appertaining to their jobs and expansive fields of interest within the province of the hospitality industry.

The provision of open inspiration for all and not just an élite

A succession of cultural and technological factors has brought the chef gastrosophers to the position they occupy today. In many ways it is the international chef gastrosophers who are the modern-day keepers of the flame for contemporary gastronomy and its reputation. Their overriding qualification is a sense of responsibility for their actions, dedication to their craft and professionalism.

Stemming from France in the late 1960s there has been a virtual revolution in culinary philosophy and practice. A new spirit of creativity and dynamism took hold of the chef gastrosophers, gastronomy and hospitality. Cuisine took on a new hybrid identity, and contemporary culinary art is a distillation of the modern gastrosopher's imagination stemming from this period. This hybridization has spurred an eclectic profusion of concept cuisines envisioned by top class chef gastrosophers. Cultural experience must be relied on to a greater or lesser extent and on those who define what is indeed perceived to be gastronomic; the gastronomes and the gastrosophers do this and it is then up to individuals to follow those in whom they place most trust and whom they most admire.

In chronicling divergent cuisines, parallels can be drawn with the top fashion houses of the world whose designers bi-annually have to produce a new collection or remodel and update existing themes or lines. Basically, in the case of the chef gastrosopher, like the designer, the ensemble takes place in the brain. This is of course a greatly simplified analogy, since the chef gastrosopher takes into account changing tastes, and food fashions of the year – current and past examples are Thai dishes on the menu, gourmet pizzas, oriental spicing of dishes, anything in a sausage skin or caul, and anything smoked. These were the chef gastrosophers' 'food' collections at the close of the last century and were just as likely to work their way across Europe and be piratically remodelled by chefs in all kinds of hotels and restaurants. In many cases the food fashion may be founded more on culinary locution (terminology), as seen in the vogue for flamboyant menu terminologies like pools of sauce, light, airy, pyramids (anything pyramidical and stemming from antiquity, particularly to do with sweets). Haunting plated geometries under the heading plated art have also been much in evidence.

The phenomenon of fame and star status in gastrosophy is not created by a single individual. It may be engendered in one individual, but it is generated by a willing and dedicated public and media. However, the true success comes as a result of a group of skilled craftspeople functioning collaboratively and fraternally, of which the chef gastrosopher is really the conductor; the 'art' is orchestral and what results from this socially conducted synthesis should be symphonic.

Most chefs and gastrosophers, if honest about it, will create few true designer creations in their lives. Most create anew that which has been worked on in the past, by remodelling, changing ingredients, cooking methods, menu terminology, but also from their own culinary repository, and from their staff's pooled ideas, from foreign travels, from other gastrosophers, and through culinary piracy. The hospitality industry, and gastronomy and gastrosophy are dynamic, and ever changing, and full of complex social action and reaction to various stimuli. As such they are ripe for social research.

Chapter 1 identified a range of callings, specialisms, professions and trades, which overlap with, and at the same time are part of, the exploration of gastronomy, and which could form a basis for respectable and rigorous interdisciplinary collaborative work. Academia has to a greater or lesser extent ignored what is truly fertile ground for social research partly because of the problems of finding appropriate research methods. However, academia might usefully remind itself of Douglas (1966), when she states: 'we must take the problems of objectively determining the social meanings of actions to the actors as the fundamental problem'. The problem for gastrosophers and gastronomes is that they must also wish to find more valid ways of approaching and portraying the meaning, symbolism and semiology which they freely use, and with which they fill their lives. Trow's quotation from 1957 (in Burgess, 1982) is useful advice: 'get on with the business of attacking our problems with the widest array of conceptual and methodological tools that we possess and they demand'. The productive array of social, scientific and anthropological research that could flow from sectors of academia collaborating with gastrosophers and gastronomes can only, and very beneficially, enrich our understanding of our nature and culture. Understanding the differences and similarities between the gastrosopher and the gastronome could commence through taking a developmental perspective. The 21st century awaits the response to the challenge.

5.6 Summary

This chapter has first considered the influences on cuisine at the beginning of the 21st century. The status of the chef in society has been examined; the need for the development of future chefs and an identification of levels has been given for a proposed stratification of chefs. The importance of design, vision and leadership to the development of food and beverage operations has been examined, as well as the necessity of entrepreneurial skills, both in the owners of food and beverage businesses and in those who are employed in them, in order to develop them beyond the ordinary. The chapter has then explored the relationship between gastronomy and philosophy in those who have contributed the most to the development of European gastronomic culture. These people have been more than chefs, gastronomes and philosophers; they are the gastrosophers, a term that recognizes the fusion of all of these things and through that, the recognition of gastrosophy as a new and legitimate science. Finally, a plea has been made for greater emphasis on and recognition for the exploration of gastronomy as a rich source of material for legitimate study.

Some significant figures in the world of gastronomy named in the text

Diane Ackerman	Writer, author of *A Natural History of the Senses* (1995)
Grace Léo Andrieu	Owner of the Montalembert Hotel in Paris
Pierre Androuet	Gatronome, restaurateur and author of the *Guide de Fromage*, the most authoritative work on the subject
Marcus Gavius Apicius	Gastronome
Archaestrate	4th century BC Greek cook, poet, philosopher, traveller and gastronome
Atheneus	Greek author
Bacchus	Classical Roman god of wine whom the Greeks called Bacchos, or more frequently Dionysus
Robert Baty	Gastronome
Antoine Beauvilliers	1752–1820. Paris chef, restaurateur and author
Dr Auguste Becart	Gastronome
Felix Benoit	Fernand Point's biographer. It was he who termed Point 'the Pharaoh of the Pyramide in Vienne'
Raymond Blanc	Chef proprietor, author, broadcaster, businessman and gastronome. Le Manoir aux Quat' Saisons, Church Road, Great Milton, Oxford, England
Jean Anthelme Brillat-Savarin	1755–1826. French magistrate, author, philosopher and gastronome

Paul Bocuse	Chef proprietor, businessman, author, broadcaster and gastronome. Paul Bocuse, 40 rue de la Plage, Place d'Illhausern, 69660 Collonges-au-Mont-d'Or, France; L'Abbaye de Collonges Quai de la Jonchère, 69660 Collonges-au-Mont-d'Or, France
Etienne Boileau	Grand Provost of Paris in the time of Louis IX – assembled the 'Livre de Metiers' (Book of Trades)
Nicholas de Bonnefons	Writer and valet to King Louis XIV
Boulanger	Proprietor of a Paris café in the rue des Poulies who, in 1765, became the first Paris restaurateur
Xaviour Marcel Boulestin	1878–1943. Writer and chef restaurateur offering authentic French haute cuisine in London. Marcel Boulestin was Britain's first television chef; amongst other things he wrote a column in *Vogue*
Alfonso Borgia	Founder of the Borgia family fortune; became Pope Calixtus III
Rodrigo Borgia	Became Pope Alexander VI
Michel Bourdin	Chef des Cuisines, philosopher, classicist and gastronome. The Connaught Hotel, Carlos Place, Mayfair, London W1Y 6AL
Richard Cantillan	18th century French economist thought to have coined the term entrepreneur
Marie Antoine Carême	1784–1833. The most sought after French chef and gastronomer of his age
Antonnio Carluccio	Restaurateur, author, broadcaster and gastronome
Alain Chapel	1939–1990. Apprenticed with Vignard in Lyons then with Fernand Point in Vienne before working with many of the top chefs in France. Responsible for a traditional country cuisine with inspiration from Japanese cuisine. He also opened a restaurant bearing his name in Kobe, Japan
Curnonsky (Maurice Edmond Sailland)	1872–1956. Prince elect of gastronomes. Author. In 1928 he founded the Academy of Gastronomes
Elizabeth David	Actress, author and broadcaster
Jean Delaveyne	Mentor to Michel Guérard, often termed his spiritual father. He set up 'La Chambre Syndicale de la Haute Cuisine Française', the French Haute Cuisine Union (CSHCF), on 16 September 1986 with Joël Robuchon assisted by Jacques Bruel
Dionysus	The Greek god of ecstasy, wine and music (*See* Bacchus)

Alain Ducasse	Chef proprietor, author, broadcaster philosopher and gastronome. Le Louis XV, Hotel de Paris, Place du Casino, 98000 Monte Carlo. Also, Alain Ducasse, SAS 'Hotel Le Parc', 59 avenue Raymond Poincaré, 7516 Paris, France
Adolphe Dugléré	1805–1874. Chef of the restaurant 'Les Provenceaux' in Paris and at the CaféAnglais
Georges Auguste Escoffier	1846–1935. Chef, author, gastronome. One of the leaders of ancienne cuisine, having a massive impact on gastronomy
Epicurus	Philosopher 324–270 BC
Sir Clement Freud	Gastronome
Paul Gaylor	Chef de Cuisine, author and gastronome. (Internationally renowned specialist in vegetarian cuisine.) The Lanesborough Hotel, Hyde Park Corner, London, SW1X 7TA
Michel Genin	Gastronome
Philéas Gilbert	1872–1925. Chef, gastronome, author. Collaborated with Escoffier on *Le Guide culinaire*
Count Erwin Graf Matuschka Greiffenclau	Viticulturist, philosopher and gastronome. Proprietor of Schloss Vollrads in Germany. A great proponent on food and wine combining and the promotion of drier wine styles in Germany. Died 1997
Jane Grigson	Broadcaster, writer, author, gastronome and cook
Sophie Grigson	Broadcaster, writer, author, gastronome and cook, daughter of Jane
Alexandre Balthasar Laurent Grimod de la Reynière	1758–1837. Gastronome, writer, critic, philosopher. Grimod de la Reynière had a massive impact on gastronomy
Michel Guérard	Chef proprietor, author, broadcaster, businessman, philosopher and gastronome. Les Prés d'Eugénie, Eugenie-les Bains, 40320 Geaune, Landes, France
Johannes Gutenberg	Developed the principle of movable type. Born 14th century
Paul, Marc and Jean Pierre Haeberlin	Gastronomes and proprietors Auberge de l'Ill, 2 rue de Collonges, 68970 Illhaeusern, Alsace, France. Gastronomes
Madhur Jaffrey	Cook, actress, author, writer and broadcaster
Hans Matthias Kann	Executive Assistant Manager, Food and Beverage, Oberoi Hotels
Kasavana and Smith	Coined the term 'menu engineering', a sales mix analysis tool which utilizes data from the sales mix and assigns to it a percentage according to overall sales signalling whether it should be replaced, repositioned, repriced or retained

Liam Lambert	Director and General Manager, Mandarin Oriental Hyde Park hotel, London
Paul Levy	Journalist, writer and broadcaster
Vincent de La Chapelle	Chef to Lord Chesterfield and to William of Orange. Author of several books
François Pierre de La Varenne	1618–1678. Founder of French classical cuisine
Lucius Licinus Lucullus	110–56 BC. Gourmet who brought back rare foodstuffs to Rome. Lucullus was a Roman general renowned for his wealth and luxurious feasting. Several dishes in the classical *répertoire* are termed Lucullus and feature elaborate preparation and costly ingredients – especially truffles
Atef Mankarios	Chairman and Chief Executive, Foresthills Hotels and Resorts. He has guided the development of some of the world's most prestigious hotels
Gualtiero Marchesi	Chef proprietor, writer, businessman, broadcaster and gastronome. Gualtiero Marchesi, Via Vittoria Emannuele II, No. 11, 25030 Erbusco (Brescia), Italy
François Marin	Chef to Prince de Soubise. He wrote *Les Dons de Comus* in 1739
François Massialot	Last premier cook of the 1600s
Catherine de Medici	1519–1589. Influential wife of one French King and mother to three kings. Introduced the Florentine art of table decoration to the court
Marie de Medici	1573–1642. French queen. Had similar achievements to Catherine's at the start of the 17th century
Giovanni de Medici	1475–1521. Became Pope Leo X. He was a theatrical epicure
Menon	Author of *La Cuisine bourgeoisie*, 18–19th century best-selling book
Helen Porter Mitchell	The diva 'Nellie Melba'. Melba was a stage name derived from her links with Melbourne. She was an Australian soprano and regular frequenter of the Savoy Hotel in London where Escoffier named 'Pêches Melba' in her honour
Marc Meneau	Chef proprietor, businessman, author, broadcaster, philosopher and gastronome. L'Ésperance, 899450 Saint-Père-sous-Vezelay, Yonne, France
Anton Mosimann	Chef proprietor, author, broadcaster, businessman, philosopher and gastronome. Mosimann's, 11b West Halkin Street, Belgrave Square, London, SW1X 8JL

Dieter Müller	Chef proprietor, businessman, author, broadcaster and gastronome. Schlosshotel Lerbach, Lerbacher Weg, Lerbach im Bergisch Glasbach, Germany
Bernard Naegellen	Long term Director of Red Guides, Michelin
Dominique Nahmias (Olympe Versini)	Chef proprietor, author, broadcaster, businesswoman and gastronome. Casa Olympe, 48 rue St Georges, 9th Arrondissement (Opéra), Paris, France
Edouard Nignon	1865–c.1934. French chef. Generally regarded as one of France's greatest culinary craftsmen
Raymond Oliver	Born 1909. Chef proprietor of 'Le Gand Vefour' in Paris, author innovator and gastronome
Louis Outhier	Chef proprietor, L'Oasis, 06210 Mandelieu-la-Napoule, France
Petronius	Emperor Nero's arbiter of elegance
Lionel Poilâne	World renowned Paris baker, author, philosopher and gastronome
Fernand Point	1897–1955. Chef and gastronome. The father of contemporary gastronomy
Dr Edouard Pozerski de Pomiane	1875–1964. French gastronome and nutritionist
Marcel Proust	1871–1922. French novelist and gastronome
César Ritz	1850–1918. His name is synonymous with luxury and good living
Jancis Robinson	Wine expert, journalist, author, broadcaster, presenter, narrator and gastronome
Joël Robuchon	Chef proprietor, author, broadcaster, philosopher and gastronome. Jamin, 32 rue de Longchamp, 75116 Paris, France
Claudia Roden	Cook and author
Egon Ronay	Gastronome
Gioachino Antonio Rossini	1792–1868. Italian operatic composer. Tournedos Rossini was named after him by Escoffier
Albert Roux	Chef proprietor, author, broadcaster and gastronome. Founder of Le Gavroche
Michel Roux	Chef proprietor, author, broadcaster, patissier and gastronome. The Waterside Inn, Ferry Road, Bray on Thames, England
Michel Roux (Junior)	Chef, Le Gavroche, 43 Upper Brook Street, London W1Y 1PF

Scotto Sisters	Cooks, authors and broadcasters
Alain Senderens	Chef proprietor, businessman, author, broadcaster, philosopher and gastronome. Lucas Carton, 9 Place de la Madeleine, 75008 Paris, France
Alexis Benoist Soyer	1809–1858. Was employed by the Duke of Cambridge and later became chef of the Reform Club in 1837. Had a great influence on the kitchen and chefs in general
Delia Smith	Author and broadcaster. She has had a massive impact on the education of an interested public in the UK on matters of simplifying and demystifying cooking
Rick Stein	Chef proprietor, broadcaster, author, philosopher and gastronome. He has successfully increased diminishing interest in fish consumption and cuisine in general in the UK
Taillevent (born Guilaume Tirel)	c.1310–c.1395. First prominent French chef to make his mark on gastronomic history
Jean and Pierre Troisgros	Chef proprietors, authors, broadcasters and gastronomes. Hotel, Restaurant Troisgros, Place Jean Troisgros, 42300 Roanne, France
Baron Vaerst	19th century German aristocrat writer and gastronome. Coined the term gastrosopher
Jean Valby	Gastronome, headed for many years La Confrerie de la Chaîne des Rôtisseurs
Norman Van Aken	Current founder of the latest version of fusion cuisine. Proprietor of 'Norman's' located in the Coral Gables area of Miami USA
Roger Vergé	Chef proprietor, businessman, author, broadcaster, philosopher and gastronome. Le Moulin de Mougins, Avenue Notre-Dame-de-Vie, 06250 Mougins, France
Anne Willan	Writer, broadcaster and proprietor of a cookery school
Eckart Witzigmann	Chef proprietor, businessman, author, broadcaster, consultant and gastronome. Palazzo dell' Arte & Gusto, Waterloo Platz, Hannover, Germany; Cas Puéres, Calle Isabel II, 39 E-07100 Sólle Mallorca amongst others
Heinz Winkler	Chef proprietor, writer, broadcaster and gastronome. Residenz Heinz Winkler, Kirchplatz 1, 83229 Aschau, Germany

Trade, professional and gastronomic contacts

Academy of Culinary Arts
53 Cavendish Road
London
SW12 0BL

Academy of Food and Wine Service
Burgoine House
8 Lower Teddington Road
Kingston upon Thames
Surrey
KT1 4ER

British Nutrition Foundation
High Holborn House
52–54 High Holborn
London
WC1V 6RQ

Cookery and Food Association
1 Victoria Parade
331 Sandycombe Road
Richmond
Surrey
TW9 3NB

Court of Master Sommeliers
1 Seaway Close
Chelston
Torquay
TQ2 6PY

Craft Guild of Chefs
1 Victoria Parade
331 Sandycombe Road
Richmond
Surrey
TW9 3NB

École des Arts Culinaires et de l'Hôtellerie
Château du Vivier
BP 25 69131
Ecully
France

École Lenôtre
40 rue Pierre-Curie
BP6 78373
Plaisir
France

École Nationale Supérieure de Pâtisserie
Château de Montbarnier
BP48 43200
Yessingeaux
France

École Ritz Escoffier
15 Place Vendôme
75001 Paris
France

European Catering Association
Bourne House
Horsell Park
Woking
Surrey
GU21 4LY

Fondation Auguste Escoffier
06270 Villeneuve-Loubet
France

Guild of Food Writers
48 Crabtree Lane
London
SW6 6LW

Guild of International Professional
Toastmasters
and
Ivor Spencer School for Professional
Toastmasters
12 Little Bornes
London
SE21 8SE

Hotel and Catering International
Management Association (HCIMA)
191 Trinity Road
London
SW17 7HN

Institute of Masters of Wine
Five Kings House
1 Queen St Place
London
EC4R 1QS

International Wine and Food Society
9 Fitzmaurice Place
London
W1X 6JD

L'Academie des Gastronomes
Brillat-Savarin
7 rue Aumale
F75009 Paris
France

La Confrerie de la Chaîne des Rôtisseurs
Association Mondiale de la Gastronomie
7 rue Aumale
F75009 Paris
France

L'Ordre Mondiale des Gourmets
Degustateurs
7 rue Aumale
F75009 Paris
France

Michelin
46 Avenue de Breteuil
F-75324 Paris
Cedex 07
France

Michelin Tyre plc
Michelin Travel publications
The Edward Hyde Building
38 Clarendon Road
Watford
WD1 1SX

RAC Motoring Services
RAC House
1 Forest Road
Feltham Middlesex
TW13 7RR

Relais & Chateaux Relais Gourmand
15 rue Lamennais
F 75008 Paris
France

Relais & Chateaux Relais Gourmand
Hannover Strasse 55/56 3100
Celle
Germany

Relais & Chateaux Relais Gourmand
28 Basil Street
London
SW3 1AT

Restaurant Association of Great Britain
Africa House
64–78 Kingsway
London
WC2B6AH

Vegan Society
Donald Watson House
7 Battle Road
St Leonards-on-Sea
East Sussex
TN37 7AA

Vegetarian Society UK Ltd
Parkdale
Dunham Road
Altrincham
Chesire
WA14 4QG

Wine and Spirit Education Trust
Five Kings House
1 Queen Street Place
London
EC4R 1QS

Bibliography

Aaron JP (1973) *Le Mangeur du XIXeme siecle* (The Art of Eating in France: Manners and Menus in the Nineteenth Century) Robert Lafont, Paris

Aaron JP (1975) *The Art of Eating in France*, Peter Owen, London

Ackerman D (1995) *A Natural History of the Senses*, Vintage Books, New York

Anderson RE (1899) *Gastronomy as a Fine Art*, by Jean Anthelme Brillat-Savarin, Chatto and Windus, London

Andrien P (1956) *Fine Bouche: A History of the Restaurant in France* (trans. AL Hayward), Cassell, London

Arcier M (1990) *Aromatherapy*, BCA, London

Arnott ML (1975) *Gastronomy. The Anthropology of Food and Food Habits*, Mouton, The Hague

Artusi P (1891) *The Science of Cooking and the Art of Eating Well*, Florence

Asch SE (1946) 'Forming impressions of personality', *Journal of Abnormal and Social Psychology*, 41, pp. 258–90

Backman W (1951) *Professional Knowledge*, Vol. III, McLaren, London

Baudrillard J (1993) *The Transparency of Evil: Essays on Extreme Phenomena* (trans. James Benedict), Verso, London

Bebe-Center JG (1949) 'Standards for the use of the gust scale', *Journal of Psychology*, 28, pp. 411–19

Beck LW and Holmes RL (1968) *Philosophic Enquiry: An Introduction to Philosophy*, Prentice Hall, London

Bennus W and Nanus B (1985) *Leaders: The Strategies for Taking Charge*, Harper Collins, New York

Berriedal-Johnson M (1996) 'A Short Biography, Alexis Benoist Soyer', part of the leaflet of the Alexis Benoist Soyer Monument Appeal, London

Black M (1985) *Food and Cooking in 19th Century Britain*, English Heritage, London

Black M (1985) *Food and Cooking in Medieval Britain: History and Recipes*, English Heritage, London

Blake A and Crewe Q (1978) *Great Chefs of France*, Mitchell Beazley, London

Balmforth H (1992) *A Chef's Guide to Nutrition*, Cambridge University Press, Cambridge

Blanc G (1987) *The Natural Cuisine of Georges Blanc*, Webb and Bower, Exeter

Blanc R (1988) *Recipes from Le Manoir aux Quat' Saisons*, Macdonald, London

Blanc R (1991) *Cooking for Friends*, Headline Books, London

Bochenski JM (1962) *Philosophy*, Reidel Publishing Company, Dordrecht

Bocuse P (1978) *The New Cuisine*, Granada, London

Bocuse P (1979) *The Cuisine of Paul Bocuse*, Granada, London

Bocuse P (1991) *Bocuse's Regional French Cooking*, Flammarion, Paris

Boddy D (1991)*Walk the Talk*, BBC Education, Scotland

Bolton B and Thompson J (2000) *Entrepreneurs: Talent, Temperament, Technique*, Butterworth-Heinemann, Oxford

Borrel A (1992) *Dining with Proust*, Ebury Press, London

Bowden GH (1975) *British Gastronomy*, Chatto and Windus, London

Brears P (1985) *Food and Cooking in 16th Century Britain: History and Recipes*, English Heritage, London

Brears P (1985) *Food and Cooking in 17th Century Britain: History and Recipes*, English Heritage, London

Brillat- Savarin JA (1899) *Gastronomy as a Fine Art* (trans. RE Anderson), Chatto and Windus, London

Brillat-Savarin JA (1970) *La Physiologie du gout*. Hermann, Paris (English translation as 'The Philosopher in the Kitchen', by Anne Drayton, Harmondsworth, Penguin, 1975)

Burgess J (1982) 'Perspectives on gift exchange and hospitable behaviour', *International Journal of Hospitality Management*, I, pp. 49–57

Buttle F (1996) *Hotel and Food Service Marketing – a Managerial Approach*, Cassell, London

Cannon G and Walker C (1984) *Food Scandal: What's Wrong with the British Diet and How to Put It Right*, Century, London

Capatti A (1990) *Le Gout du nouveau: origines de la modernité alimentaire* (The Taste for Novelty: Origins of Alimentary Modernity), Albin Michel, Paris

Centrale Marketinggesellschaft der Deutscher Agrarwirtschaft. (1992) *Central Marketing Organisation of German Agricultural Industries*, Wimbledon

Ceserani V, Kinton R and Foskett D (1999) *Practical Cookery*, 9th edn, Hodder and Stoughton, London

Christian VA (1979) *The Concept of Hospitality*, International Jubilee Conference, Hogere Hotel School, The Hague

Clark KE and Clark MB (1994) *Choosing to Lead*, Leadership Press, Geensboro, NC

Clarke HC (1969) *Menu Terminology*, Pergamon Press, London

Cobb R (1975) *A Sense of Place*, Duckworth, England, p. 4

Conway H (1998) 'Last word in luxury', *Caterer and Hotelkeeper*, 28 May, p. 52, Reed, London

Coon, Carlton S (1962) *The History of Man: From the First Human to Primitive Culture and Beyond*, Cape, London

Cooper R (1983) *Spirits and Liqueurs*, Hamlyn, Middlesex

Cousins J, Foskett D and Gillespie C (2001) *Food and Beverage Management*, 2nd edn, Pearson Education, Harlow

Cullen NC (1996) *The World of Culinary Supervision, Training and Management*, Prentice Hall, Englewood Cliffs, NJ

Davies J (1990) *The Victorian Kitchen Garden*, BBC Books, London

Davis B (1983) *Food Commodities*, Heinemann, London

Dennis-Jones H (1972) *Zones of Cuisine*, Letts Travel Guides, London

Dixon R (1993) *The Management Task*, Butterworth-Heinemann, Oxford

Douglas M (1966) *Purity and Danger: An Analysis of the Concepts of Pollution and Taboo*, Routledge and Kegan Paul, London (MIT Press, Cambridge, MA, 1980)

Drayton A (1975) *The Philosopher in the Kitchen*, Penguin, London, and Hermann, Paris

Drucker P (1992) 'Leadership – more doing than dash', in *Managing for the Future*, Butterworth-Heinemann, Oxford

Dubois U (1870) *Artistic Cookery: A Practical System Suited for the Use of the Nobility and Gentry and for Public Entertainment* Longmans Green and Company, London

Dubois U and Bernard E (1881) *La Cuisine classique*, E Dentu, Paris

Duby G (1973) *Guerriers et paysannes* (Warriors and Peasants), Gallimard, Paris

Durkan A and Cousins J (1995) *The Beverage Book*, Hodder and Stoughton, London

Edwards J (1984) *The Roman Cookery of Apicius, translated and adapted for the modern kitchen*, Rider Books, London

Engen T (1982) *The Perception of Odours*, Academic Press, New York

Escoffier A (1903) *Le Guide culinaire: aide mémoire de cuisine practique*, Flammarion, Paris

Escoffier A (1934) *Ma Cuisine*, Paul Hamlyn, London

Escoffier A (1979) *The Complete Guide to the Art of Modern Cookery* (trans. HL Kracknell and RJ Kaufmann), Butterworth-Heinemann, Oxford

Farb P and Armagelos G (1980) *Consuming Passions: The Anthropology of Eating*, Houghton Mifflin, Boston, MA

Fine GA (1996) *Kitchens: The Culture of Restaurant Work*, University of California Press, Berkeley, CA

Flandrin JL (1982) 'L'ancien service à la française', in *Chronique de platine pour une gastronomie historique*, Odile Jacob, Paris, pp. 90–2

Forster R and Ranum O (1979) *Food and Drink in History: Selection from the Annales economies sociétés civilisations*, Vol. V, Johns Hopkins University Press, Baltimore, MD and London

Geldard FA (1972) *The Human Senses*, John Wiley and Sons, New York

Gillespie C and Morrison A (2000) 'Symbol, sign and senses: a challenge to traditional market communication?', *The Hospitality Review* (Threshold Press Ltd, Newbury, UK), 4, pp. 12–18

Gillespie C (2000) 'Anton Mosimann: from chef to cook to businessman', *The Hospitality Review*, 7 (Threshold Press Ltd, Newbury, UK)

Girardet F (1985) *Cuisine Spontanée* (trans. S Campbell), Macmillan, London

Gostelow M (1992) 'Changing passions: food trends', *Great Hospitality*, 10, 1 (Motivate Publishing Ltd, London)

Guérard M (1978) *Michel Guérard's Cuisine Gourmande*, Macmillan, London

Guérard M (1992) *Minceur Exquise*, Mitchell Beazley London

Guy C (1966) *Une histoire de la cuisine française*, De Groot, Paris

Handy C (1992) *The Empty Raincoat*, Century Business, London

Hanneman LJ (1971) *Patisserie*, Butterworth-Heinemann, Oxford

Hanneman LJ (1981) *Bakery and Confectionery*, Butterworth-Heinemann, Oxford

Harin F (1739) *Les Dons de comus ou les delices de la table*, Paris

Harrison AF (1982) *Gastronomy*, New Horizon Books, Sussex

Henry J and Walker D (1999) *Managing Innovation*, Sage Publications, London

Hinchliff S and Montague S (1988) *Physiology for Nursing Practice*, Baillere Tindall, London

Hooker D (1990) *Art of the Western World*, Foreword by Michael Wood, Channel Four Books, London

Hubert-Bare A (1991) *The Heritage of French Cooking*, Ebury Press, London

Jackson M (1992) *The Great Beers of Belgium. A complete guide and celebration of a unique culture*, 'By the Beer Hunter', Media Marketing Communications, MMC, Fcankrijklei, Antwerp

Jellinek P (1951) *Die Psychologischen Grundlagen der Parfumerie*, Huthig, Heidelberg

Jesee J (1982) *The Sense of Smell Awakens Nostalgia*, Dragoco report, 3, p. 76

Johnson H (1990) *The Story of Wine*, Mitchell Beazley, London

Jones P (1988) *Food Service Operations*, Cassell, London

Kasavana M and Smith D (1982) *Menu Engineering: a Practical Guide to Menu Analysis*, Hospitality Publications, Lansing, Michigan

Katz D and Kahn RL (1952) 'Some recent findings in human relations research', in E Swanson, TN Newcomb and E Hartley (eds), *Readings in Social Psychology*. Holt Reinhart and Winston, New York

Ketchan-Wheeton B (1983) *Savouring the Past: The French Kitchen and Table from 1300–1789*, Chatto and Windus, London

King JR (1983) *Have the Scents to Relax*, World Medicine, 19, pp. 29–31

Koffmann P (1990) *Memories of Gascony*, Pavilion, London

Kotas R (1986) *Management Accounting for Hotels and Restaurants*, Surrey University Press

Kracknell HL and Kaufmann RJ (1989) *The Illustrated Escoffier*, Pavilion, London

Kracknell HL and Nobis G (1985) *Practical Professional Gastronomy*, Macmillan, London

Kracknell HL, Kaufman RJ and Nobis C (2000) *Practical Professional Catering Management*, Macmillan, London

La Nouvelle Maison rustique ou économi general de tous les biens de campagne (1740), Paris

Langley A (1987) *The Selected Soyer*, Abolute Press, Bath

L'Art culinaire française, par Nos Grands Maitres de la Cuisine (1957) Flammarion, Paris

Lashley C and Morrison A (2000) *In Search of Hospitality: Theoretical Perspectives and Debates*, Butterworth-Heinemann, Oxford

Lazareff A (1992) in Michel Guérard, *Minceur Exquise*, Pyramide Books, London

Leach E (1985) *Levi-Strauss*, Fontana, London

Leeming M (1991) *A History of Food*, BBC Books, London

Leto MJ and Bode WKH (1985) *The Larder Chef: Food Preparation and Presentation*, Heinemann, London

Levi-Strauss C (1958) *Anthropologie structurale*, Paris (translated as *Structural Anthropology*, Doubleday, New York, 1967)

Levi-Strauss C (1966) *The Savage Mind*, Weidenfeld and Nicolson, London

Levy P (1984) *The Official Foodie Handbook*, Ebury Press, London

Lillicrap D, Cousins J and Smith R (1998) *Food and Beverage Service*, 5th edn, Hodder and Stoughton, London

Lipinski RA and Lipinski KA (1992) *The Complete Beverage Directory*, Van Nostrand Reinhold, New York

Lockwood A and Jones P (1984) *People and the Hotel and Catering Industry*, Cassell, London

Lodge N (1992) *The International School of Sugarcraft*, Merehurst, London

Logue AW (1986) *The Psychology of Eating and Drinking*, State University of New York and W.H. Freeman and Company, Stony Brook, New York

MacClancy J (1992) *Consuming Culture*, Chapmans, London

MacDonough G (1987) *A Palate in Revolution*, Grimod de la Reynière and the Almanach des Gourmets, Robin Clark, London

McDonough G (1987) *A Palate in Revolution: Grimod de La Reynière and the Almanach des Gourmands*, Robin Clark, London

McGee H (1991) *On Food and Cooking: The Science and Lore of the Kitchen*, Harper Collins, London

McGreggor Burns J (1978) *Leadership*, Harper Row, New York

Maude B (1978) *Leadership Management*, Business Books Ltd, London

May J M (M.D) (1966) *The Ecology of Malnutrition in Central and Southern Europe*, Studies in Medical Geography, Vol VI, Hafner Publishing Company, New York

Medlik S (1989) *The Business of Hotels*, Butterworth-Heinemann, Oxford

Mennell S (1985) *All Manners of Food: Eating and Taste in England and France from the Middle Ages to the Present*, Basil Blackwell, Oxford

Mennell S, Murcott A and van Otterloo A (1992) *The Sociology of Food: Eating Diet and Culture*, Sage, London

Menon (1807) *La Cuisine bourgeoise*, New Edition, Paris

Merrick W and O'Sullivan J (1990) *The Human Body* (Action Science), Oxford University Press

Mintzberg H, Quinn JB and Ghoshal S (1998) *The Strategy Process*, rev. European edn, Prentice Hall Europe, Hemel Hempstead

Mitchell D (1975) *The Politics of Food*, James Lorimer & Co, Toronto, Canada

Montagne P (1938) *Larousse Gastronomique*, Larousse, Paris

Montagne P (1971) *Larousse Gastronomique*, rev edn, Paul Hamlyn, London

Montagne P (1995) *Larousse Gastronomique*, ed. Robert J. Courtine (new edn, Engl. trans.), Paul Hamlyn, London

Montaigne M (1958) *1595a, Essays*, Penguin, Harmondsworth

Montignac M (1989) *Dine Out and Lose Weight: the French Way to 'Savoir Vivre'*, Montignac Inc, USA

Morris H (1938) *Portrait of a Chef: The Life of Alexis Soyer*, Cambridge University Press

Morrison A, Rimington M and Williams C (1999) *Entrepreneurship in the Hospitality, Tourism and Leisure Industries*, Butterworth-Heinemann, Oxford

Mosimann A (1981) *Cuisine à la Carte*, Northwood Books, London

Mosimann A (1981) *Cuisine Naturelle*, Papermanc (Macmillan), London

Mosimann A (1988) *Fish Cuisine*, Mitchell Beazley, London

Mosimann A (1988) *Fish Cuisine*, Papermac (Macmillan), London

Mosimann A (1989) *Cooking with Mosimann: The Cookbook of the TV Series*, Guild Publishing, in association with Channel Four, London

Mosimann A (1990) *The Art of Anton Mosimann: Culinary Works of Art for All Who Appreciate Fine Food*, Waymark, London

Mosimann A (1991) *Anton Mosimann Naturally*, Ebury Press, London

Mosimann A (1992) Interview at Mosimann's, *Inside Hotels* (1992/3) Vol. II, Dec./Jan., pp. 336–8, Blakebeck Magazines, London

Mosimann A (1992) 'Serving it right', *Great Hospitality*, 12, 1, p. 22, Motivate Publishing Ltd, London

Mosimann A (1993) *The Essential Mosimann*, Ebury Press London

Moulin L (1989) *The Ceremonies of Dining*, Albin Michel, Paris

Müller D (1988) *Das Dieter Müller Kochbuch*, Heyne, Munich

Müller D (1992) *VIF Gourmet Journal*, Hamburg

Nahmias D (1986) *Les Parfums d'Olympe*, Paris

Nahmias D (1988) *La Cuisine d'Olympe*, Paris

Neirinck E and Poulain J P (1988) *History of Cooking and of Cooks. Culinary Techniques and Eating Habits in France from the Medieval Period to the Present Day*, Jacques Lanore, Paris

Nicolello LG and Dinsdale J (eds) *Basic Pastrywork Techniques*, John Wiley, Chichester

Open University (1985) *An Introduction to Sociology*, Open University D207, Milton Keynes

Page EB and Kingsford PW (1971) *Master Chefs: A History of Haute Cuisine*, Edward Arnold, London

Peters R (1992) *Essential Law, for Catering Students*, Hodder and Stoughton, London

Peterson J (1991) *Sauces, Classical and Contemporary Sauce Making*, Van Nostrand Reinhold, New York

Peynaud E (1996) *The Taste of Wine: The Art and Science of Wine Appreciation*, 2nd edn (trans. Michael Schuster), Wiley, New York

Portmann G (1982) *Contacts et pensées: souvenirs recueillis par Rene Massot et Anne Portmann*, Editions Biere, Bordeaux

Prentice WCH (1961) 'Understanding leadership', *Harvard Business Review*, Sept/Oct, 39 (5), p. 143, Harvard Business School Publishing, Massachusetts

Ramanumurthy PSV (1969) Phsiological effects of 'hot' and cold' foods in human subjects, *Journal of Nutritional Diet*

Ranke L von (1952) *History and Historians in the Nineteenth Century*, 2nd edn, Longman, London

Ranke L von (1973) *Theory and Practice of History*, Bobbs Merrill, Indianapolis

Reber SA (1968)) *Dictionary of Psychology*, Prentice Hall, Englewood Cliffs, NJ

Relais Gourmand (1992) International, Regie Publicaire, Paris

Rival N (1983) *Grimod de la Reynière, Le Gourmand Gentilhomme*, Le Pré aux Clercs, Paris

Robinson J (1992) *Vines Grapes and Wines*, Mitchell Beazley, London

Robinson J (1999) *The Oxford Companion to Wine*, Oxford University Press, Oxford

Ronay E (1991) 'Cooks or Svengalis?', *Great Hospitality*, 8, 1 (Motivate Publishing Ltd, London)

Ross R (1957) *Symbols and Civilisation: Science, Morals, Religion, and Art*, Harbinger Books, New York

Sadler P (1997) *Leadership*, Kogan Page, London

Salinger P (1986) *Dining in France* (book of the TV series), CEL Communications/Initial Groupe FR3, Paris

Sanjur D (1982) *Social and Cultural Perspectives in Nutrition*, Prentice Hall, Englewood Cliffs, NJ

Saulnier L (1982) *Le Répertoire de la cuisine*, 17th edn (reprinted 1991), Leon Jaeggl & Sons Ltd, Middlesex

Scharfenberg H (1987) *The German Kitchen*, Papermac, London

Simon J (1996) *Wine with Food*, Mitchell Beazley, London

Simpson LF (1859) *The Handbook of Dining, or How to Dine*, Longman, London

Sirotkin V (1991) *Walk the Talk*, BBC Education, Scotland

Soyer A (1847) *The Gastronomic Regenerator: a Simplified and Entirely New System of Cookery*, 3rd edn, Simpkin Marshall, London

Soyer A (1849) *The Modern Housewife*, Simpkin, Marshall and Co, London

Stead J (1985) *Food and Cooking in 18th Century Britain*, English Heritage, London

Steel J (1985) 'The Nature of Prescription in Cuisine', PhD, University of Strathclyde

Stevenson T (1991) *World Wines*, Dorling Kindersley, London

Stevenson T (1997) *Sothebys World Wine Encyclopedia*, Dorling Kindersley, London

Taillevent GT (1892) *Le Viandier* (The Cook's Notebook), Jerome Pichon and Georges Vicaire (revised and enlarged by S. Martinet, Slatkine, Geneva, 1967)

Tannahill R (1973) *Food in History*, Stein and Day, New York

Tannahill R (1975) *Food in History*, Paladin, London

Taylor J (1989) *The Wine Quotation Book*, Robert Hale, London

Taylor J (1990) *The Gourmet's Quotation Book*, Robert Hale, London

Telfer E (1996) *Food for Thought: Philosophy and Food*, Routlege, London

Titterington R (1987) *Growing Herbs*, The Crowood Press, Dorset

Tosh J (1992) *The Pursuit of History*: *Aims, Methods and New Directions in the Study of Modern History*, 2nd edn, Longman, London and New York

Unwin T (1991) *Wine and the Vine: An Historical Geography of Viticulture and the Wine Trade*, Routlege, London

Uttal WR (1973) *The Psychobiology of Sensory Coding*, Harper and Row, New York

Vaerst Baron von FCE (1851) *Gastrosophie oder die Lehre von den Freunden der Tafel* (The Art of Enjoying Good Food), Leipzig

Valby J (1993) *Gastronomie*: *Amitié et Gastronomie Font la Joie de Vivre*, Alex Morton, Florida

Vallejo S (Press Officer) (1992) *Food and Wine from France*, French Tourist Office, Piccadilly, London

Van Toller S and Dodd G (1991) *Perfumery: the Psychology and Biology of Fragrance*, Chapman & Hall, London

Vergé R (1986) *Entertaining in the French Style*, Webb and Bower, Exeter

Verlag Herder KG (1962) *Wege Zum Philosophischen Denken*, Verlag Herder, Freiburg im Breislau

Viard A (1828) *Le Cuisinier royal, ou L'Art de fair la cuisine*, Barba, Paris

Weishaupl G (1988) *Incentive Travel Manual*, Munich Tourist Office

West A and Hughes J (1991) 'An evaluation of hotel design practice', *The Service Industries Journal*, 11 (3), p. 363

Westley F and Mintzberg H (1989) 'Visionary leadership and strategic management', *Strategic Management Journal*, Vol. 10, p. 17

Willan A (1992) *Great Cooks and their Recipes*, Pavilion, London

Wilson CA (1990) *Food and Drink in Britain*, Constable and Co., London

Wood R (1991) 'The Shock of the New: a sociology of nouvelle cuisine', *Journal of Consumer Studies and Home Economics*, 15, pp. 327–38

Worral Thompson A (1991) Interview, *Inside Hotels*, Vol. I, April/May, pp. 86–90, Blakebeck Magazines, London

Wright, P (1996) *Managerial Leadership*, Routledge, London

Youell T and Kimball G (1992) *Pocket Guide to French Food and Wine*, Carbery, London

Yudkin J and Mackenzie C (1964) *Changing Food Habits*, MacGibbon & Kee, London

Yukl, GA (1981) *Leadership in Organizations*, Prentice Hall, Englewood Cliffs, NJ

Zaleznik A (1966) *Human Dilemmas of Leadership*, Harper Row, New York

Zeeman F (1983) *Clinical Nutrition and Dietetics*, The Collmare Press, Lexington, MA, pp. 164–5

Glossary of terms

à la carte | From the card. Term used for menu style of, sometimes largish, selection and individual pricing (F)

à la mode | In fashion (F)

Aestheticism | Belief that beauty is the basic principle of prime good in life and underlies morality

Aetiology | Study of causes. The philosophical investigation of causes and origins (L, Gr)

Amphitryon | A person who entertains guests at his table, and undertakes responsibility for their happiness while under his roof

Autodidact(e) | Person with no formal training, who is self-trained (Gr)

Avant garde | Pioneering, ahead of the times (F)

Beau monde | Fashionable society (F)

Beaux-arts | Fine arts (F)

Behaviourism | The doctrine that behaviour, rather than mind or consciousness, is all that can really be known or studied about human nature (F)

Belle époque | 'Beautiful period', the era preceding the First World War (F)

Bon vivant | A person who enjoys luxurious living (F)

Carte blanche | Unconditional authorization, i.e. free hand (F)

Carte du jour	Literally card of the day. Applied to menu with a number of courses (F)
Cause célèbre	Interesting and controversial public issue (F)
Cognoscent/e(i)	Connoisseur(s) (I)
Concept cuisine	The *idea* of a chef producing clearly recognizable dishes or cuisine(s) which are truly their own. Helps to reinvigorate the market. There needs to be a theme behind the concept however, making it unique
Connoisseur	A critical judge in matters of taste (F, L)
Coup de grâce	Deathblow: conclusive stroke (F)
Coup d'état	Sudden overthrow of government (F)
Cri de coeur	Heartfelt cry of appeal (F)
Cuisine ancienne	Ancient (old style) cuisine (F)
Cuisine maigre	Lean cuisine (F)
Cuisine du marché	Market cuisine (F)
Cuisine aux mille senteurs	Cuisine of a thousand aromas/perfumes (F)
Cuisine minceur	Exquisite slim cuisine (F)
Cuisine moderne	Modern cuisine (F)
Cuisine naturelle	Healthy style cuisine devised by Anton Mosimann (E)
Cuisine nouvelle	Meaning new style; there have been many throughout the ages but the term chiefly applies to the latest version attributable to the 1970s in France that later travelled around the world (F)
Cuisine parfumée	Highly aromatic or perfumed cuisine attributable to Dominique Nahmias (Olympe Versini) (F)
Cuisine réussie	Successful cuisine (F)
Cuisine sans frontières	Cuisine without boundaries, in terms of geographic, socio/cultural or historical limitations (F)
Cuisine de sensibilité	Sensitively balanced cuisine (F)
Cuisine du soleil	Cuisine of the sun, devised by Roger Vergé (F)
Cuisine spontanée	Spontaneous cuisine (F)
Cuisine du terroir	Earthy cuisine (F)
Dark Ages	Period of European history before Middle Ages, between the fall of the Roman Empire, from AD 395 and about the end of the 10th century, for which there are few historical records, and during which life was comparatively uncivilized (E)
Demonde	Out of fashion: out of date (F)

De rigueur	Required by fashion or social custom (F)
Dernier cri	Latest fashion (F)
Élitism	In the sense used, indicates recognition as a kind of social badge, associated with a certain life style, bound up with personal status symbols
Eminence grise	Influential person behind the scenes (F)
Empiricism	The doctrine that knowledge can only be gained through sense perception and experience (Gr)
Enlightenment, age of	Period before the French Revolution. Term used to indicate trends in 18th century European thought and letters which were believed to be 'enlightened' by reason, science and respect for humanity (F)
Epicure	Epicurean (obsolete). One given to sensual enjoyment; a person of refined and fastidious taste, esp. in food and wine etc. An individual who is choice and dainty in eating and drinking (L)
Epicurean	Pertaining to Epicurus (341–272 BC). The Greek philosopher, who taught atomic materialism in physics and hedonism in ethics: misrepresented by opponents as brutish sensuality, given to luxury. A follower of Epicurus – a hedonist, an Epicure (L)
Epicurianism	The doctrines of Epicurus, attachment to these doctrines (F)
Epistemology	The study of nature, origin and validity of knowledge (Gr)
Esprit de corps	Good spirit or morale (F)
Etymology	The study of the origins of words or parts of words and how they have arrived at their current form and meaning (F, Gr)
Fait accompli	Irreversible fact (F)
Fusion cuisine	Coined by Norman Van Aken (chef). It is an evolution in cuisine, taking account of the harmonious blending of foods of various origins as a consequence of the convergence of contrasting cultures
Gastro-geography	Implications on cuisine as a result of location of the European continent and the specific location of the individual countries within it. Includes consideration of: climatic zones, temperature, geology, precipitation, natural vegetation, land and water, agriculture, farming and food production, population density and culture and tradition, diet, nutrition and health and diseases (F, Gr) (L, Gr)
Gastro-history	Implications on cuisine and eating habits and traditions as a result of the history of Europe and the individual countries within it, the influences of the countries that surround it, and

also those beyond with which Europe has been and is involved. Takes account of the socio/cultural, economic, political, legal, ecological and technological influences, and developments over time, those that are current, and those that are on the horizon (F, Gr) (L, Gr)

Gastrology	Cookery, good eating (F)
Gastronome	From the Greek *nomos*, meaning (law). A judge of cooking (F)
Gastronomer	An epicure (F)
Gastronomic	Pertaining to gastronomy (F)
Gastronomist	*See* Gastronome (F)
Gastronomy	The art or science of good eating. The study of food and beverages (F)
Gastronomy, the art of	To prepare food in a pleasing way (F)
Gastrosoph	From the Greek *sophos*, meaning wise. One skilled in matters of eating (F, Gr)
Gastrosopher	Professionals who combine theory and practice in a general spirit of reflection. The gastrosopher can be an individual with a great and private love of food and drink or the prophet, writing about and sharing meditations and philosophies on food and beverages for the greater good of people and society (F, Gr)
Gastrosophy	The process of enjoying, and reflecting on food and drink. The practical and academic interwoven, and complementary (F, Gr)
Genetically modified organisms (GMOs)	Modern method of biotechnology used to improve yields of particular foods and ingredients. Common GM foods are maize and soya; 15 per cent of soya is now genetically modified. Together these derivatives are found in up to 60 per cent of all processed foods including cakes, biscuits, meat substitutes, bread, peanut butter and chocolate, and tomato puree made from genetically modified tomatoes. There is considerable public concern over health and environmental safety and it is probable that all consumers are now likely to encounter GM foods (G)
Gourmand(e)	A person who is gluttonous. Fond of eating. It can mean gluttonous and an epicure in the French dictionary (F)
Gourmet	One who is a connoisseur of table delicacies. Title of honour confirming certain skills, which have been learned through study and practice (F)
Grande cuisine minceur	The highest expression of slim cuisine
Haute cuisine	High class cooking (F)
Haute monde	High levels of society (F)

Hedonism	The belief that pleasure is the basic principle or primary good in life, and underlies morality or determines one's actions (Gr)
Historicism	The doctrine that history is governed by inevitable processes; theory that a past age should be judged on its own terms rather than by modern values (F)
Historiography	The art or employment of writing history (F)
Medieval	Of the Middle Ages: relating to, involving, belonging to, or typical of the Middle Ages. Period 100–1400 AD and broader sense 600 to 1500 AD (L). Also appears as mediaeval
Middle ages	*See* Medieval
Millenarianism	Belief in a perfect future period or society (L)
Idée fixe	Obsession (F)
Irradiated foods	Foods that have been subjected to electromagnetic radiation in order to prolong shelf life (L)
Mot juste	The exactly appropriate expression (F)
Nouveau riche	Newly and ostentatiously rich person (F)
Partie system	Specific historical phenomenon credited to Escoffier. Division and stratification of kitchen staff into 'parties' or sections, each more or less separated. Comprises highly skilled, semi-skilled, and manual operators including those who are involved in prolonged training, the latter spending this period progressing from one partie/corner/section to another within the system, as a desired standard is achieved. Teamwork and the interdependence required is a major feature of the 'partie' system (F)
Perspectivism	The doctrine that there can be no absolute knowledge of truth, since rival conceptual systems produce different views; the theory that several points of view are needed to understand reality (F, L)
Phenomenalism	The doctrine that the only thing knowable for certain is our set of sense perceptions or sensations (L, Gr)
Pièce de resistance	Outstanding item (F)
Plat du jour	Dish of the day (F)
Reductionism	Analysis of a subject or problem into its components, often by oversimplifying it (F, L)
Renaissance	Revival of, period of progress in, art and letters under the influence of classical models – 14th to 16th centuries (F). Also as Renascence (L)
Rich meaning	Meaning which is self-defining and impacts deeply into the conscious or sub-conscious level

Rococo period	Period roughly corresponding to the reign of Louis XV of France (1715–1774). Refers to highly ornamented or florid 18th century style
Savoir-faire	Knowledge of appropriate behaviour (F)
Scholasticism	Medieval Christian philosophy and theology associated with the Church Fathers, sometimes influenced by Aristotle
Semiotics	The study of signs and symbols in various fields
Semiotic carriers	Refers to the way symbols, signs and senses are woven together to create a meaningful, common language
Sense	Faculty of receiving sensation, general or particular; immediate consciousness; inward feeling; impression; opinion; mental attitude; discernment; appreciation to become aware etc. (F, L)
Sensibility	Sensitiveness, sensitivity and capacity of feeling or emotion: readiness and delicacy of emotional response (F, L)
Sommelier	Professional wine waiter, ordering, storing and serving wine and other beverages (F)
Sybarite	An inhabitant of Sybaris, a Greek city in ancient Italy, on the Gulf of Tarentum, noted for luxury; one devoted to luxury (L, G)
Symbol	Usually anything representing, signifying or indicating anything else. It can also be a gesture, artefact, sign or concept standing for, signifying or expressing anything else
Symbolism	Generally, the act or practice of using symbols
Synergy	The working together of two or more things, people, or organizations, especially when the result is greater than the sum of their individual effects or capabilities (L, Gr)
Table d'hôte	Table of the host. Used to indicate type of menu, usually at set price and with a number of courses and choice within each course (F)
Terroir	A French concept. Insisting the quality of a wine stems from the combination of soil, exposition, climate and wine-making (F)
Terror	September 5 1793–July 27 1794. The period of the French Revolution when through civil and foreign war the revolutionary government would make 'Terror' (September 5 Decree) the order of the day. In Paris a wave of executions followed (17,000 were officially executed, many others died in prison) against those suspected as enemies of the Revolution (nobles, priests and hoarders)
Tour de force	Outstanding feat of achievement (F)
Tout court	Plainly and simply (F)
Vade mecum	Literally 'go with me'. Old name for a guidebook (L)
Vis-à-vis	Compared with: in relation to (F)

Index